Bodies & Souls

A Down-to-Earth Guide for the Human Experience

First published by O Books, 2007
O Books is an imprint of John Hunt Publishing Ltd.,
The Bothy, Deershot Lodge, Park Lane, Ropley, Hants, SO24 0BE, UK
office1@o-books.net
www.o-books.net

Distribution in:

UK and Europe
Orca Book Services
orders@orcabookservices.co.uk
Tel: 01202 665432 Fax: 01202 666219 Int. code (44)

USA and Canada
NBN
custserv@nbnbooks.com
Tel: 1 800 462 6420 Fax: 1 800 338 4550

Australia and New Zealand
Brumby Books
sales@brumbybooks.com.au
Tel: 61 3 9761 5535 Fax: 61 3 9761 7095

Far East (offices in Singapore, Thailand, Hong Kong, Taiwan)
Pansing Distribution Pte Ltd
kemal@pansing.com
Tel: 65 6319 9939 Fax: 65 6462 5761

South Africa
Alternative Books
altbook@peterhyde.co.za
Tel: 021 447 5300 Fax: 021 447 1430

Text copyright Sue Minns 2007

Design: Stuart Davies

ISBN: 978 1 84694 053 8

A CIP catalogue record for this book is available from the British Library.

Printed in the US by Maple Vail

Bodies & Souls

*A Down-to-Earth Guide for
the Human Experience*

Sue Minns

BOOKS

Winchester, UK
Washington, USA

The world was made to be free in.

Give up all the other worlds
except the one to which you belong.

Sometimes it takes darkness and the sweet
confinement of your aloneness
to learn

anything or anyone
that does not bring you alive

is too small for you.

David Whyte
from 'Sweet Darkness'

ACKNOWLEDGEMENTS

MY MOST GRATEFUL THANKS TO

my dear friend and meticulous editor, Logan Lewis Proudlock, for all her unstinting help, suggestions, clarity and research. Not to mention wine and laughter.

Cheryl van Blerk, not only for introducing me to John Hunt, but for her incredible aliveness, encouragement and more wine and laughter.

John Hunt himself, for being such an author-friendly publisher, and for his dedication to creating an organism with his business rather than a soulless organisation.

Abigail Robinson for her beautiful contribution; for who she is and what she does.

the College of Psychic Studies for all that I learned during my years there; and to Brenda Marshall, who, as President, held the note of the College with absolute integrity for so long.

And you, Moustapha, for your guidance on the heart of Islam and the deeper meanings of the Qur'an; for our discussions, and too many other things to mention. As you say,

> "We have only one heart
> for the love that hurts us
> and the love that is beyond us.
> Trust is the Friend of the heart;
> We will never have Love without trust".

CONTENTS

preface

This book is not intended to be another How to Sort Yourself Out Manual, but more of a personal guide to help you navigate the waves of information available on the ocean of this New Age of Aquarius. Some of these waves have the substance to move you, whilst others are like bursts of foam that confuse rather than clarify and have as much spiritual nourishment as a stick of candyfloss.

And there is something else to be aware of on journeys of self-discovery in these extraordinary times. Whilst investigation of our personal archives is a prerequisite to sifting out the faulty information and beliefs that have informed our lives, it's important not to get stuck in past wounds. These wounds, once identified and understood for what they are, need to be left to heal. Going over old ground again and again actually reinforces the neural pathways of grief, loss, anger, betrayal and every other variety of suffering. These wounds are the battle scars on the journey to find our soul. Not that it was ever far away; just waiting to make its presence felt.

All 'difficulties' are nudges, prods or sometimes hammerings from our soul who is trying to attract our attention to the wonder of what we might be beyond our biographies and looping karma.

Perhaps over 20 years in the Mind Body Spirit 'business' has made me a bit cynical, and extremely selective in what is out there that I believe has lasting real value. My bookshelves are full of books hardly touched, and there are others that are tagged, marked and dog-eared through constant use. As I peer back down the time-line of workshops and trainings I've been to and through, there have been some remarkable punctuation marks – signposts that certainly gave a clear direction – but the rest have faded beyond recollection. The ones that made a difference I could probably count on one hand. I don't think I even really knew what it was that I was searching for, in the beginning. I stumbled rather than walked along the path to Self Knowledge; turning over stones that often didn't reveal even an atom's worth of knowledge, waiting for some

Enlightened Being – even a two-legged teacher would do - to reveal themselves to me and hand me the keys to wisdom.

What I have learned though, is that there are two useful litmus tests available to help us navigate the ocean of information and experience now on offer for the spiritual seeker. The first of these is to ask the simple question 'So what?'. Because whilst it may be a dizzying experience to be told (and this is the bit to watch – being *told*) that you are about to enter the 9th dimension or that an Ascended Master has cleared all your karma, what does this really mean to you in the here and now? Does it help you cope with your divorce or deal with your laundry? Does it put you in touch with the deep feelings of your own soul? Or is it just more second-hand information? For the last couple of thousand years, we have had the 'path to god' delivered to us by 'those in the know' to the rest of us 'who are not'. A true mentor is concerned with your soul (not their own status); is interested in making themselves obsolete, and will guide you to *your own* understanding of what is true for you. It was Socrates who advised that an unexamined life was not worth living. In these days where belief systems are creating havoc on the Earth, perhaps we should redefine this, as John Lamb Lash suggests, to:

an unexamined belief is not worth holding.

The second useful tool is what's become known as an 'Aha!'. It's that sense that you have discovered, recognised or remembered something that has value for *you*. Like re-discovering something you once owned or knew, but may not even have been aware was missing. 'Ah, yes! That's right, I understand' something inside you acknowledges. This is the soul letting the personality know that it's on the right track.

I have distilled my experience and the knowledge I have gleaned over the years into the following pages. But don't believe a word of it unless it makes sense, unless you feel a 'resonance' (important word) with it. Ultimately all roads lead to the same destination and of course it's up to you to choose whether you would prefer the scenic to the direct path.

There's nothing 'wrong' with a diversion into a fairground; just so long as you are aware of the nature of who it is entering the fairground, how long you want to spend there, and where the exit is. The path to your Soul doesn't have to be a slog – rather it can become an exciting exploration – but it requires commitment if you really want to feel the change. There will be ups and downs, too, when you might think you just want to be 'normal'. But just hold on to the knowledge of what happens to the caterpillar.

There are four phases in a butterfly's life cycle: first an egg from which emerges the larva or caterpillar; the third stage is in its chrysalis or cocoon from which, finally and miraculously, the *imago* or butterfly emerges. No one quite knows how the caterpillar transforms in such a dramatic way, but what is known is that inside the caterpillar's body there are clusters of cells called – of all things – *imaginal* buds. Now there's an interesting word. The Oxford English Dictionary notes that as well as "pertaining to an insect imago" it was also first used circa 1647 in the following context "That inward life's the impresse imaginall of Nature's Art". Nowadays, psychologists use the word *imago* to mean an idealised image of your self or a loved one. So these imaginal cells deep inside the caterpillar are holding the vision of colourful flight. The caterpillar's immune system believes these cells to be foreign and tries to destroy them – it is after all busy being a gravity-held creature, stuffing itself with leaves – we might even call it a gross consumer. Inevitably, in the caterpillar's case but unfortunately not in human beings, it weaves a cocoon around itself, it shuts its shop as a caterpillar, and the imaginal buds link up. Its immune system breaks down and the caterpillar literally goes into liquidation. The buds then begin to build a butterfly from the fluid contents of the chrysalis. A human being's imaginal buds – or soul seeds - may never link up in a lifetime, to realise the soul's presence, either because the everyday caterpillar life is too comfortable or we are too afraid of change.

The most important part of the journey, from the limited view of our everyday personality to multidimensional awareness, is to distil any information into your own personal 'knowing'. Anything less just won't work.

The call from your soul may feel like a rumble of sky-shattering thunder, or it may drip its raindrops slowly into your conscious awareness, but we ignore its signals at our peril. No one has ever said this was easy. We are attached with super-glue to the masks that we wear and the personalities we have developed in order to take our place in a conditioned world that is run by power and money hungry warmongers and religious fanatics. As we began to turn away from the old hierarchical, patriarchal religions we have looked for - and found - a more inclusive way of seeing our world. But we must go deeper still. So much that is on offer in the name of 'spirituality' still does not take us to soul – just candyfloss. It encourages people to say they are 'too sensitive' to watch the news, too 'spiritual' to rock and roll – they just want to go 'Home' as they don't really belong here. What they are really saying is that they are not present in their bodies or in touch with the juice of their souls. We are all here for a reason and the reason may be simply to engage fully as a soul in a physical body in these difficult but transformative times. Souls know what is going on and why. Perhaps there has never been such collective suffering – in all its different expressions – as there seems to be in the world at the moment. But denying its existence and the reasons for it will not heal it or make it go away. Nettles must be grasped. Our souls wait to help us understand and navigate our unravelling world. And here I would like to explain how I understand the difference between 'Spirit' and 'Soul'.

Defining the undefinable and understanding concepts that it seems our mind-computers are not equipped to encompass could make this a bit difficult. But a map is required for the following pages, and since I myself need things simplified in order to understand them, this is how I see it (at the moment) and how Bill Plotkin in his book *Soulcraft* precisely describes it ...

Soul calls us to express what is most unique in us;

Spirit encompasses and draws us toward what is most universal and shared.

Distilling it down to basics, it is as if there are three aspects to our selves. Our Soul, our Everyday Personality, and Spirit. Many people live their lives asleep to the conscious awareness of the first and last of these aspects. Their lives from start to finish, like the caterpillar, are lived in the third dimensional world of physical matter – it's all that matters. Their souls wait for the opportunity to express themselves through the individuals' human experience, and Spirit remains ineffably invisible and unknown. Throughout the world, with its different religions, cultures and philosophies, those who believe that there is more to life than just existing as a human being, have chosen mostly to focus on the transcendent path to Spirit. Less acknowledged is the spiritual path to Soul, a path which has been taken by those from shamanistic traditions and indigenous cultures, and now by 20th century depth psychologists such as Carl Jung, Roberto Assagioli, Marie Louise von Franz, Robert Johnson, Marion Woodman and many others.

Both the Soul and Spirit are transpersonal, which is to say beyond (and yet within) the Everyday Self. Spirit existed before souls because all exist within it. Spirit is everywhere and within everything and throughout the world It has acquired many different names, God being the most universal. It is also known as the One, the Divine, the All That Is, Unity Consciousness, the Great Spirit, the Source, the Creative Mind. It's referred to by quantum physicists as the 'Sea of Implicate Order'. Christians call this spiritual force God the Father, Muslims say that Allah has 99 names one of which is *Al Malik* meaning the King, the Sovereign, whilst Judaism's patriarchal god 'out there' is called YHWH, originally a War God. This god force (you might note that it is always masculine) is arrived at or returned to by transcendent means – It is 'up there', 'out there'. In fact, It is 'in here' too – It's everywhere. Spirit is the Great Mystery behind the stars, the universe, the strange life of a dragonfly. It is the Great Unknowable that simply Is. It is eternal and infinite –

fuse-popping concepts for our limited capacities - and we exist as minuscule micro-dots within the vast body of this Creative Force. We are like specks of foam on a wave of an infinite ocean, appearing and disappearing in less time than it takes to wink an eye. So how might our souls have any significance, you might be asking yourself?

The soul is like a snowflake, a totally unique, individual particle. Spirit is the cloud which formed it and from which it fell. We have emerged from the Being of Spirit – created by It – in order that it may *know* what it has created. Each individual soul is like a sensor-cell for the All That Is. Ideas and plans on drawing boards are all very well, but how do they work 'on the ground'? It's the down-to-earth experience that is important. The sweet fragrance of a rose, the full moon against a dark velvet sky, murder, torture, a green tree frog, acts of compassion and courage – all of creation experienced through individual sensors: our bodies and souls. For Spirit to know about the particular, to truly under-stand Its creation, It needs to experience it through Its soul agents. A vehicle and equipment for this experience is required. Enter the human body – a miracle of engineering that is anchored to the third dimensional reality and subject to the laws of the physical universe. The energy vibrations of the body are, obviously, much denser and slower than that of the soul. It is a basic, instinctual creature made of the same building blocks as everything else on Earth. It has needs, desires and functions that are all totally natural to it, but taken for granted, denied or embarrassing to the Everyday Personality.

Every soul coming to Earth – like a seed – contains the ingredients, the qualities, the potential for its particular unique flowering. Our souls are our essential natures, the very heart of us, our natural talents. They are also the custodians of our past experiences in human form and at this point in time, most souls have incarnated many times before. They carry the memory of their deeply felt previous experiences both painful and ecstatic. Souls, it seems, constellate in groups in order to work together with a particular aspect or theme during their visits to earth. Because one of the laws that governs physical reality is duality, or relativity –

up/down, pain/pleasure, day/night, good/bad etc – we need, as souls, to collect experience from both ends of the pole. The operative word is 'experience'. However, once the soul has left 'Home' for its next earthly assignation, gone through the ring-pass-not of forgetfulness and engaged with the little foetal body that will be its partner for this experience, it starts to be 'conditioned' by the events that follow.

This conditioning creates our Everyday Selves or Personalities. We learn to do up our shoes, ride a bike, eat spaghetti and write our name – and then forget about it. It goes into the body's everyday working manual and doesn't have to be re-visited once it is learned. Other information goes in too, in these early learning years; it sinks into the sub-conscious mind and then goes on automatic. Some of this information we would be better off without. What gets stored is what we perceive to be the sort of behaviour that gets love and attention for a start and which bits of life – and which people – make us feel safe and those that don't and so on. The soul is present in a child – preoccupied with the fascinating things it is discovering, living in the present, making mud pies, drawing, watching a spider in its web, but it can receive some paralysing shocks at this time too – as you will discover later in this book. We need our Everyday Selves to deal with the practicalities of life as a visitor on the Earth, but unfortunately many people spend all their lives in this band between Spirit out there, everywhere; and the soul deep down in here - scarcely aware of their bodies either. Where are we then?

Since Descartes stated "I think, therefore I am" and Darwin proposed his theory of evolution, it's been a bit grim, soul-wise, for the last few hundred years – but this is all part of the cycles that make up the clockwork of the physical universe. Our society now could hardly be called soul-centred. The cult of the personality just about rules the world. But the clarion call has sounded. The opportunity for Earth-bound experience is now limited by the demise of the planet herself. Time's running out, and an epoch is drawing to its close.

Fr. Pierre Teilhard de Chardin (1881 – 1955) was a French Jesuit priest trained as a palaeontologist and philosopher whose work was denied publication by the Roman Holy Office during his lifetime. These words of his hit the nail on the head:

We are not human beings having a spiritual experience.
We are spiritual beings having a human experience.

The soul wants the deep down and juicy experiences that this garden Earth has to offer, the experiences that can only be felt through the sensory equipment of a human vehicle. The sights, the sounds, the sensations – everything that makes us feel alive, curious, passionate and creative in whatever way that turns on our lights.

You are unique! Not a clone, not a robot, not a carbon copy. Listen to your soul. It gives you permission to be – it requires you to be – fully present as a shimmering representative of the Great Creative Spirit. Throw the rule book out of the window; give your soul some time; dare to be different. You might even hear laughter as your soul – on behalf of its Creator – begins to live through you.

We are not here just to survive
and live long ...
We are here to live and know life
in its multi-dimensions
to know life in its richness, in all its variety.
And when a man lives multi-dimensionally,
explores all possibilities available,
never shrinks back from any challenge,
goes, rushes to it, welcomes it,
rises to the occasion
then life becomes a flame,
life blooms.
Bhagwan Shree Rajneesh: The Sacred Yes

SM

introduction

Only within yourself exists that other reality for which you long.
I can give you nothing that has not already its being within yourself
I can throw open to you no picture gallery but your own soul
Herman Hesse

Around and within us everything is changing at a speed that makes us feel
as if something has happened to Time itself. In the past we have relied on
others to inform us on everything, trusting their intentions to be clear. But
from parents to priests, governments to history books, we find this trust
has not always been respected. It feels as if we are sitting on a tea tray that
is hurtling down a very steep hill – beyond anyone's control. In order to
try and make sense of what is happening to us and our world, we turn to
something – anything – that will mask our feelings of fear and uncertainty. We accumulate more and more belongings in our search to find a sense
of belonging – always searching outside ourselves for something to make
us feel safe. We swallow, smoke or snort something that will numb reality and blur the edges. Perhaps the next workshop, journey to India, Tarot
reading or Reiki healing will do the trick and give us the key to our freedom. And whilst the new Age of Aquarius has opened many windows, it
has not always put back authority where it belongs – *within our Selves.*
Perhaps this is because it has offered us many ways to 'get out' of our
bodies, when the truth is we are not going anywhere until we have
arrived. There may be the odd epiphany for the fortunate few, but there
are no quick spiritual fixes for the rest of us. We've got used to others
being responsible for our welfare – the nanny state – and to blaming every
and anyone if we don't get what we want, or some accident befalls us.
This approach has leached into our search for meaning, as we expect
teachers, gurus, masters, even spirit guides to take responsibility for us
and our destinies. Centuries of conditioning by those who used religion to
manipulate and control the populace using the ultimate power tool of fear

has created people who feel safe only when toeing the party line – or others who would seem to have thrown all the babies out with their bathwater.

It's time to grow up now. The game's over and the chips are down. The clock is about to strike midnight and we will discover that all the world is truly only a stage and the coach is a pumpkin after all. In fact it is not only one clock striking midnight, but several all at about the same time – now. Everything in the universe moves in cycles. We can calculate the movement of tides on our seashores, but are not so aware of the larger tides that affect us all. Being 'asleep', as we have been, for a few thousand years is all part of our tidal cycle. But perhaps deep down we are aware that history repeats itself, like James Joyce, when he gets one of his characters to say:

History is a nightmare from which I am trying to awaken.

One of the huge clocks now about to strike midnight is known in Hinduism as the Cycle of the Yugas. This great repeating loop of time is divided into four quarters, each with its own characteristics. The soul journeys round the cycle, starting its life-on-earth experience in the first quadrant, the Golden Age, or *Satya Yuga,* and then repeating incarnations through the Silver, Bronze and finally the current Iron Age, known as the *Kali Yuga.* By the time the soul reaches this quarter, it has collected many experiences and quite an attachment to the world of matter. Some of the characteristics of this last portion of the cosmic pie have been outlined in the sacred Hindu texts thus:

Rulers will no longer see it their duty to promote spirituality or to protect their subjects. Instead, they will become a danger to the world. People will start migrating; seeking countries where wheat and barley form the staple food source.

Avarice and wrath is common, men will openly display animosities towards one another. Ignorance of Dharma (moral justice) will occur.

Lust will be viewed as being socially acceptable. People will have thoughts of murder for no justification, and they will see nothing wrong with their mind-set. People will no longer follow the science of reason and instead be led by their emotions instead of their minds. Family murders will also occur. People will see those who are helpless as easy targets and remove everything from them. Many other unwanted changes will occur. The right hand will deceive the left and the left the right. Men with false reputation of learning will teach the Truth and the old will betray the senselessness of the young, and the young will betray the dotage of the old. Cowards will have the reputation of bravery and the brave will be cheerless like cowards. People will not trust a single person in the world, not even their immediate family. Even husband and wife will find contempt in each other.

In the Kali Yuga there will be teenage pregnancies. The primary cause will be the social acceptance of intercourse as being the central requirement of life. It is believed that sin will increase exponentially, whilst virtue will fade and cease to flourish. People will take vows only to break them soon.

Alongside death and famine being everywhere, men will have lustful thoughts and so will women. People will, without reason, destroy trees and gardens. As previously mentioned, men will murder. There will be no respect for animals, and also meat eating will start.

People will become addicted to intoxicating drinks. Men will find their jobs stressful and will go to retreats to escape their work.

Gurus will no longer be respected and their students will attempt to injure them. Their teachings will be insulted and followers of Kama [not to be confused with Karma, this is one of the 4 goals of life according to Hindu tradition] *will wrest control of the mind from all humans.*

Throughout the age, humans become shorter in height and weaker physically as well as mentally and spiritually.

According to the *Surya Sidhanta*, an astronomical treatise that forms the basis of all Buddhist and Hindu calendars, the Kali Yuga began at midnight on 18th February 3102 BCE. Curiously, at the opposite end of the globe another 'clock' began to tick only 12 years later. This is the *T'zolkin*, or Long Count Calendar of the Maya, who were like Lords of Time, their knowledge of cosmic clocks being so extraordinary. They divided periods of time into portions of equal length and the Long Count – a period of 1,872,000 days (5,125 years) – is divided into 13 *baktuns*. The Long Count started in August 3114 BCE and concludes in December 2012. There seems to be a slight disparity in contemporary calculations regarding the start and end dates, but the difference is only a matter of a couple of days. And by the way, December 2012 does not herald the End of the World – but the end of the world as we have known it.

As far as the Maya were concerned, it was a very significant point in time. Perhaps this was because they were also very keen on Venus as a deeply influential celestial body, and as you might know we are in the middle of a 'Venus Sequence', when this bright planet makes a double transit across the face of the sun. The first crossing was in 2004 and the second will be on 6th June 2012. Each of the 13 Maya baktuns was given a headline, and this last one that we are now in was known as the baktun of 'The Transformation of Matter'. This becomes even more interesting when you see what the celestial or cosmic line-up is around that time concerning our own sun and the Galactic Centre. Through their books and research, John Major Jenkins and Geoff Stray have brought us the facts about the hoo-ha surrounding 2012 and what it might mean for us all (references at the end, together with the website of a fascinating up-coming film titled *Time of the 6th Sun*).

"...the human race will unify as a single circuit. Solar and galactic sound transmissions will inundate the planetary field. A current charging both poles will race across the skies, connecting the polar auroras in a single brilliant flash" is what Jose Arguelles – controversial author of *The Mayan Factor: Path Beyond Technology* – has to say about this event.

What is striking (apart from clocks) are the parallels between a diversity of cultures and world views on the times we are in. Emissaries from many different ancient traditions are speaking about their beliefs and handed-down prophecies concerning what's happening on Earth at this point in time. The Maoris say that as the veils between the physical and spiritual worlds dissolve, they will merge. The Zulus believe that the whole world will be turned upside down (a pole shift?). The Aztec call this the Time of the Sixth Sun, a time of transformation which will give birth to a new race. The Dogon speak about the spaceship of the visitors, the Nommo, who will return in the form of a blue star. The Cherokee say their ancient calendar ends exactly at the year 2012, like the Maya. The Tibetan Kalachakra teachings are prophesies left by Buddha, predicting the beginning of the Golden Age, and in Egypt the stone calendar encoded in the Great Pyramid ends in 2012. But let's just have a quick look at what might be behind the Maya understanding of all this, since it is the revelations from their Long Count Calendar that seem to have triggered all the interest.

The Maya civilisation had a relatively brief flowering, between 270 and 900 CE in Meso-America, and has been historically noted for producing the only known fully developed written language of the pre-Columbian Americas, as well as its spectacular art, monumental architecture, and sophisticated mathematical and astronomical systems. They also knew their onions as far as celestial clocks were concerned. It's evident that they understood the approximately 26,000-year cycle of the precession of the equinoxes – the cycle which marks the Earth's point of its wobbling axis move through the twelve signs of the zodiac – since they seemed preoccupied with a date that is over a thousand years after they just appeared to vanish.

The Milky Way represented the Great Mother to the Maya, and at its centre is a dark rift, which they believed represented her vagina. Astrophysicists now believe that a Black Hole exists within the centre of our Galaxy, and Black Holes are these still-mysterious 'singularities' in which space and time break down – they are trans dimensional portals to other universes. Our Galactic Black Hole is literally from where everything in our Galaxy, including us, originated. There is clear evidence that the Maya were aware of the Black Hole at the Galactic centre and they considered it to be intimately involved in cosmic evolution. The Galaxy, like the Earth, has an equator which divides its north and south hemispheres. On Earth we experience distinct field-effects on the two sides of the equator. For example, water spins down the drain counter clockwise north of the equator, and clockwise south of it. Hurricanes also spin in different directions depending on which side of the equator they are. Any spinning body will exhibit these effects. The Earth is a spinning body that exists within a spinning Galaxy. John Major Jenkins, in *Maya Cosmogenesis*, has this to say:

In general the solstice sun will be in conjunction with the great bulge of the Galactic Centre, which we understand as a rare conjunction of Earth, the local sun [ours] and the Galactic Heart. More importantly, however, in AD 2012 the solstice meridian will cross over the Galactic Equator.

He continues by emphasising the date as the Zero Point location as we 'cross the line', and believes that this is all about a field-effect energy reversal – our basic orientations will be inverted. But let's not worry about the direction our bath water might go down the plug-hole because even though the Maya named this loaded moment 'the Transformation of Matter' my guess is that it means what *matters* to us will be turned around. It has already started in fact, as we move into countdown. The old paradigms have run their course. We've gone about as far as we can go into materialism, corruption, violence, industrialisation and separation from nature and each other, not to mention abuse of the 'innocents' in our care – children and animals. All systems are on overload. Minds need to be spun in a different direction as we have completed a cycle. Coming to the end of a road of a particular expression of humanity means the opposite orientation begins to appear and a New Day dawns.

Round and round the celestial cogs turn, with everything repeating itself until awareness of the true meaning of life on Earth filters through into our consciousness, at which point we, as souls, are released from the cycle of karma and reincarnation. Until we realise that we are all individual expressions arising from the same Source, we continue to sleepwalk through the dream to which we have become so attached.

In the meantime, it appears as if we, as visitors on this once-beautiful way station we call Earth, or Gaia, have not respected our hostess and so she will probably not tolerate our presence for much longer. And she herself is going about her own business apparently. According to Gregg Braden, earth scientist and researcher into ancient wisdoms, we are being affected by something that is producing widespread low-level states of anxiety - a sense that something big is about to happen that goes beyond 9/11 and what is happening in the Middle East. He attributes this to changes in two parameters concerning the Earth's own 'physiology'. Firstly, the magnetic fields surrounding her are in rapid decline. They reached their peak about 2,000 years ago and are heading towards a zero point. This is not new in the Earth's history − it has happened 14 times during a period of 14½ million years, according to geological records. It heralds a reversal in the magnetic fields and from a human being's point of view, affects our own electromagnetic field, our sleep patterns, and our dream states and creates a sense of not really being anchored on the ground. Secondly, in 1899 a pulse, or heartbeat, was detected within the Earth herself. This was measured at 7.8 Htz (cycles per second) and communication systems and military weapons were based on what appeared to be a constant. But by the late 1980s this rate was increasing relatively rapidly. It affects our rhythms and cycles as well as our perception of time, and perhaps more significantly our own hearts are entrained to that of the Great Mother. Western scientists seem not to know the significance of these changes, but indigenous ancient wisdoms have known about this 'awakening to zero point' for ages.

Something has to change for certain. Our numbers have increased in the last 60 years from a sustainable 1 billion to a toxic nearly 7 billion.

We've poisoned her seas beyond recall and removed most of her lungs – the forests – like a cancer that ultimately murders its host. We have been asleep for too long, living in a dangerous dream. James Lovelock, the earth scientist responsible for the Gaia hypothesis, has forecast that it will take the Earth 100,000 years to recover from the damage that we have wreaked during the last 300 years. It's time to remember those imaginal buds and hold on to the words of the wise:

I say to you: "One must have chaos in oneself in order to give birth to a dancing star".
Friedrich Nietzsche

As the industrial revolution assisted in the propulsion of humanity towards its Armageddon, and the volume of human beings on the earth increased exponentially, there were other things besides fossil fuels that were being found in and on the ground. In the last 200 years archaeologists and anthropologists have revealed some astonishing facts as they attempted to piece our history together through their excavations, which has helped us begin to rub the sleep of some 2,000 years from our eyes. Evidence began to surface that has proved that ancient people around the world were not 'hairy barbarians', but had an understanding of medicine, astronomy, mathematics, geometry, architecture and building skills that were far in advance of our own. And what's more they knew that all things 'in Heaven and Earth' are interconnected. Their science and religion were two parts of the same whole.

There has always been what's known as Perennial Wisdom available to those with eyes to see, ears to hear and a mind to understand. This is a universal body of truths and values common to all peoples and all cultures – changeless, timeless knowledge about the nature of reality and the meaning and purpose of existence in a material world that is not the only reality. This fundamental wisdom has run like an underground stream throughout history, available to replenish the wells of those seeking true sustenance. Esoteric teachings have traditionally been handed down from master to student in the confines of the temples, the ashrams and other cloistered teaching schools. This secrecy was to ensure that the power of the ancient wisdom was not abused. It also enabled the initiate to explore his or her expanding awareness with guidance and in safety. This practice, even if it were available, is not an option for most of us. Sacred knowledge has now become widely available to us here in the West, but in order for this knowledge to be transformed into something more than just more information that we carry around, it is of utmost importance that we approach the subject with the sense of reverence and sacredness that this exploration deserves. It is not a game, a new fad or something to dabble in. It requires commitment and, most importantly, the right intention. Spiritual masters move quietly through the world, their energy is contained and they are aware of the power of this energy which is not about *who*, but *what* they really are. Simple acts, in the context of 'being spiritual', are just as important as great deeds.

Whilst archaeologists were busy revealing our collective history out there amongst the sands and ruins, we have been busy digging around in our own personal archives, releasing mummified feelings, paralysing patterns and frozen moments when the soul stood still in time and a protective armour was placed around it.

And one day the eyes of your spirit shall open
And you shall know all things.
The Essene Gospel of Peace

This day is now. And these times are pregnant with potential for making the changes required of us if we can stir ourselves out of our comfort zones. With the dawning of the Age of Aquarius – marking the beginning of yet another cosmic clock striking midnight – a new cycle begins. For just over 2,000 years we have been in the Age of Pisces, the final sign in the zodiacal circuit which takes some 25,000 years to complete as the equinoxes precess. Aquarius represents freedom and reform, liberation from process and packaging, understanding the laws of thought and the principles of things; it's about friendship, group life and shared ideologies.

And as the energies of this new cycle begin to filter in we have begun to realise that we have been straightjacketed by our tribal conditioning, our karmic residues, second- hand belief systems and genetic inheritance. Things are not what they have seemed to be. And, like the butterfly, we are emerging from our dark cocoon, discovering that we are free to fly after all A bit of help is useful as we cast off our history as a caterpillar and begin to know that everything has changed, whilst seeming to remain the same. Hopefully, these pages offer that little bit of help.

The subjects that follow are in a sort of structured sequence, although each chapter is complete on its own. There would not be much point, for example, in going to the chapter on psychics without first having understood about the aura and chakra system.

"I have no special gift. I am only passionately curious" Einstein modestly remarked. Since the journey of the soul cannot be a half-hearted affair, besides a burning curiosity and sense of exploration, a sensitivity and reverence is no more than it deserves, knowing that *whatever* is in front of us at this moment has significance. Hopefully this book will provide you with a useful map – but it is only a map – to help you explore the territory of your Self and what on Earth it is you are doing here. You can then make up your own mind about whether you want to carry on incarnating for another 26,000 years in this dream (fast becoming a nightmare) we believe to be reality, or to move on to the next experience in store for you as an expression of an infinitely Creative Mind.

How to use this book

We have become used to doing everything at speed. Unfortunately this approach does not work if real change is to be effected on behalf of the soul. Perhaps the first question to ask yourself is 'Do I really want to know and understand more about my Self?' ('Self' with a capital S denotes the Higher Self, the Soul or Psyche – the one that is You beyond the everyday personality or ego self). Quick fixes won't work in this department. Commitment (another word that is loaded with resistance) is essential if you **really** want changes to occur. Truth is like a multifaceted lantern. Its unchanging eternal flame may be observed through myriads of different panes, each reminding the soul of its Lightness, of its connection to the Heart of this lantern and of its eternal nature. An encounter with Truth generates a feeling in us, and this feeling results in a 'knowing'. This is the Aha! There is no other way to truly know, and no one can do this for us. Here are a few suggestions as to how you might help your Self.

Give yourself time and space to explore or 'test drive' each subject. This sends a message to your Self – like firing an arrow of intention – that you are open for discussion and from which there will be a response. The amount of attention you give to anything can be measured by effects. Time and thought spent on the creation of a garden enables something beautiful to appear. Little attention means it gets overrun with weeds and dead leaves.

Keeping a special notebook to write down your thoughts and reflections helps you crystallise in a more specific way the information that will start 'downloading' from your psyche, your soul, your higher Self or whatever you wish to call that Power beyond the personal. In this journal you might also like to record your dreams (more information from the Out There/In Here realms) and the changes you notice in your awareness.

You will find a '**Soul Focus**' box in each chapter. You can use this as a focus to take you into a contemplative space, or to use as a daily affirmation – something you say to yourself before you join the daily busyness of life. It will act as a compass, helping to keep you on course as you navigate the day.

There is also a **REMINDERS** section at the end of each chapter, which gives a summary of key points to re-mind you, literally, of the focus of each chapter. Take it slowly, don't practice too many new things all at once and give yourself time to digest and test the information.

And finally, under **Resources**, you will find books, websites and any other information you might need if you want to explore the topic in more depth.

It is also important to remember that nothing changes in isolation. When one thing moves, everything around it is obliged to move. Although there is now more general awareness of 'spiritual' matters, those who don't want to change may feel uncomfortable when we start using a 'new' vocabulary to interpret events. Don't make waves, just keep going. This may mean that some of your friends and acquaintances will change. You have just switched TV channels, so don't expend valuable energy trying to tune back into theirs. Soaps are fine, but that is all they are. Don't let anybody else define who and what you are, but instead set off on the path that will widen out into a road with an infinitely more interesting view.

That is at bottom the only courage that is demanded of us; to have courage for the most strange, the most singular and the most inexplicable that we may encounter. That mankind has in this sense been cowardly has done life endless harm; the experiences that are called 'visions', the whole so-called 'spirit-world', death, all those things that are so closely akin to us, have by daily parrying been so crowded out by life that senses with which we could have grasped them are atrophied. To say nothing of God.
Rainer Maria Rilke

Resources
The Reign of Quantity & Signs of the Times: **Rene Guenon** (Sophia Perennis)
Beyond 2012: **Geoff Stray** (Vital Signs Publishing)
Maya Cosmogenesis 2012: **John Major Jenkins** (Bear & Co)
A Monument to the End of Time: Alchemy, Fulcanelli & The Great Cross: **Jay Wedner and Vincent Bridges** (Aethyrea Books)
Awakening to Zero Point: **Gregg Braden** (Radio Bookstore Press)
www.timeofthesixthsun.com

chapter 1

minding the body

Understanding the Faithful Servant

Our own physical body possesses a wisdom
Which we who inhabit the body lack
Henry Miller

Before exploring the outer reaches of experience and beyond, it makes sense to understand more about the place from which we start any journey - whether inner or outer - in other words our body. It is the house in which we live, the vehicle we drive and contains the map we will be using as well as the territory we will be exploring. Within it is a space-time travel capsule, a magic child, a barometer, a pharmacy complete with pharmacist and a library full of archives. It is a universe, and also an atom within a universe. It contains over 50 trillion cells and is itself a cell within an incomprehensibly vast body. In short, it's a miracle, and without it we would have no idea what it means to be a human being.

If we think about our bodies at all, we may feel that they are just physical vehicles that keep us glued to the face of the earth, full of appetites and desires that continually need resisting or fulfilling. Religion has done a good job on conditioning us to believe that this miraculous container is what will lead us astray. 'Denial of the flesh' was advocated – which seems a bit senseless when you think about it. 'Sin' was another loaded word that was intimately involved with our poor, naturally instinctual, sensual, tactile bodies who were given instructions to keep eyes focused on heaven since that's where we'd be going when we vacated this temporary and cumbersome source of distraction. These days it would seem that bodies are staging their own revolt. They are certainly making their presence felt. Bodies and what they can get up to are out of their closets nowadays, but the pendulum has swung to its other extreme. It seems as if they are insisting on making their presence felt by increasing their volume in some people, a trend that is moving parallel with the whole 'body beautiful' cult of nipping and tucking the bits that don't fit the mind's image of how it 'should' look. How many friends (especially if you are a woman), if you asked them what they thought about their bodies would say they were happy with their size and shape?

How would you feel if you were a breast, continually hearing the message: "You are too small, I hate you," or a belly that is told: "You are big and revolting!". Criticism never makes anything feel good about itself. Every body is perfect in its own unique way, like your thumbprint, and what is more it is your greatest ally and essential companion on the path of spiritual exploration. Why? Because it lives in the present moment, in the Now. It gives you invaluable feedback on whether you are acting according to your soul purpose – or not. It informs you on your negative, destructive thoughts, shows you where you are storing unexpressed feelings and is the vehicle that can create transcendent experience as well as take you to the depths of your soul. It's your means for crossing from the level of physical 3D reality to the expanded conscious awareness of who you are BEYOND your body. It also houses the internal computer you need to connect to the quantum information highway whilst having your earthly experience.

Just **STOP** for a moment. Imagine what your body might look like if it were a car. Mini Cooper, 4 x 4, Porsche or 2nd hand car auction wreck?

What does the driver know about this car? Do you just jump in and hope it will get you from A to B as quickly as possible? Do you know and understand what goes on under the bonnet? Obviously it needs fuel, or you won't be going anywhere. Do you pay attention to the odd knock or rattle – or just hope that they will go away? Many people ignore the rising needle on the temperature gauge until steam gushes out of the bonnet and the car comes to a grinding halt. Perhaps you're trying to make a Porsche go through a ploughed field, or your 4 x 4 win on the race track? Maintenance work is only carried out because of a looming MOT. Let us now have a look at our vehicle, this body, and know that the attitude and awareness of the driver is essential for the smooth-running of its performance. This miracle we take so much for granted is our 'earthing' device. Every electrical gadget needs an 'earth' and we are no exception. If we are not earthed or grounded, we will not be able to handle the higher voltages – or energy charges – that we will access on our spiritual journey. It's all about frequencies, and recognising the different levels that exist beyond our every day 'channel'. Making sure we are properly earthed is a fundamental requirement in preventing blown fuses or becoming too airy-fairy.

Your body has its own consciousness. It has a mind of its own. It hears every word you say, or rather *feels* every thought you think, and translates those thoughts into reality. It metabolises your thoughts in the same way that it metabolises an egg sandwich – by turning them into something else. Each of the trillions of cells in your body has over 3 million different ways of communicating – creating an information super highway. Life and death at a cellular level are the same as night and day to us. Each cell that dies is replicated by a new cell stored with the identical information of the deceased, so a scar continues to be a scar even though the wound was experienced long ago.

Hair just keeps on growing, waste gets disposed of, hearts keep beating, baked potatoes get digested and every cell gets replaced when it has reached its cell-by date, all without our conscious knowledge. The you that is reading this will be totally different from top to bottom, head to toe, skin to bone cell in the space of seven years. There will not be one cell that is the same as it is at this moment. In his fascinating book, *The Biology of Belief*, Dr Bruce Lipton writes about his transformation from an atheistic scientist into a cell biologist who now knows that we are immortal, spiritual beings who exist separately from our bodies. His epiphany came – as it does with all major breakthroughs – with a super 'Aha!' moment when he realised that we are not frail biochemical machines controlled by our genes, but powerful creators of our lives and the world in which we live. This realisation emerged from the results of his research which produced evidence that genes and DNA do *not* control our biology, but are turned on and off by signals from outside the cell, which include the waveforms created by our positive and negative thoughts.

But let's now take a look at how the body speaks to us. Or rather how it responds to the messages it receives. Do we need a dictionary or glossary of terms? No, but we do need to recognise that the body works closely with the unconscious mind and the language of the unconscious mind is image and metaphor. You will probably not be able to access the body's messages and information through literal interpretation – it uses a different tongue.

One of the ways that the body speaks its mind is through posture. When a person is depressed, the body becomes lethargic, it wants to slump and hide. And when it feels challenged, or needing to protect itself, it acts on the unconscious instructions from the 'control tower' in the head to cross its arms, thus protecting the solar plexus – the power centre of the chakra system – from a perceived threat. Avoiding eye contact is another way that our bodies will maintain defence. To look someone in the eye may mean that they will 'see' who you are, and that is something that might feel frightening. Lie detectors register body signals to detect whether the truth is being told, since bodies never lie. Conversely, it is easy to identify people who feel 'on top of the world'. Their whole body looks as though it's enjoying being alive. And even though the world seems to be collapsing on the global stage, being around them is like taking a tonic.

The most obvious way the body speaks to us is by expressing its disease, its discomfort about the way we are living our lives, and about the thought patterns and emotions that are not in line with our soul's expression. We have been accustomed to rushing to the doctor to fix a symptom, but this effectively silences the messenger that's bringing an important message. When the car blows up, we rush to the garage to get it sorted, so that we can continue to hurtle from here to there. Perhaps it would be more useful to stop and wonder why your car overheats in certain situations, why it continually refuses to start because its battery is flat or why the windscreen wipers keep packing up when the weather gets extreme. By taking the approach that disease is a message from someone who is trying to get our attention and communicate that there is an imbalance that needs to be addressed, we will eventually uncover the *cause* behind the symptom. Obviously that's not a suggestion to take no action in emergencies.

Swedenborg, the 17th century Swedish visionary and scientist, said "Every natural physical manifestation has a relationship to a corresponding non-physical state of being". In other words the invisible and the visible, the unconscious and conscious, spirit and matter are all inextricably linked. Until relatively recently, science has embraced a different train of thought, subscribing to the Cartesian view that mind and body are separate, and that the universe and everything in it is a machine that will gradually run down – from Big Bang to Big Crunch. But there is radical change afoot, as some of the world's 'frontier' scientists observe something remarkable through their electron microscopes. In his inspiring book already mentioned, Bruce Lipton tells us that:

> *our new understanding of the Universe's mechanics shows us how the physical body can be affected by the immaterial mind. Thoughts, the mind's energy, directly influence how the physical brain controls the body's physiology. Thought 'energy' can activate or inhibit the cell's function-producing proteins via the mechanics of constructive and destructive interference ....*

In a nutshell, he's saying that through his research he has discovered that it is the membrane – or interface – of each of our trillions of cells that is responsible (or even response able) for our experience. In other words, we are informed *externally*, rather than genetically, and our cells take action based on the information that is filtered through their membranes. In any living cell there are ten thousand molecules of water for each molecule of protein. Our bodies consist mostly of water, so this massive presence in our biological make-up leads us to consider another man's research which would make it seem that science and magic are finally starting to shake hands after a several hundred year breakdown in communication.

An average adult body is 50 to 65% water - that's roughly 90 pints. Surprisingly, men are more watery than women. A man's body is 60 to 65 percent water, compared to 50 to 60 percent for a woman. In infants, the figure is a whopping 70 percent according to statistics compiled by the International Bottled Water Association. Water content differs throughout the body. Blood is made up of 83 percent water, bones are 22 percent water, and muscle is 75 percent water. Armed with these facts then, the work of Dr Masaru Emoto must grab our attention. He has been studying water around the planet and is the author of several books on the theme of the 'hidden' messages that water contains. Think of snowflakes. Every snowflake is completely unique, like our own fingerprint. Snow is frozen water – crystallised water in fact. The bee in Dr Emoto's bonnet concerns the nature of vibration, and how every vibration 'tells a story'. The vibration of guilt or hatred for example is totally different from that of love, kindness or compassion. His experiments with water, using frozen-water crystal photography, have revealed something astonishing. The crystalline components that make up water change their shape according to their 'environment'. (Is something repeating itself here?) So if you shout angrily at a glass of water, its crystals take on the 'shape' of anger, which is totally different from those in a different glass of water which have been treated with loving kindness. Think about the implications of this, living as you do, in a watery container. What messages are you sending to your water crystals? What shape – literally – might they be in?

Dr Emoto's experiments with prayer have also been fascinating. He was lecturing in Israel, at the Sea of Galilee, where he asked his audience all to send words of prayer from their hearts to a glass of tap water in his office in Tokyo. Japanese tap water, because of the processes it has been through, has no crystalline structures. After the prayer energy had been transmitted from Galilee, the Tokyo tap water was then frozen and photographed, and the results e-mailed to the lecture hall where his computer was ready to project the images on to a screen for all to see. The power of their prayers had indeed reached Tokyo and changed the shape of the tap water from an indistinct content to snowflake-like crystals. The conclusions that Dr Emoto has drawn from all his experiments are that illness is primarily caused by distortions of vibrations at the level of elementary particles. He suggests that if all of us just took a few seconds out of each day to put our hands together, close our eyes and say to ourselves, using our name, *I love you; I thank you; I respect you*; it would help our bodies feel more appreciated and less likely to express their feelings of unease through illness. Perhaps you would like to stop and try it now? And say it as if you really mean it.

Every part of our body gives us specific information about ourselves, if we care to pay attention. Because it can't actually spell out what's making it feel so uncomfortable, it will get our attention through the only language available for it to express itself – in symbols as symptoms. So hands, for example, speak not about holding kettles or gripping pens, but more about being 'in touch' with life. Hearts and the whole cardio-vascular system may tell us about 'going with the flow', being 'open hearted' or 'loving with all your heart'. The waste disposal department gives us clues about whether we hold on to old unwanted 'stuff' or shoot things through without digesting and assimilating. Feet and legs may let us know about stepping out into life and whether or not we have our feet on the ground. The body's job is to keep things in balance, or homeostasis, and it will keep going until the pressure creates a 'breakdown' at the weakest link.

Our bodies are obedient to the edicts coming from the control tower.

As you will see in the next chapter, thoughts actually create waveforms and it is these messages that are received and then become actualised. And now we know how – through the cell membrane and the effect on the crystalline structures of our watery ingredients. An anorexic continually tells her body "It's not safe to get bigger – I don't want to be a woman". The gut of someone worried and frustrated hears "I'm sick and tired of this situation" and produces an ulcer to prove the point. The eyes of someone stuck or confused may get the message, "I can't see things clearly" and need ever-stronger spectacles. Imagine what your body might do to draw your attention to imbalance if it was continually hearing the following messages:

> I feel heart-broken about his/her death
> I'm going out of my mind with worry/grief/fear
> I am dead on my feet
> Something is eating away at me
> I'll give him/her the cold shoulder
> Don't bite off more than you can chew
> He/she's a pain in the neck
> I can't see my way out of this
> I'm losing my grip
> I just don't want to hear what they are saying

It makes no difference whether these thoughts or statements about things going on in your life are conscious or unconscious. The waveform or 'energy' charge of each thought or feeling will be heard by the faithful body, and acted upon. Repetition of the same feeling (with the same energy charge or waveform) piles static onto static until it becomes an aggregation, or complex of energy held in the subtle, non-physical anatomy, which then downloads onto the body itself.

Matter and energy are entangled. The logical corollary is that the mind (energy) and body (matter) are similarly bound, though Western

medicine has tried valiantly to separate them for hundred of years.
Dr Bruce Lipton: The Biology of Belief

In order to understand our body's language, we need to know a bit about its make-up. There are three primary substances into which cells are formed – hard tissue, soft tissue and fluids. How do these messengers speak about their welfare?

Hard tissue cells make up our bones. Our bones are our core structure, the very skeleton on which everything else hangs. Our spinal column is the central axis of our being, supporting the rest of us. Millions of people suffer from back pain these days. What are their bodies trying to tell them about feeling unsupported? Certainly many people lead sedentary lives which do not encourage healthy posture, but perhaps there's something more behind that chronic lower back pain. What does a broken leg have to say about a deep-seated fear of stepping forward? What split at our core level is being manifested by the body to draw attention to a need that it is time to address?

Our bones are clothed with thoughts and emotions, and these are represented in the body by soft tissue and fluids.

Soft tissue is flesh, fat, muscle, nerves, skin and organs. The soft tissue of our bodies reflects our mental energy, our hidden mental patterns, attitudes, behaviour and experiences. We build fat to protect us from painful memories. Many women seem to have a disposition to accumulate weight round their hips and thighs. Is this their bodies making a literal statement about the need to protect a vulnerable sexuality? Might an increase in volume reflect body's message that it has to 'add weight' to its right to exist and make choices about what fuel is shovelled in under the influence of the control tower? What about tension and stiffness in the muscles? Those shoulders that feel as though they are made of concrete? Is it difficult to 'shoulder' all those life burdens? The mental stress that we impose on ourselves gives the body the message that it is necessary to be on continual 'red alert', ready to fight – brace the upper torso, tense the neck and shoulders – or flee, with buttocks, abdomen and thighs tightened for action. If this state of tension is maintained throughout the day, the muscles never get a chance to relax and release the toxic by-products of being on emergency stand-by. This is because the tension is not turned into action and the adrenaline just keeps on pumping, in accordance with the message from the mind that 'our safety is under threat'. Our skin is the interface between our inner and outer worlds. Eczema, allergic rashes and psoriasis may be telling us about the body's discomfort at our interaction with the outside world. Where this appears on the body also has significance.

Fluids represent our emotions. Like the planet we live on, over 75% of the human body is liquid: water, blood, urine, lymph, sweat, saliva, tears, endocrine and sexual secretions. We came into physical being in the waters within our mothers' wombs. Every single cell is bathed in fluids which move within us like a great sea, tides surging with our desires, waves of feelings and impulses. These fluids literally change their nature to reflect the emotions we are experiencing as Dr Emoto has now proved. Blood can 'freeze' with fear or become 'red and hot' with anger. It is our liquid life force. Hardening of the arteries can indicate a resistance to and hardening of our emotional energies. Clots in the cardio-vascular system may mean we are blocking the flow of life through us in some way. Lymph is the garbage collector of the body and swollen glands may be the body's way of saying, "I'm getting congested with toxic thoughts in here, so please pay attention". Dripping noses, weeping eyes – anything to do with the liquids in your body is related to the waveforms of your emotions, which are either blocked out or creating ripples of disturbance in your electromagnetic field which then impacts on your physical being.

Every aspect of your body will give you clues, in metaphoric language, that will direct you to what is needed to bring balance into your life. The respiratory system indicates your ability to breathe in life. The cardio-vascular system speaks about the flow of life. The lymphatic system is the messenger of waste and toxic thought forms, and the gastro-intestinal system will tell you about your ability to digest life itself. Your eyes might have something to say about what it is you are not looking at, and your back will tell you about what you might be trying to put 'behind' you and whether you feel supported.

Each hemisphere of the brain is connected with a side of the body and there is a neural crossover behind the eyes, which means the left brain is concerned with the right side of the body, and vice versa. So, discomfort expressed in the right side of the body may be connected to the masculine, yang aspect of your nature – the positive, out-going, active side of you – governed by the left brain. Anything amiss on the left hand side of your body, conversely, may be connected to the feminine, yin, motherly, receptive aspect of your Self – governed by the right brain.

> **STOP** and think about the times when you or somebody you know experienced any of the illnesses that have been mentioned. See if you can make the connection between the symptom and the cause that might lie behind it.

Our bodies also have the most phenomenal capacity for memory. Stored in the body-memory is everything from the colour of the shoes you wore at your third birthday party, to every car registration number in the supermarket car park you were in yesterday. It remembers how to ride a bike, drive a car and eat spaghetti, so that you do not have to learn these skills anew each time. It may also store the memories from previous life-times, and produce birthmarks where there were wounds before, or physical disabilities that echo past body trauma.

There are many well-documented stories of the experiences of transplant patients who receive not only a 'new' organ, but some of the psychological traits and habits of the deceased donor. This will be mentioned again later but perhaps the strangest story of them all is that of a young girl who began to have nightmares about a murder after her heart transplant. Her dreams were so vivid that they led to the capture of the murderer who killed her heart donor.

Something like the trunk of a tree, our body stores the memory of what happens to us year by year, moment by moment. If you cut through the trunk of a tree, you will find it has rings which indicate its annual growth. You can also tell from the rings whether the year was a good one for the tree, with plenty of rain and sun to encourage its growth, or whether conditions were hard and difficult. As with a tree, our early years of growth are instrumental in forming the nature of who we become later in life. If we did not have a very good reception on arrival, then we may not have felt safe in coming fully into our bodies. If our first relationship with others left us feeling controlled, abandoned or not worthy of love, we will experience the same challenges in our adult relationships. What happened to us as children is registered, and our body will respond physically if those woundings continue to be reinforced.

Remembering that we are spiritual beings having a human experience, and not the other way around, helps us keep a more balanced perspective on the nature of this earthly 'reality'. Bringing about balance in a physical world of opposites is the soul's ultimate objective. What could be more opposite than physical bodies and souls? So rather than denying our bodies, they need to be recognised as essential vehicles for our soul's experience. We have become obsessed with the power of mind and intellect and their ability to accumulate more and more skills and information. This has not only led to a distorted understanding of our own bodies, but the body on whose face we have had the privilege to walk – Gaia – who now, if looked at from space looks like a dog with mange, since her natural coverings have been destroyed and her waters polluted.

So it's time to value and respect these physical vehicles whatever shape and age they are, as they are like faithful servants who will respond to consideration and sensitivity to their needs and requirements.

Soul Focus
My body is the vehicle for my soul's experience on Earth. It is a living, conscious being through which my soul may experience the physical universe.

REMINDERS ....

- Be aware of how and where you hold your feelings. Where do you feel grief or guilt? Is there any anger or resentment tucked away in your upper thighs or clenched teeth? What is your blocked nose trying to tell you?
- Notice how you walk and sit. Be more conscious of your body rather than treating it like a robot.
- When you eat your meals, don't do it standing in the kitchen or watching TV – pay attention to the fuel going into your tank, ask your body what it feels like digesting and be mindful as you eat.

Resources:

Why People don't Heal and How They Can: **Carolyn Myss** (Harmony Boos)

Your Body Speaks Your Mind: **Deb Shapiro** (Piatkus)

The Biology of Belief: **Dr Bruce Lipton** (Cygnus Books)

Messages from Water: **Dr Masaru Emoto** (Hay House)

The Endorphin Effect: **William Bloom** (Piatkus Books) www.williambloom.com

Frontiers of Health: **Dr Christine Page** (C W Daniel & Co)

9 Ways to Body Wisdom: **Jennifer Harpur** (Harpur Collins)

Everything you always wanted to know about your body

But so far nobody's told you: **Chris Thomas & Diane Baker** (Capall Bann Publishing)

Heal Your Body A_Z: The Mental Causes for Physical Illness & the Way to Overcome Them: **Louise Hay** (Hay House)

Your Body's Many Cries for Water: **Dr F Batmaghelidj** (Global Health Solutions Inc.)

chapter 2

meditation

Contemplating Your Navel

If you want to find God,
hang out in the space between your thoughts.
Alan Cohen

The Great Eastern Takeaway

The Beatles did it for my generation. Suddenly it seemed as if we were all looking for gurus to teach us how to do this thing called 'meditation'. Waves of strange Eastern words flooded the vocabularies of spiritual seekers. Chakras appeared, yoga, kundalini, ashrams and karma, on the same menu as korma, vindaloo and poppadoms. If you could scrape the money together, you'd trek to the other side of the world to seek out the elusive Meaning of Life, returning in sandals, with a *bindi* dot to mark the spot of your ajna chakra, and chanting Oms at every given opportunity. It was mostly all very positive and marked a major post-war paradigm shift. And although experimentation with altered states of consciousness careened about like a wild, riderless horse, at least the Church began to lose its grip on the mandate for our souls, and we were beginning to wake up to what is what and what was definitely not what. The Kali Yuga was drawing to a close. But the old powers do not give up their thrones easily.

With freedom in the air, rules and regulations were broken, changed, ignored, recapitulated. Of course there were casualties from acid–fuelled explorations, and addictions and substance-dependency emerged as part of the shadow of the 'New' Age. As things became lighter, an equal amount of dark appeared both in individuals and on the global stage.

Suddenly we became more aware not only of freedom in the air, but of the air itself. It might sound like a superfluous comment, but breathing in and breathing out is another of the millions of things we take for granted and without which we surely wouldn't be here. One of the most valuable practices we acquired at the Eastern Takeaway was a consciousness of the value and abilities of our breathing patterns to change many things in our lives. We learned – or rather remembered – that our breath is our inspiration for life on earth. It's the first thing that happens when you arrive and the last thing you do on departure. Breathing. As well as being your constant, unrecognised, trusty companion, it also has other applications besides transporting clean and dirty air in and out of your nostrils. Becoming aware of how you breathe opens up more than the alveoli in your lungs. It gives you the power not only to live in the world of the five senses, but also to experience life from a deeper, wider and fuller perspective of consciousness. Once you recognise that breathing not only keeps you alive, but also makes you *feel* more alive, you can use it as a vital tool to access your inner world. Using your breath, you can get in touch with the stillness that is always there beneath the choppy and turbulent waters of the 'market place'.

Let's look at how this freely available commodity can improve your well-being and be used as a tool for a more alive body, mind and soul.

Breathing and Your Body

If you have ever watched a baby breathe, you will have noticed that its little diaphragm moves rhythmically and peacefully (when it's asleep), using the entire capacity of its tiny lungs to re-oxygenate its blood, its abdomen expanding and contracting like a balloon. Now go and have a look in the mirror, and watch yourself breathe. What happens to your shoulders? Do they look as if they are attached to your ears in some invisible way? Does the air ever get a chance to go right down to your belly? A baby breathes naturally and freely, but as soon as the stresses of life begin to thrust into its awareness, its breathing will become shallow and restricted by the fears and anxieties it will face concerning love and safety. Our breathing is influenced by our moods, and our moods are mostly influenced by our state of mind. In fact you have your own personal weather system operating within you on a daily basis. The simple act of paying attention to your breath can prevent an emotional hurricane from spinning you into overwhelm, or it can help you focus and be calm before confronting a difficult situation. Our bodies also suffer from the effects of our attention always being focused on what is happening around us and never on what is going on within us.

There's a way of breathing
that's a shame and a suffocation
and there's another way of expiring,
a love breath,
that lets you open infinitely.
Jelaluddin Rumi

Every emotion and significant thought has an associated breathing pattern. When you are stressed, anxious or fearful you breathe in shallow, rapid breaths – sometimes hardly breathing at all. This is the body's response to having the fight or flight button pressed. You might heave a sigh of relief when the tension has passed, which is the cue for the body to relax again, but most of the time you just pile tension onto tension. This means you become used to breathing with only the top part of your lungs – and your body suffers. Your heart starts to struggle to cope with the situation, your food doesn't get digested properly, your blood does not get fully oxygenated and, even worse, you remain in emotional tension. Holding your breath enables feelings to be controlled, but the healthier option is to consciously breathe through them rather than over the top of them.

> **STOP** now and put one hand on your upper chest, and the other hand on your belly. Close your eyes and think of a recent situation which made you feel upset or agitated. Notice which of your hands is moving in response to your breathing ...... now let the memory of that situation dissolve. Bring to mind a situation, a place or event where you feel calm and relaxed and glad to be alive. Notice any difference?

Breathing and Your Mind

The mind cannot penetrate meditation;
where mind ends, meditation begins.
Osho

How could breathing possibly affect your mind? Minds have become our masters, telling us that we need to become more and more efficient. Filling us with circling repetitive thoughts, we get furrowed brows with tension and anxiety in the solar plexus. It has been said somewhere that we think over 30,000 thoughts a day, and 75% of those thoughts we thought yesterday. Not the most creative use of an incredibly sophisticated piece of equipment. We can get ourselves into a state of fear and resistance at the drop of a hat. Stuck in traffic, your mind can give you a major production about the consequences of being late. Tense and anxious, you stay stuck in the jam. Thinking about doing your income tax returns, writing that letter, making the phone call you keep putting off or doing something that you are dreading can encourage your mind to produce endless excuses, or come up with worst-case scenarios. By doing some conscious breathing, you can shift the frame of reference and choose what you want to think. At that moment you have gone beyond your mind. Take a breath in, and then a big sigh out. Say to yourself .... "I breathe in......... .and I breathe out .... I breathe in peace ...... I breathe out tension .... I breathe in ...... peace .... And I breathe out ..... tension."

Just focusing on breathing in peace, and breathing out tension for a few moments allows the mental static to calm, and you will find yourself operating from your centre, rather than the periphery of your circle. Practise conscious breathing in moments of thought-induced stress, fear, anxiety or procrastination, and notice what happens.

Breathing and Your Soul

Breathing and spirit have been synonymous for literally ages. Perhaps we could say that the soul is like the axis of a wheel. Each spoke of the wheel represents an aspect of our personality, a role we play or a mask we wear. Jung referred to these aspects as 'sub personalities'. When you are with your father, are you still his Little Girl? In front of your Team Manager are you still the Boy at School? Who are you with your own children? When the going gets difficult do you become The Dreamer, or The Organiser? Victim, DIYer, photographer, computer buff, artist, mother, company director, yoga teacher or activist – whatever ....

> **STOP** for a moment and think of a few of the characters that are involved in your own personal soul drama. I wonder how many you will find?

All these roles make up the personality of who you are, but who is the wearer of the hats, the One behind the roles?

Here is the axis of your wheel. The central core of your Being and who you truly are. Whilst you may spend more time and energy focused on one or other of these roles – parent or business person for example – the nature of the One behind remains constant. By becoming aware of that One behind, you can play all your parts in a different, more soul-full way, and this is where breathing comes in. Conscious breathing is the key to connecting with that still, small voice that cannot be heard above the cacophony of sound that fills our daily lives and is generated by the actors on our stages. All your different roles may be played with the guidance that is to be found at the axis of your wheel. When you feel you are getting too caught up in one of your roles, conscious breathing will remind you of the central axis of the wheel – that place where you have a wider, wiser perspective.

Of course you have thoughts (30,000 a day), but are you your thoughts? You have emotions too, but are you your emotions? You also have a body, but are you your body? Minds think, emotions feel and bodies sense, but the soul simply 'knows'. Knowing about this 'knowing' is the perennial wisdom referred to in the Introduction which remains a constant stream underneath the turbulent waves of history, available to those looking for meaning in the human experience. This wisdom goes beyond the confines of religious dogma and is sometimes referred to as '*gnosis*' from the same Greek word meaning 'knowledge'. Those who follow this path were – and still are - called 'Gnostics'. A Gnostic is a spiritual mystic who believes that knowing yourself fully enables you to know 'god' directly, without the mediation of rabbis, priests, bishops, imams, or other religious officials. Gnosticism was alive and well long before the advent of the great monotheistic religions that appeared on the scene and crushed it out of existence. Gnostics, the knowers, were initiated into their knowing in the Mystery Schools – the most revered religious tradition of antiquity. The initiate became endowed with special knowledge in divine matters, and an expert on theology and cosmology. They practised sexual equality and in their meetings they would throw lots to see who would lead the current session, with women equal to men in their ability to guide and instruct the group. In the words of John Lamb Lash:

"Mysteries were initiation rituals of a voluntary, *personal,* and secret character that arrived at a change of mind through *experience* of the sacred." (My italics) This experience renewed and recharged the initiate through the revelation of some kind of supernatural luminosity – a Mystery light – that was interactive with the experiencer. This is similar to the radiant Shakti of Brahma and the White Tara in the Buddhist tradition – a feminine divinity clothed in 'animated currents of white light'.

Although the Gnostics were persecuted out of existence and the wisdom of the Mystery Schools claimed as heresy, this stream of perennial wisdom has not been lost. It is emerging once again, thanks to contemporary 'heretics'. They are helping us dismantle our old hierarchical, patriarchal belief systems on this stage, which we believe to be the only reality and where we have given away our right to make choices to others.

When you rid yourselves of guilt and shame
And tear off your old rags and trample them beneath your feet
Like children.
Then you'll see the Son of He who is the living God.
The Gnostic Gospel of Thomas
(part of the Nag Hamadi Scrolls discovered in Egypt in 1947)

One of the keys to becoming a 'knower' yourself is by expanding your awareness beyond the limits of your everyday self to into the Oneness that is the sky beyond the clouds - and conscious breathing will help you. It will also be doing your body a favour by supplying it with more energy and therefore helping it to keep healthy. You will be able to consciously influence your thoughts and feelings and make considered rather than reactive responses to a situation. To further convince you of the need to pay more attention to what is happening between your nostrils and your lungs, consider the following uses to which your breath might be put:

- **Building up energy:** Breathing can energise your body by building a charge of energy, which is created with sharp inhalation and exhalation techniques, sometimes known as the 'Breath of Fire'.
- **Directing attention**: Breathing can help you focus and direct attention to specific parts of yourself. This is useful for helping pain and discomfort.
- **Accessing information**: Controlled breathing allows you to gain information from the unconscious mind more easily.
- **Altering thoughts and feelings**: Changing the way you breathe

allows you to change your thoughts and feelings.

- **Changing consciousness**: Controlled breathing, as used in some meditation practices and certain forms of therapy, induces a shift to a non-ordinary state of consciousness.
- **Linking conscious and unconscious mind**: Breathing provides a gateway between the conscious mind and the deep sea of the unconscious mind – the world wide web of information.

Yes, there's more to breathing than meets the eye. Becoming aware of it brings you right into your body in the here and now and immediately anchors you in the centre of your wheel with a fundamental awareness of the rhythmic flow of life.

All journeys start here.

Soul Focus
Breathing is the key to peace and stillness.
In peace and stillness, I am my soul.

On the way to the topic that this chapter is all about – meditation – there is something else that needs to be understood, and that is the nature of our minds.

Where is your mind actually located? If our bodies have minds of their own, then is there an overseeing – 'overthinking' – mind? We are taught that thinking is a function that takes place in the head, the home of the super computer, our brain. But Dr Rupert Sheldrake, a frontier scientist recently awarded a Scholarship by Cambridge University for his work in parapsychology and psychical research, is suggesting that our minds extend far beyond our brains. They stretch through fields that link us to our environment and to each other. He calls this process of the influence of like upon like through time and space, 'morphic resonance', and suggests that:

Descartes believed the only kind of mind was the conscious mind. Then Freud reinvented the unconscious. Then Jung said it's not just a personal unconscious but a collective unconscious. Morphic resonance shows us that our very souls are connected with those of others and bound up with the world around us.

We could call it wireless technology. Forgetting that we have these astonishing internal communication abilities, we have created the external tools which mirror our internal capabilities.

In its bony capsule (remembering that bone is as tough as steel and as light as aluminium) sits The Brain. And whilst we might assume that we think with a single mind, this is not the case. There are twin 'travellers' living beside one another in our cranium – the left and right hemispheres of our brain – and they each have very different functions and very different ways of experiencing, translating and storing information about the world. Usually one of the two hemispheres is dominant, and in our current society we have been encouraged to use and trust the processes of our left brain whilst referring to input from the right sides of our minds as 'only imagination'. This is an unbalanced view of the world.

To simplify, imagine that you are about to do a jigsaw. The right brain holds the picture on the lid of the box, while the left brain sorts out the pieces and works out what bits go where. Obviously you need the input from both of these two working together, to complete the puzzle.

Unfortunately we do not usually allow these partners to collaborate in making sense of the puzzle that is life, and we value the functions of one side more than the other. Perhaps we have become overly concerned with sorting out which bit goes where without holding the overall vision of our lives. Or we may live 'in the clouds' and be totally out of touch with the practicalities that have to be dealt with – so involved with the dream that we forget that bills have to be paid and doors have to be locked.

Listing the different functions may give you an idea of which side of your brain you use predominantly ...

LEFT HEMISPHERE:

Masculine   Proof through Logic

Active	Sequential	Classified	Judges	Detail
Rational	Labels	Time-conscious	Factual	Analytical
Enjoys puzzles and crosswords		Verbal	Outward	Relativity
Looks at cause and effect		Linear Looks at the view and counts the trees		

Qualities: Day Fire Heaven Sun   Spirit YANG

RIGHT HEMISPHERE:

Feminine   Proof through Experience

Passive	Inward	Fantasy	Colour	Feeling
Creative	Form & movement		Receptive	Intuitive
Sees the whole picture		Timelessness	Likes metaphor & pun	
Pattern, image & symbol		Sensory	Emotional	
Sense of meaning and purpose				

Qualities: Night   Water   Earth   Moon Soul YIN

Both of these twins think and reason – but as you can see – in very different ways, and it is obvious which one of these we are educated and encouraged to use predominantly. Whilst there are obvious advantages to the route we have followed, it makes it clear how we have become disconnected from our souls. The more we develop our left-brain faculties, at the expense of the right, the more separate we see ourselves from the world and all it contains. Indigenous cultures – the Aborigines for example – have used and developed the faculties of their right mind, rather than the literal, analytical abilities of the left. They do not perceive time in a linear way, but see it as either 'Dreamtime' or 'Now'. They also use the psychic super highway – the Universal Energy Field – to communicate non-verbally with one another, and to perceive weather, effect healing and locate sources of food and water. In other words, they are totally in tune with, and part of, their environment.

The potential available to us if we were to use both these two hemi-spheres in our head with equal respect, is literally mind-boggling. Like two leads from a battery, one positively the other negatively charged, when they are connected real power is activated. One of the many reasons why it is important to recognise the different functions of each side is that the left-brain has an extremely active critic, which is always ready to mut-ter "It's only your imagination" or "You're making it up" when your soul is attempting to communicate. Only your imagination? What a judgement against the most creative, inventive and diverse resource we have avail-able to us. It was Einstein, no less, who said that imagination was more important than knowledge, and he should know since his ground-break-ing theories floated in when he was relaxing in his bath.

Those who operate almost exclusively in the left-brain mode have difficulty in letting go of the need to rationalise everything that happens to them. They do not trust their feelings as valuable guides and their intu-itive faculty is marginalised. They may deny the value of this faculty, but experience vivid and bizarre dreams as the soul tries to catch the attention of the personality. Often the denial of the value of the imagination and its partner, intuition, stems from early childhood experiences where feelings were things to fear because they overwhelmed or that stories, drawings and imaginary games were not seen to be powerful fertiliser for the child's mind. When we are small we have wonderful, unfettered imagina-tions. Perhaps this was not fostered or encouraged if the focus of our par-ents was on educational accomplishment, where being top in maths or sci-ence was more important than writing stories or poems. Our educational systems are based on the storage of facts and figures – working things out, logical conclusions, cause and effect and tremendous value is accorded to those who are skilled in mastering the mind in this way. They are essen-tial and valuable skills to help us navigate this plane of existence, but they are only part of the story.

The soul is not interested in statistical proof of anything.

As we turn **IN**ward (for we are surely not going to find our souls on the outside) we must respectfully ask the left brain to take time off (which it will not always agree to do) whilst we listen for information coming from outside the box. We need to lose our mind, so to speak, and come to our senses, and from there we can move beyond the issues of right and wrong (or left), black and white, good and bad, into that place where there is no judgement, no words – only experience – *your* experience.

What lies behind us and what lies before us
are tiny matters compared with what lies within us.
Oliver Wendell Holmes

Millions of words have been written on the subject of meditation and there are possibly equally as many ways of getting to the same place. The thing to remember is that it is not about DOING anything. Meditation is a state of BEING. We have become accomplished human Doings (left brain again). What is it like to be a human Being?

In a meditative state, you will experience a distinct change in the whole atmosphere and vibration of your body. It is as if your body dissolves as your focus becomes internalised. With the help of conscious breathing, your brain waves slow down from beta (the level of wakeful, decision-making consciousness) to alpha, which is the frequency of light trance and day-dreaming. You develop a different perspective on the problems of life after you have taken them into – or rather set them free - in meditation. Sometimes the things that mattered to us before seem to become inconsequential and not really as important when they are considered from a place of balance and alignment. This place of alignment is sensed only when your body is calm and relaxed and your mind has become still – which is the essence of meditation.

Meditation is not about going to sleep. It is about allowing your body to feel calm and relaxed, but your mind is focussed and aware. Focused on what? Focused on nothing. "Nothing?" says the left brain. "Impossible! How can you focus on nothing?"

This is a classic example of the way the left brain sabotages anything that threatens its autonomy, and it will probably try to continue sabotaging by interrupting the process with intrusive, incessant thoughts – like a child that wants attention. Buddhists call this the 'monkey mind'. When you recognise this as simply the left brain trying to retain its control, doing anything in order not to 'disappear', then you can move away from the struggle of wrestling with these thoughts, and just wait for them to settle.

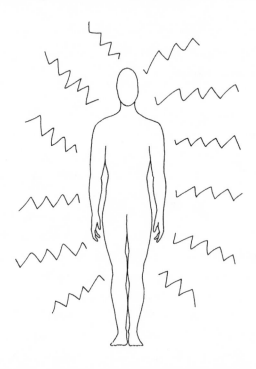

Before meditation : energy field full of static

Because your mind thinks it is essential for survival in the physical world, it is at first reluctant to get out of the driving seat. It insists on popping thoughts into the space you are creating. Because space and nothingness are anathema to the mind and ego, help is needed at this moment, and this is where conscious breathing is your ally. In fact you have two allies to help you focus on nothing – breathing is one of them, and the other is your posture.

It may be possible to meditate in a crumpled heap, and also lying down, but it is more effective when you become aware of yourself 'sitting like a mountain'. This means finding a chair that supports your back and is reasonably comfortable. Feet need to be on the ground with no crossed legs and hands resting on your thighs. Or you might prefer to use the traditional yogi position of sitting on a cushion or meditation stool with your legs folded in front of you.

The important thing is to have a sense of a central core or axis in your body, then with your head resting comfortably on the top of that axis you can begin to become aware of your breathing. All you have to DO is notice the breath moving in and out of your nostrils – this is the beginning of taking your attention inwards. Just breathing and knowing that you are breathing. That is all. As your attention begins to let go of the external world you may begin to notice which parts of your body are holding tension.

Mind is like a candle flame; unstable, flickering, constantly changing, fanned by the violent winds of our thoughts and emotions. The flame will only burn steadily when we can calm the air around it; so we can only begin to glimpse and rest in the nature of mind when we have stilled the turbulence of our thoughts and emotions.

Sogyal Rinpoche: The Tibetan Book of Living and Dying

Once your body has been taken care of, the next department that will need – probably demand – attention will be your mind. There's little point in ordering your mind not to think, this just creates conflict or rebellion. Like saying "Don't think about ice cream" – what happens? The best approach is just allow it to think its thoughts and let it settle itself. Imagine watching a stream that has become stirred up and muddy – you don't jump in to try and make the stream clearer, you just sit on the bank and wait. There is nothing to be done because whatever you do will make it more muddy. Just watch and wait.

As your thoughts settle themselves, start to be aware of how your mind works. The moment you become aware of the functioning of your mind, you realise that you are not the mind, and that this very awareness means you have gone beyond the mind – you have become the witness. You no longer identify yourself with that thought – you are the thinker of the thought. You have moved your awareness from the foreground to the background, from the clouds to the sky itself. The more aware you become, the more you will be able to see the gaps between the experience and the thoughts or words. Between two words there is always a gap. Between two notes of music there is always a gap, a silence. That silence is always there but you have to be really aware and attentive to feel it.

After meditation : energy field in harmony and open to receive

The more 'aware' you become, the slower the mind becomes. The less aware you are, the faster the mind is. It is always relative. Heightened awareness means that the mind slows down and the gaps between the thoughts widen. As you come to understand the subtle workings of your mind, you will perceive a great sense of awareness welling up inside, which is accompanied by a feeling of intense joy. This feeling of joy which comes from meditative experiences is the original joy of consciousness in its pure form, without attachment to any thing. Meditation is sometimes referred to as a state of nothingness – or no-thing-ness. So sitting like a mountain, with your body relaxed and calm, just noticing your breath move gently in and out through your nostrils, you become the observer of your thoughts.

Most schools of meditation state the necessity for consciousness to be focused between and behind the eyes. This is the location of the pineal gland, and is the place of the third eye or brow chakra – the centre associated with insight, intuition and inner vision. It is also known as the 'Throne of the Soul' or 'Gateway to the Void'. It is an appropriate place to review events and issues with the discernment of an observer, without judgement and with the clarity that comes from that one still voice.

Don't go outside your house to see the answers,
My friend, don't bother with that excursion.
Inside your body there are flowers.
One flower has a thousand petals.
That will do for a place to sit.
Sitting there you will have a glimpse of beauty inside the body and out
*   of it before gardens and after gardens.*
Kabir (c.1440-1518)

Different Ways to Meditate

As already stated, there are many different routes to the same destination and you need to find the one most suitable for you. Some people find it easier and a more powerful experience to meditate with others in a group. You may prefer it to be a solitary experience. Whatever you choose is really only a training for approaching every moment of life as a meditation, conscious awareness that provides a bridge between our different 'worlds'.

Centering Prayer: This way of meditating has its roots in the fourteenth century mystical Christian work, The Cloud of Unknowing. A holy word was chosen and repeated in the mind – similar to the mantra that is used in Eastern traditions, and whenever attention drifts, you bring it back to the word. This repetition creates a vehicle to move you beyond the stuff of everyday concerns and acts like an arrow to penetrate the 'cloud of forgetfulness' – through the gap – and into the sky itself. The word you choose these days might be Peace, Love, Thank You or Tenderness, a word that has a beneficent universal connotation and meaning for you personally that is linked to the highest good of all. Just keep on repeating the word, until the word itself falls away and you become the quality, the sense of the word, as it infuses your being.

Holy Moment Meditation: After you have gone through the preparation of posture, breathing and body relaxation, bring to mind the memory of one of those moments when you felt a deep sense of connection. Perhaps it was a sunset, the smile of a baby, a view from a cliff top or a special moment with a loved one … involve all your senses in this recollection ….. remembering how that sense of being connected infused your whole being. Then let the memory go but just stay with the feeling that was linked to that moment and let it become your meditation. Meditation, as you've probably gathered by now, is all about going beyond what we perceive to be reality.

Walking Meditation: Sometimes our minds just will not settle down, especially if there has been some bad news or there is a major event on the horizon. In a situation like this you might like to try the practice of walking meditation that has been popularised by the wonderful Vietnamese Buddhist monk, Thich Nhat Hanh. Find somewhere quiet to walk, preferably in natural surroundings, although it works on pavements too. Begin by focusing on your breathing, as usual. Then notice the movements of your feet – each one lifting, moving forward in space, and then coming down again. Then let your awareness expand beyond the physical sensation of walking to the environment around you. Keep a quarter of your awareness on breathing and the other three quarters on the space around you – everything you see, hear, feel and smell. If thoughts from the left brain intrude, don't pay them any attention, they will pass. Just concentrate on the rhythm of your breathing and each movement of your feet, taking you into a different awareness.

There are plenty of other ways, too, which don't involve sitting and contemplating your navel, and can be done wherever you are. Gardening – if you're lucky enough to have one – painting, drawing, anything creative, and even polishing your furniture or cleaning your car can take you into that place where time seems to disappear and somehow you feel more expanded. While it may seem as if these are 'active' ways to meditation, they can take you through that gap, beyond the activity. Runners and joggers say they experience this when they get into their 'rhythm'.

There is one really important point to remember here, and that is when you have been in a different state of awareness, however that might have come about, it is important to remember to 'earth' yourself again, or return your energy system to Everyday Maintenance level. Once you have become familiar with its practise, it can be done in the wink of an eye, simply by your intention.

Coming Down to Earth

- Be aware of your feet on the ground
  Imagine invisible roots growing from the soles of your feet down into the Earth
- Draw the Earth's energy up through your roots into your feet and legs – the root chakra
- Get a sense of, or imagine, it centralising at a point between your legs
- Using your in breath, draw the Earth's energy up through the next two chakras to the Heart
- Now focus on a point of Light way above your head. Imagine this as your Soul Star, your link to the Divine Mind or Great Spirit
- Allow the light from this now to come down through the top of your head, through the Third Eye and Throat centres to the Heart
- The energies of Heaven and Earth come together at the Heart, melding and merging to create a column of Light, a column which

is anchored in the Earth and connected to your Soul Star
- This column of Light, which is energy and information, brings balance, guidance and stability.

The point of meditation is to shift your awareness. Throughout the ages Gnostics, shamans and sages have all used it as a way to bring about a change in consciousness, which in turn brings about the realisation that the physical world, with all its opposites of day and night, right and wrong, rain and shine, is not the only reality. We are having this human experience in order to reach the understanding that we, with our bodies, minds and souls are the ultimate paradox - dense earthly bodies and also multidimensional, non-physical beings that are all expressions of a Divine Mind.

You yourself are your own obstacle - rise above yourself.
Hafiz

Soul Focus
Meditation takes you to the place where you experience your
Soul being and its connection to Spirit

REMINDERS….
- The more you practise meditation, the easier it becomes to move through the gap into expanded awareness.
- Make meditation part of your daily routine – even if you can only manage 10 minutes. Five minutes of attention to your meditation is more valuable than 50 minutes of mental wandering.
- Make a space that is sacred for you. Light a candle, or put a flower in a vase. A ritual, however seemingly insignificant, if done with intention, marks a transition from one state of being to another. Make sure you will not be interrupted. Turn off your phones. Even

yogis find it difficult to meditate at a railway station.

- Try different methods of meditation until you find one that suits you. Using music such as Gregorian chant, Bach or Mozart can also take you into spaciousness by just following the notes. Focusing on the flame of your candle might be another way of going within. Sitting with your back to a tree, or under the stars or anywhere in nature, just breathing and being away, can also open up the sense of connection to what is more than your individual self.

- Make sure you are not too tired when you begin your meditation practice, and also not too warm and comfortable, or you'll go to sleep.

- If you are in emotional pain or turmoil and cannot get outside to do the Walking Meditation, yet find it impossible to sit and be still because the thoughts and feelings just seem to intensify, then perhaps it is time to pay attention to how much time is spent running away from anxieties and uncomfortable feelings. Sticking with it, and allowing yourself the time and space to really feel the emotions that frighten you, enables you to become the observer of your feelings, rather than the victim of them. This helps us make friends with frightening feelings and enables us to transform the fear that we will be overwhelmed by them.

- Don't try too hard! It will happen when you let it BE.

Resources:

Heart of Wisdom, Mind of Calm: **Christina Feldman** (Element Books)

Peace is Every Step: **Thich Nhat Hanh** (Rider & Co)

Moon Over Water: **Jessica MacBeth** (Gateway)

The Tibetan Book of Living and Dying: **Sogyal Rinpoche** (Rider & Co)

Lucid Living: **Timothy Freke** (Books for Burning)

www.timothyfreke.com

The Gnostic Bible: **edited by Willis Barnstone & Marvin Meyer** (New Seeds)

Not in His Image: **John Lamb Lash** (Chelsea Green Publishing)

chapter 3

auras and energy fields

There's More To You Than Meets The Eye

The aura given out by a person or object
is as much a part of them as their flesh.
Lucien Freud

If you were able to see your aura, you would see a pulsating, shimmering, multicoloured energy 'field' surrounding your body. Observed by mystics, artists and healers throughout the ages, it was described by the Pythagoreans of ancient Greece as a 'luminous' body, a light body. Everything that has an atomic structure has an energy field. Everything from a pea to a planet has an aura. Because the energy of animate life is more vibrant, it is easier to sense the energy field of a chipmunk than it is to sense that of a chair.

Before going into more detail about the nature of your own personal aura, it is useful to put it into a wider context. Like the student fish that asks its teacher, "What is this sea that people talk about?" we swim about in a 'space' that supports and nourishes us and connects us with everything else in the sea. One of the names for this sea that we find ourselves in is the Universal Energy Field. It is a vast ocean of energy radiating in all directions. It is the ultimate information highway. Your link to this, your computer or telephone, is already installed – it's just a matter of activating the line.

The flute of interior time is played whether we hear it or not....
It penetrates our thick bodies, it goes through walls –
Its network of notes has a structure as if a million

Suns were arranged inside ...

I don't know if Robert Bly was referring to the Universal Energy Field when he wrote these words, but he might as well have been.

Einstein proved that energy and matter are interchangeable. Matter is simply energy that has slowed down. Forms are built from energy, they collapse and then re-form. Newtonian physics are based on the observation of solid, everyday objects of ordinary experience and they provided us with tried and tested laws for predicting physical behaviour. But as physicists began to investigate into the tiniest realms of matter, they discovered that Newtonian Law could neither explain nor predict the results of the researchers. Quantum Theory had arrived. The term *quantum* was first applied to this branch of science by the German physicist Max Planck in 1900, and is used to mean the smallest unit of any physical property, such as energy or matter. So there are two sets of laws which govern the universe: Newton's and Quantum. The most fundamental difference is that one offers absolute certainty and the other no guarantee of how a specific thing will turn out.

Imagine a stunning Rembrandt hanging in the National Gallery, and yourself as a myopic fly strolling over its surface. You are only able to take in a tiny, fly-sized part of the whole at one time. The part of the picture you have already walked over lies in the past, and the part you have still to walk over lies in the future. Meanwhile, what's present is this dark and dismal patch of brown. You are disturbed and take off, whilst still looking at the picture. Of course you discover by taking off that you can take more in, and what you couldn't see as the stationary fly has revealed itself to you.

This is like our own ability to perceive the world we live in when we are aware only of our Everyday Selves. For a start we know that our perception of colour and sound is restricted to a narrow band. There are ultraviolet and infrared bands on either end of our visible colour spectrum, which we cannot see, and sounds that animals can hear but we cannot. There are sounds that can shatter a wineglass, put you into a trance, raise your spirit or drive you insane. No doubt there is a reason for our radically limited perception of the world. Perhaps our minds would be blown if we were exposed to much more, so it's important that we understand something about the interfaces between the different levels we might access. Then we can consciously and safely navigate the different frequencies between the slow vibration of physical form and what will begin to reveal itself. Becoming familiar with an expanded version of what we thought we were makes us realise how our senses have become dulled and we are no longer 'in tune' with the world in which we live, and helps us understand the Hermetic maxim which states

That which is Below corresponds to that which is Above,
And that which is Above corresponds to that which is Below,
To accomplish the miracles of the One Thing

In other words everything replicates itself from the microcosm to the macrocosm. We are part of a holographic universe, and in a holographic 'something', every piece of the something mirrors the whole something.

The Universal Energy Field – the ocean in which we consciously exist – holds all information, which is a difficult concept to grasp. Because we have been educated to believe only in that which is provable, the magic of the universe is denied us. We need to become magicians again. Strange, when you consider the magic that goes on around us every day with our wireless connections to each other across the globe, our electrical source of light and, most astonishing, the existence of the world wide web 'out there' in cyberspace. We have created an external technology which replicates our own astonishing capabilities both individually and as part of an infinite universal web.

Our brain, our computer, seems not to be designed for certain tasks – understanding infinity being one of them. As children we might have asked the question "Where does the sky end?" – a question which will remain unanswerable till the day we die. Our souls have come from an Infinite Source to experience a time-bound, gravity-held reality. Our focus needs to be in the here and now. There will be plenty of opportunities to explore infinity when we are no longer anchored to the earth by a physical body, and in the meantime there are miracles under our very noses which remain unexplored.

Carl Jung, the psychologist, visionary and father of modern psychotherapy, believed that contained within this Universal Energy Field was what he termed 'the collective unconscious'. Dr Rupert Sheldrake, whose work has already been mentioned in the previous chapter, believes that this infinite library contains what he calls morphogenetic fields, or pockets of information – perhaps we might even call them websites. When enough individuals have accessed the information from one of these fields of information, it becomes available for everyone else. This is sometimes referred to as the '100th Monkey Syndrome'. This term was coined after observing the behaviour of monkeys on an island, part of an archipelago in the southern seas. One of these monkeys, having stolen a yam from the field of a local inhabitant, inadvertently dropped it into the sea, and noticed that it tasted more delicious without earth on it. This monkey showed her baby, was observed by others in her troupe, and before long they began to follow her example. The remarkable thing was that within a matter of weeks, troupes of monkeys on the other islands also began to wash their stolen yams. How had they got this information? All sorts of experiments have been carried out to further understand this phenomena. Using a crossword puzzle was one of them. A certain number of people were given a crossword to complete, and once this had been done, another set of people were set the same crossword. This second group were able to complete the crossword in a much shorter space of time than the original puzzlers. So if enough of us expand our awareness – create a website – there will come a certain point (known as 'critical mass') when it will happen to others by default. The more we learn, the easier it is for others to follow in our footsteps. This theory helps explain such phenomena as simultaneous scientific breakthroughs – the discovery of DNA by different scientists in different parts of the world, within days of one another is one example. Clusters of brilliant composers and musicians seem to appear together, or artists (as in the Impressionists) or thinkers (as with Blavatsky, Gurdjieff, Alice Bailey and co.).

When we understand that everything is connected, we can see that nothing ever happens in isolation.

Quantum physics tells us that if two particles have been part of the same quantum system and are separated in space, they retain a mysterious connectedness. Einstein called this 'spooky action at a distance' and couldn't believe the implications of such a finding. In fact a recent experiment found that one particle could be in up to 3,000 places at once. Even more baffling is the fact that the same quantum 'object' may appear to be a particle in once place, or a wave – spread out over time and space. And they seem to have the ability to communicate *instantaneously* over any expanse of space, thus confounding Einstein's theory that nothing can travel faster than the speed of light. A change in one separated part of a system can affect another instantaneously. This phenomenon is known as quantum non-locality or non-separability. It demonstrates the fact that nothing changes in isolation and also enables us to actually realise how we are able to have a hand in the creation of our lives – co-creators in fact – within the cycles of time-bound reality. There is order and chaos, movement and rhythm in the sea in which we live. Birth, life and death of cells and bodies, the days, months and seasons – everything moves in cycles.

As the Earth and planets move around the sun, so the entire solar system has its own precise cyclical movement within the galaxy. Everything has a precise order. In our own bodies there are rhythms and cycles that move in time with one another. We do not stand outside the laws and principles that govern the entire cosmos. Nothing is exempt from this universal order. Indigenous cultures – sometimes ignorantly referred to as 'primitive' - such as the Aborigines and Bushmen understand these laws and rhythms, and live their lives in accordance with them. Our preoccupation with the material world has led us away from the knowledge that we are part of this wider whole. By ignoring these laws we are now in danger of extinction, by taking the Earth to the point where she can no longer sustain our presence. Nature is abundant – she always makes too much! And if we had respected the power and energy of the Natural Laws instead of trying to conquer and manipulate them, that abundance would always be available for us too, as visitors on this planet. Becoming aware of ourselves as part of the living universe both visible and invisible – even at this late stage – gives us a different perspective and allows us to send a different message into the collective sea of information.

What does this mean, then, to us as the ants at ground level or the fly on the painting? It means that at the very least we can begin to grasp the significance of Krishnamurti's statement "We are the world". We are not separate from our surroundings. There is a continual exchange of information going on through interfaces – at a cellular level, through the cell's membrane (as Bruce Lipton has discovered), and also through a much more expanded interface – our aura. We have access, therefore, to any and all information that the psychic world wide web contains. Everything, every possibility, every experience is 'out there' in this field of pure potential, and like logging onto the world wide web on our own computers, we can access into whatever we feel inclined.

The Universal Energy Field also supplies us, as individuals, with vital, life-sustaining nourishment. In the East, (where they have never lost sight of these fundamental principles), it is referred to as *prana*, or *chi*. T'ai Chi and Qi Gong are practices that encourage the free flow of this life force into and around our physical beings. It is important to encourage this free flow, because we are no different from our own planet, whose energy field, or aura, has now become congested, punctured and contaminated with humanity's negative emissions: physical, mental and emotional. Imagine what the daily collective emissions of fear, violence, greed, guilt and suffering might look like if we had the ability to see them. Just because we can't, doesn't mean they don't exist. No wonder the Earth's feeling sick.

What is an Aura?
Your aura is like a halo surrounding your whole body, a cloak of moving

colours that expands and contracts according to how you are feeling. The colours vary according to your physical health and also depending on what you are thinking as well as what you are feeling. Remember the expressions 'green with envy', 'seeing red', or 'feeling blue'? Your aura is made up of several levels, known as bodies – something like a Russian doll – except that each layer interacts with and interpenetrates the others. Being aware of the interaction between your body and your thoughts and feelings means that there will be a freer flow of energy between the different levels, or frequencies, that make up your 'subtle' anatomy.

Each 'body' or level has a different vibration, starting with the physical body which has the slowest frequency and is the densest, to the outer levels of the auric field, which are much finer and have a much faster vibration. These subtle bodies alter according to what goes on inside us. They reflect the state of our physical body, our feelings, our minds and our spiritual presence. They are also affected by what goes on outside. Environmental stressors such as noise, pollution and electromagnetic fields (VDUs, overhead cables, underwater streams, geopathic stress, radio and satellite transmitters) affect our auric field and may result in physical disease. More about this in Chapter 9.

Our auras REFLECT the state we are in. They PROTECT us, they NOURISH us, and the health of our subtle anatomy AFFECTS the health of our physical body. Since our thoughts and feelings affect our aura, it follows that they therefore affect our bodies. If you feel down and depressed, your aura will become grey and contracted. The auric field of a depressed alcoholic will look murky, depleted and might even have rents or holes in it. If we have a rigid approach to life and need to be in control, our auric field will reflect this, resulting in lack of flow and movement in the subtle anatomy and manifesting in inflexibility and stiffness in our physical body. On the other hand, the aura of someone like the Dalai Lama is extended, clear and sparkling with his humour and spiritual presence.

How do you know you've got an aura? If you answer yes to any of the following questions, then you have experienced the interplay of an outside energy field upon your own ...

- When you are with certain people, do you feel drained?
- Have you ever 'felt' someone staring at you?
- Do you associate certain colours with people?
- Have you ever taken an instant liking or disliking to someone?
- Are you able to sense how someone is feeling, in spite of how this person is behaving?
- Have you been able to sense another person's presence before you actually saw or heard this person? Ever thought of someone and at that instant they phone you?
- Do certain colours and sounds make you feel more comfortable than others?
- Do you pick up 'vibes' in a place when you enter it?
- Can you 'sense' when something is wrong?

Becoming more aware of your own auric field means you will begin to notice how it interacts with outside forces and energies. You also need to learn to recognise the limits and strengths of your own energy field, so that you can pay attention to its health and welfare, in the same way that you look after your physical body. You will begin to be more aware of how you affect and are affected by the energy of others and the places you find yourself in. Being able to recognise those times when you need to strengthen, balance or clean up your aura will give you the chance to take action before you become depleted and also make you conscious of your whole being.

Drains & Radiators: Be aware of the situations and people that 'drain' you, and what it is that makes you radiant. Another point to remember is that energy always flows from strong to weak. We talk about being 'in tune' with another person – 'on the same frequency'. These are the people who resonate with our own frequency, who are on the same wavelength, but we don't always find ourselves with like-minded souls. Become aware of how your energy gets drained away by others. Every time we come into contact with another person, two energy fields meet and because of the electro-magnetic properties of the aura, you may give energy (the electrical part) or you may absorb (the magnetic aspect). The more people you interact with, the greater the energy exchange. Unless you are aware of this exchange, by the end of the day you can accumulate debris that is not yours, causing you to feel drained and washed out. On the other hand, if you allow yourself to 'sink' into nature by taking yourself out to a wood, a river or whatever natural landscape you feel at home in, you will become aware of how everything is interconnected, giving your body and soul a breather from the striving and struggle of everyday life. Nature is both balancing and cleansing. Your soul loves being in the natural world because it is *natural*. Trees are definitely radiators and have a particularly dynamic energy field, each with its own unique frequency, just as individual human beings do. Sitting under a willow tree, for example, helps remove headaches. Pine trees have a particularly cleansing effect (that's why we find pine in domestic cleaning fluids) since they draw off negative emotions, and an oak tree will offer strength and support. Walking by the sea, or a river, will also have a balancing effect on your energy field. If you live in an urban environment, it becomes an imperative to take time out in a park or somewhere quiet, and preferably green, to re-balance and re-establish a sense of the sacred in your inner and outer environment.

The ancient Egyptians, with their extraordinary wisdom, recognised that we were more than just this physical vehicle. Their hieroglyphs tell us that they believed we were made up of no less than nine 'subtle' bodies, each with its own particular function which enabled the soul not only to have a human experience, but also to navigate what happened after the physical body had switched off its lights.

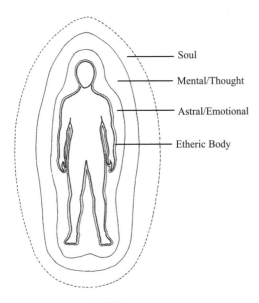

The following labels appear on the diagram:

- Soul
- Mental/Thought
- Astral/Emotional
- Etheric Body

The Auric Field

The Etheric Body

If we had the ability to see the different levels and frequencies that make up the different 'bodies' of our auric field, starting from the most dense – the physical body itself – the first layer we would notice is the etheric body, or double. Being closest to the physical, this is also the most easily sensed. It projects an inch or two beyond and all around our bodies. It is composed of matter vibrating at speeds just above the velocity of light, which makes it invisible to our everyday senses. In 1939 a Russian called Semyon Kirlian discovered a method of 'photographing' this energy field which showed that there is an energy blueprint or matrix from which every living thing develops. It's like a map for the physical body, not only for us humans but all physical manifestations. This matrix defines our size and shape and is what stops a cow from growing into the size of a dinosaur, a tree to the size of the Eiffel Tower or humans growing two noses. Using this method, Kirlian photographed leaves, which showed up as outlines of themselves, but not as a single echo of their shape rather an 'alive' field with peaks and troughs. He then experimented by cutting off part of the leaf and then re-photographing it, which revealed that although part of the leaf had gone, the matrix of where it had been was still intact. This is known as the phantom leaf effect and perhaps accounts for why many people who have had limbs amputated still experience sensations in the part of their body that no longer physically exists. What is interesting and also useful about Kirlian photography is that disease could be detected in the leaf before it had appeared in the plant or tree itself. Obviously the ramifications of this are far reaching when it is applied to the human body. However there is considerable argument about this method and it has not been accepted by any scientific body as a reliable or accurate diagnostic tool.

So, as the old Chinese proverb advises

He who reads, forgets
He who sees, remembers
He who does, knows.

Try it for yourself and then you, at least, will know, so here's a little exercise ....

Energy-Sensing Exercise

Sit comfortably, with your palms facing one another, but not quite touching.

Slowly move your palms away from each other. Then bring them together.

Establish a gentle rhythm - moving together, then apart - as though there was an invisible elastic band connecting them. You might notice that it feels as if you are 'holding' something.

You may begin to 'feel' an energy field building up between your hands.

Just close your eyes and breathe in an even, relaxed way.

Notice how far apart you can take your hands before you lose the sense of the ball of energy that you have created.

The etheric body is not only the matrix for the physical form, but it is also the interface between matter and non-matter. Like the chakras (see Chapter 4), it acts as a step-down transformer, a membrane between the visible and invisible worlds. And in the light of what Dr Lipton has revealed through his cellular research, we know what a crucial role membranes play in our experience of life on earth.

The Astral or Emotional Body

Whilst it seems as if I am going through the aura layer by layer, in fact the outer, higher frequency levels move freely throughout the entire aura and the physical body itself, but each field is defined by the level at which it vibrates. So the next field, having a finer frequency than the etheric double, also extends further. It is governed by the Law of Attraction, which means that, through the energy of our emotions, we will attract towards us all that is needed for our soul's experience and growth. It is through the astral field that the soul draws towards us the unfinished business of the past. So whilst the etheric body senses things, this level of our aura 'feels'.

Every feeling we experience has a different energy charge, or wave form. Depression, for example, obviously has a different frequency from that of anger. We metabolise these feelings as we metabolise a plate of pasta – they are turned into something else. Your emotions register on the astral body of your aura. Similar to the effects brought about by feeling directed at water in Dr Emoto's experiments, compassion, love, joy, peace and trust will make your aura look and feel quite different from the charge of fear, guilt, anger and hate. All feelings need to be felt and expressed – appropriately – otherwise they become held in the auric field and metastasise into blocks, or pockets of stuck energy that will prevent free flow around you. Continuing to suppress or hold on to these feelings over a period of time will then affect the etheric field and finally impact on the cells in your physical body, which will begin to express this congestion as discomfort – dis-ease. Understanding the connection between thoughts and feelings and their effect on our bodies is now becoming the recognised branch of orthodox medicine known as psychoneuroimmunology, or PNI, a term coined in 1975 by two professors at the University of Rochester, researching into the placebo effect and psychosomatic illness.

There is another aspect to our astral field. Because its vibratory rate is finer than that of our dense physical body, it is possible to travel at will using the astral body as a vehicle – hence astral travel. Astral travel is achieved by moving your consciousness from your physical body into your astral body, thus enabling travel into what has been known about for hundreds of thousands of years and is sometimes referred to as the 'astral plane'. These experiences are known as OBEs (out-of-body experiences). Sometimes they happen spontaneously, but they can also be consciously induced. The work of Robert Munroe, who was spontaneously plunged into having out-of-body experiences, seemed to be the beginning of many others travelling in the astral plane. Perhaps he was the 100th monkey to open up this field of information for others, certainly it is all part of human consciousness widening the scope of its understanding of the nature of reality. In the astral plane and without our physical bodies (to which we are attached by what has been perceived by some as a 'silver cord') we have the ability to move out of time-bound, gravity-held physical reality. Shamans induce this ability by going into a trance-state often invoked by the use of psychoactive plant substances, or the use of sound and dance. Some healers in the Western world do a great deal of work using their astral bodies, which accounts for reports of them appearing in their patients' homes at all times of the day or night and also appearing to them in their dreams. These experiences often go hand-in-hand with an opening of the psychic faculty. For more information on this, and also psychic protection, have a look at Robert Bruce's website (under **Resources**) and Judy Hall's excellent book *The Art of Psychic Protection.*

Astral travel is perhaps a more glamorous aspect of the astral body's abilities than what goes on at home base. Some of the challenges presented to us at this level are:

- Being over emotional and letting emotions rule your life. Of course it's better to feel than repress but, although you have emotions, you are not those emotions.

- Conversely, suppressing your feelings in case they overwhelm you – and then stuffing them away somewhere creates congestion in your astral body and by now you know what results this creates.
- That there are usually choices about how you want to feel, and how you might express these emotions. Tit-for-tat karma acts out at this level.

E-motion is simply energy in motion, and is largely re-active, in other words it comes as a result of thinking about something, seeing something, often assuming something. Feelings that are connected to the soul have a different quality. For example:

- They are unconditional, and don't need acknowledgement
- They invoke a feeling of centredness
- They allow you to live in the 'dream' world, knowing that every-thing is connected to everything else
- Soul feelings are compassionate, enthusiastic, passionate and 'alive'
- They are stable regardless of feedback
- They widen your perspective

The Mental Body

As the etheric double is the interface between the physical body and the first 'invisible' layer around us, the mental body is how and where the soul integrates its intelligence with the personality inhabiting the relative-ly dense physical body. It is where the impulses of the soul or higher self become thoughtforms, which may then impel us to action. These thought-forms may come during sleep in the form of dreams, during meditation and contemplation when everyday static is quieter, or may slowly devel-op as an idea, which enters the conscious mind as something that 'needs to be done'.

Therefore go forth companion, when you find
No highway more, no track, all being blind
The way to go shall glimmer in the mind.
John Masefield: The Wanderer

If our actions in life are determined without listening to the voice of the soul, everything is seen as black or white, right or wrong. This is our left-brain view of the world, in cahoots with our ego and believing that there is only a three-dimensional reality that has to be rationalised in order to feel safe. This is the limited perspective from which we will respond to situations according to what we have filed away in our memory banks under the heading of 'belief systems'. These belief systems, about who we are and how we 'should' behave, may have been appropriate for our development earlier in this life, or they may be outdated scripts carried forward like tapes looped into our minds. "Could do better", "It's not safe to trust people", "We'll never have enough" or "Sex is dirty" are examples of the negative, restricting myths that we are often quite unaware that we carry with us and which prevent us from living life. These scripts may also have their origins in past life experiences. It's not difficult to see what our collective belief systems are doing to humanity as a whole and history seemingly repeats itself.

On one level the mental field or body is capable of producing useless repetitive thoughts and on another level it is responsible for brilliant feats of intellectual genius – and everything in between. Our minds can become our masters, as our emotions can create havoc in our lives, until we realise that these are like two horses pulling our chariot (the body) through this Earthly experience.

As the information highways increase in volume and velocity on a daily basis out there in the world, it's as well to be mindful of whether our own internal information highways are approaching overload and whether our mindfield is beginning to resemble a mine-field. Stepping on a thought that scatters our focus and mental acuity can happen in a moment, triggering the astral/emotional field to react and blowing the chariot off-course. There is just too much noise in our worlds these days. Whatever happened to the value of silence? If turning off your music machine/radio/TV/mobile phone makes you feel like a castaway, you need to take a serious look at why you find silence uncomfortable. Perhaps you could try a different sort of sound to settle your energy fields. Some peaceful, gentle music, the sound of running water or birdsong will help bring you to a state of calm. But really, minds need space and quiet or they begin to resemble a ball of wire wool, making clarity and fully conscious decision-making difficult, since there are no pathways for the soul to communicate through all the static.

Try this imaging exercise before you go to sleep at night, to clear any unwanted mental or emotional junk that you might have collected during the day. It is particularly useful if you have been in an environment where another person, with whom you are in close contact, seems to be affecting you in a negative way and depleting your energy. If you can do this while you are actually having a shower, it is even more effective, since the tremendous cleansing energy of water is not only physical as we have already seen.

Waterfall Cleansing Exercise

I focus on my breathing, taking some deep easy breaths.

I imagine, or get a sense of, a beautiful, crystal-clear waterfall splashing down.

The water has a diamond-like quality to it.

Now I imagine that I am standing underneath this waterfall. It is going right through my auric field, taking with it any slow-frequency energy, any blocks of static that I might have accumulated during the day. Its clarity and refreshing coolness feel invigorating and refreshing.

Now I imagine that this water enters in through the top of my head. It goes right through my body and out through the ends of my fingers and toes.

I notice that the water coming out from my toes and fingers might seem cloudy and dark.

So I continue to allow the water to move through me until the colour coming out through my toes and fingers is as clear as the waterfall itself.

When this has happened, I then imagine that I am filling my inner space with this water .....

Clear and clean, invigorating and revitalising .....

Now I step out from under the waterfall and find a white cloak or coat that is there for me.

Putting this on, and wrapping it around I notice that it has a hood which I gently put over my head. This ensures that my personal space is protected from invasion. I take a deep breath, move my fingers and toes, and then open my eyes, feeling refreshed and lighter.

The Soul Body

This field that surrounds us and also permeates through us is sometimes referred to as the Causal Body. Extending further out now from the physical 'yolk' and the previous three bodies that make up our aura, it vibrates at a level far beyond the frequencies so far described. At this level, we just 'know'. The feelings that belong to the soul are different from the emotions of the astral body. They are stable, centring and unconditional – in other words non-judgemental. They are based on the soul's desire to communicate to the personality its ability to rise above the turbulence of everyday life and to recognise that we are in this world, but also not of it.

Out beyond ideas of wrong-doing and right-doing
There is a field
I'll meet you there.
When the soul lies down in that grass

the world is too full to talk about.
Ideas, language, even the phrase each other,
doesn't make sense.
Jelaluddin Rumi (Translation by Coleman Barks)

Our bodies carry around our biographies, imprints of many lifetimes acted out on the stage of planet Earth. Our genes carry ancestral patterns and the memory of experiences that have been significant enough to 'make their mark' on us. Dying with a powerful thought or feeling – betrayal for example – may be carried onward into the next lifetime as an echo of that event and will be experienced as an unconscious and possibly unfounded mistrust of people. The soul needs to clear that belief, knowing that there is no 'right' or 'wrong' – only experiences that we go through on our way to remembering what this is really all about.

The soul body, or field, like all the others we have already looked at, has access to other realms beyond most people's current comprehension. Its task, if you like, is to continually remind the personality, through the vehicles of thought and feeling, of its presence. Not only its presence, but of its knowledge of the contract it drew up before its time-bound, earthly experiences. It's said – I'm not sure by whom - that these experiences in a gravity-held chariot with all its history and drawn by two very different horses is so difficult and challenging that all souls are not able to manage it. For some it is enough of a challenge simply to enter the density of physical matter – and then leave. Perhaps it's the possibility of forgetting entirely the soul's perspective and presence that makes it so challenging. Memories from previous experiences 'down here' would also add to what might appear to be a punishment posting in these times of the Kali Yuga. But all mythologies tell of the hero's journey in search of a golden fleece, a pot of gold, the key to eternal life, and all these stories are parables about the soul's (or hero's) sojourn on Earth. Confronting obstacles, demons and dragons, coping with every manner of deprivation and personal pain imaginable, the soul goes through initiations and tests until it finally finds its holy grail. The grail in this case is not a chalice or a palace, a prince or queen, but the *knowledge* of the nature of duality and polarity and to express its unique qualities *whatever* they are. It is the knowledge that we have been in soul dramas once as a slave, another as a master, once rich, another poor, once loved and another abandoned. We have had experiences at opposite ends of the see-saw of polarity and at some point the soul stands in the centre, saying 'I have been both and yet I am neither'. This is the great Aha! which takes us beyond horses, chariots, stages and dramas.

This realisation can only come by experiencing the ultimate paradox of being a soul in a physical body. There is not much point in being an angel if you need to work out a control issue with your mother-in-law. It's all about moving to the point where you can say 'does it really matter?'. We are here to collect *experience* and by understanding both ends of a story we can finally come into balance and bring an end to our incarnations.

Thankfully, the soul has an ally for the work to be done in a body, and this ally is the heart. The heart, like the soul body, is an interface between the Source and physical reality. Truly heartfelt actions are not directed by mental or astral bodies, thoughts or feelings – they have a different quality to them, a different waveform. This is so important that you will find a whole chapter on the subject of The Heart later on in this book in chapter 13.

So, we are leaving the Age of Pisces, where for just over 2,000 years the focus has been on personal power and control of others. "I believe, therefore I experience" has been the maxim for this period. Religions and belief systems have stood between us as individuals and our soulfulness. The intermediaries have been predominantly male and the methods of this control have been based in fear. However, the dawning of the Age of Aquarius follows the maxim of the Gnostics by saying "I experience, therefore I believe". In other words, the quality of soul is something that we must experience for *ourselves* in order to truly know. Following doctrines and creeds, unless we have had experience of soul, is like reading a map without exploring the territory itself.

Soul Focus

Bodies, feelings and thoughts are the means for your soul's
earthly experience.

The soul's desire is to illuminate our aura.

REMINDERS....

- Before going into energy threatening situations, mentally set your boundaries, so that you are not 'invaded' or 'overwhelmed'. Imagine yourself contained within your own energy egg.

- Your aura is your multidimensional interface with the Universal Energy Field or the field of quantum non-locality.

- EXPRESS your feelings. Don't stuff them away to metastasise into illness. If they are feelings you are afraid of, write them down, bash a pillow or get help, but get them out. If it is grief, allow yourself time and space. Forget about this stiff upper lip business and allow yourself to plummet to the depths of it. It will be painful, but you won't be overwhelmed.

- Be aware of the different levels of your experience:

  'I *sense* this is right' (Body + Etheric Double)

  'I *feel* this is right' (Astral/Emotional Body)

  'I *think* this is right' (Mental Body)

  'I *know* this is right' (Soul Body)

- Notice how different colours affect you.

- Practise the Energy-Sensing Exercise regularly, so your hands become more sensitive and sensitised to energies. 'Feel' the energy around your plants, your cat and your friends.

- Please, give your Self some still, soul time.

Resources:

The Sense of being Stared at, and Other Aspects of the Extended Mind:
Dr Rupert Sheldrake (Arrow) www.sheldrake.org

What the Bleep do we (k)now!?: **William Arntz, Betsy Chasse and Mark Vicente** (Heath Communications Inc)

Far Journeys: **Robert Munroe** (Bantam Doubleday)

Astral Dynamics: **Robert Bruce**: (Hamptom Roads) See also: www.astraldynamics.com

Principles of Vibrational Healing: **Clare G Harvey & Amanda Cochrane** (Harper Collins)

Hands of Light: **Barbara Ann Brennan** (Bantam Books)

Vibrational Medicine for the 21st Century: **Dr Richard Gerber** (Piatkus)

The Art of Psychic Protection: **Judy Hall** (Findhorn Press)

chapter 4

the chakras

Microchips of Soul Information

And remember,
No matter where you go,
There you are.
Confucius

Carl Jung thought that it would take Western culture 100 years to grasp the concept of the chakra system and the subtle anatomy of man. He had clearly underestimated the impact of the Great Eastern Takeaway with its menu of practices ranging from acupuncture and T'ai Chi to Buddhist meditation and yoga. Now we have hi-tech equipment able to discern the auric field, the chakra system and the energy meridians which are the invisible circulatory network used by acupuncturists to effect healing. This invisible network is like an energy grid, spinning vital life force, prana or chi, into the extremities of our physical being. We actually take in more energy through this system than we do through our mouth or nostrils.

Dr Harry Oldfield, inventor, scientist, thinker and somewhat eccentric seeker after new and forgotten knowledge, is an explorer of undiscovered realms. In his words, 'not possible' generally translated into 'let's have a look'. This is the quality that Einstein was referring to when he commented "I have no special gift. I am only passionately curious". One of Dr Oldfield's main developments has been a photo-imaging system that reveals the human energy field – the aura. This has become known as PIP standing for Polycontrast Interference Photography.

Dr Oldfield suggests that the human energy field is like a template or network of energy points with which the physical molecules of the body are aligned. When he first began measuring the energetic fluctuations around the body with his Electro-Scanning Method, he always found energy concentrations at seven places. He was mystified as to the cause of this until a professor suggested that he may have 'discovered', that is, rediscovered, the chakra system of ancient Ayurvedic medicine.

In some quarters of the so-called New Age 'enlightened' scene, chakras have been relegated to a back seat in importance, a sort of 'been there and done that' attitude prevails, and they are considered to be simply different coloured energy points which act as interfaces between the Universal Energy Field and our own individual place within it. This is a gross oversight, as the deeper one peers into the world of the chakra, the more it reveals to you about levels of consciousness from the basic instinctual level of survival and reproduction through to the finer vibrations of insight, intuition and illumination. As a system, it offers us keys to understanding what thoughts and emotions are affecting our physical body and how that comes about. Understanding the deeper meaning of the functions of each chakra helps you respond to life with awareness, rather than being unconsciously re-active.

The soul on its journey through earthly experience has an intention, a purpose for being here. This purpose is decided before becoming incarnated and then seemingly 'forgotten' as we pass through the different planes to finally make a connection with our embryonic bodies. We have decided what will offer the best opportunities for understanding and finding that balance between the dualities. We decide which culture, geographical location, parents and others from our soul 'family' will provide us with the situations required to bring us to the realisation of who and what we really are. The soul leaves Home, calibrating and constellating its energy to enter into the tiny physical form that will be its vehicle for the next incarnation. It enters through the crown chakra at the top of the head, which is open to receive it and evident in the fontanel in babies. Even though the plates of the cranium come together as we grow up, this place of entry is our connection to where we came from and will never completely close no matter what life throws at us and how 'disconnected' we may become later on. The other chakra that is open is the root, since we need to engage with our physical bodies, or nothing much will happen. All the other chakras are like little buds on the stem of a flower which will open as we develop into adults, and their opening and healthy flowering will depend on what experiences we encounter and how we are affected by these experiences.

Since the purpose of the soul's journey on earth at this point in time is to clear its karmic backlog, and find freedom from the wounds of the past – how on earth are we supposed to know what it's all about since we have passed through the ring-pass-not of forgetfulness? The stuff that needs to be looked at – and moved beyond – is encoded into our chakras. Our biology does indeed contain our biography and a genetic biography that is ancestral, which contains not only physically inherited traits, but also the ancestral patterns that have been the work of the soul to bring into balance through its many incarnations. Unfortunately we are not given a handbook of instructions for our earthly visits and live in ignorance of what this work is until we understand the clues that will take us into freedom from the patterns and conditioning installed in our early years. These clues, like the buttons on a tape-playing machine, activate the stored information that lies hidden in the repository of your unconscious mind. Some of these buttons will activate pleasant, familiar experiences, and others will produce the opposite. So which of these buttons is pressed will send a clear message to you about what needs to be addressed, and if we don't get it the first time, then it will go into repeat mode until we understand the content and can then erase it. If we still haven't got it by the end of one lifetime, then we'll have to deal with it in the next and subsequent incarnations. The soul has infinite patience, but because we are now in these times of rapid acceleration it seems that our karma needs to express itself in more extreme ways to get our attention. Our chakras will provide us with invaluable information about the nature of what needs to be addressed now.

So what exactly is a chakra? Chakra is the Sanskrit word for wheel, although if you could see one, it would look more like a spinning, funnel-shaped energy vortex than a wheel. The wider, spinning end interacts with your auric field, whilst the stem would appear to be embedded in your spine with a nerve plexus and endocrine gland nearby. There are seven major chakras which are aligned with your spinal column, and many other minor ones ranging from those in the palms of the hands, soles of the feet, behind the knees and elbows, to others scattered throughout the body at strategic positions relevant to the energetic functioning of our physical and etheric bodies. In the Eastern traditions, these 'whirlpools' of energy were often depicted as flowers with different numbers of petals. The root chakra has four, for example, while the crown is known as the 'thousand-petalled lotus'. The number of petals is thought by modern researchers to be evidence that these ancient people knew something about the harmonic frequencies of the chakras.

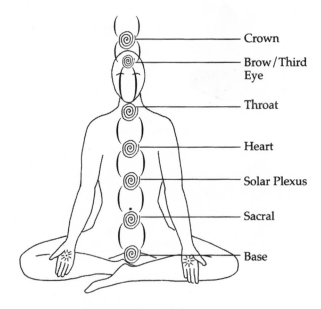

Crown

Brow / Third Eye

Throat

Heart

Solar Plexus

Sacral

Base

Chakras: Front View

These flowers are the sense organs of the soul
Rudolph Steiner

Imagine, then, an invisible network or grid that exists within you, with the chakras as the major filling stations at critical intersections within this grid. They are step-down transformers, the interface that enables the intake of vital life force, without which we would cease to exist, since it is utilised by the hormonal, nervous and cellular systems of our physical body. Chakras function as a system, not individually, and are affected by the health of the body and our emotional 'weather'. But they are not only linked to the physical functioning of our bodies, they also hold the keys to understanding our relationships, our strengths and weaknesses and the patterns that keep on repeating.

Focusing on the chakra system in general and each one in particular we find that each one has:

- A direct connection with a nerve plexus, an endocrine gland and an important body system – excretory, reproductive, digestive, circulatory, respiratory and cognitive – and is thus directly implicated with the health of the body.
- A different age at which it develops or 'opens'.
- The capacity to be over- or under-active according to the specific thoughts and feelings that affect it. This will affect our bodies if continuously out of balance.
- An association with a specific colour, which reflects its rate of vibration. The red of the root chakra, for example, spins slower than the amethyst of the crown.
- A correspondence with a different physical, emotional and spiritual issue.
- Information about our past lives 'encoded' within it.

Going through the chakras one by one is like inspecting the instruments in an orchestra. They operate as a whole system under the direction of the conductor, the Third Eye chakra. The conductor did not write the symphony nor can he play every instrument, but he needs to know what the composer (the soul) had in mind and how best to express the essence of the music. He needs to know if the flautist has flu or the percussionist a tendency to go over the top because of family problems.

Just like a small orchestra, the health of each player is vital to the harmony of the whole. Our individual chakras may get out of balance and become over- or under-active, which affects the whole system. If this situation endures, eventually the physical body will be affected. Another indicator, therefore, that there is work to be done and issues to be addressed, will be the body itself becoming ill at ease with the thoughts or feelings that are affecting that chakra. Those with continuous throat problems need to ask themselves what it might be that they are not saying, not expressing. Heartache is not the physical heart weeping, but the energy of the heart chakra coming into focus. Digestive problems will tell us that the solar plexus chakra is struggling with issues of power and control, and so on.

The seven major players in the chakra orchestra that, when playing in harmony, will sound your own very particular note are the root, the sacral, solar plexus, heart, throat, third eye and crown. As you go through the information on each of these microchips of the soul, be aware of which one strikes a chord with you.

The BASE or ROOT Chakra: Colour – Red

Surely a man needs a closed place wherein he may strike root and, like the seed, become.
Antoine de Saint-Exupéry

Position on the body:	Perineum (central point between the legs).
Relates to:	Feet, legs, lower abdomen and its contents.
Body speaks through:	Constipation, IBS, colitis, piles, problems with the rectum, hips, legs and feet.

Thoughts that affect:	It's not safe to be here. I can't stand my ground. I don't belong. I might not survive. I'll never have enough.
Feelings that affect:	I'm not really here. I'm not in my body. I feel disconnected. I'm afraid of the earthy side of life.
Past life themes:	Physical or emotional trauma which makes it unsafe to fully engage with the body in this incarnation. Lives of physical deprivation, starvation, suffering, torture and insecurity.

Through my own personal experience and observing others who come for sessions and workshops, it is as if most of us are not really 'here' and it's not difficult to learn why this is so. Once your soul has gone through the business of sorting out its contracts with others, and what it wants to address, gone through the ring-pass-not of forgetfulness and engaged with the little physical body it will be inhabiting, the next thing that happens to us is that we begin to experience our mother's feelings. It has been proven that a stressed mother produces a stressed baby, and that children born in countries where there is war, whether personal or international, will feel more anxiety about arriving than those being born into a peaceful environment. Our very delicate sensory equipment, from the moment the soul engages with the little body it will inhabit, is like a satellite dish, receiving the frequencies or atmosphere around it. What's happening to and around your mother will be transmitted to you, and will determine the health of your Root chakra. As the name implies, it is all about feeling 'earthed' and safe.

The first and most crucial challenge is to survive. The Root or Base chakra is concerned with survival, and endocrine glands to which it is connected are the adrenals. These are involved with our 'fight or flight' response – a survival mechanism that helps us in life-threatening situations. Not that a baby is going to do much fighting or fleeing, but these are two basic human instincts, and it is at this time of our lives that the first seeds of fear get imprinted onto our sensitive soul. If there is no welcoming committee when we arrive – if we are not greeted with loving contact (a fundamental need) – we will not feel safe in our little bodies, and the Root chakra will not develop in a healthy way. We will not 'earth' ourselves, because we do not feel safe, and our soul may not fully connect with our physical being, since it all feels a bit too much. So those born during times of stress or conflict (in the home or out of it), will have picked up the vibrations of tension and fear which will undermine their sense of safety at having arrived here. It is much more traumatic for the soul to be born into a dense earthly vehicle than it is to leave it – which is returning Home, after all.

Without a sense of belonging or feeling safe here, we build feelings of insecurity, which have unfortunate consequences in later life. To relieve this sense of insecurity we grow into adults attached to external sources of security – home, jobs, material possessions, or mask the feelings of 'separateness' through sex, drugs, food or alcohol. Of course it is all right to enjoy nice things, to live in a pleasant environment and to have money – but not to rely on these things for our sense of security. Always feeling that 'there will never be enough to support me' brings the need to acquire more and more or work harder and harder – but somehow we still never feel safe. This fear has bred a race of achievers and perfectionists for whom 'failure' is a cardinal sin – perhaps they grew up in an environment where being 'loved' was attached to doing well. Even before we learn to speak, we learn that smiling or crying will give us attention in one form or another. Born into a situation where there was little nurturing means the soul has never really felt at home on earth.

Pause for a moment and ask yourself these questions:

- Why did I choose these parents and this culture?
- What might my mother have been feeling when she was carrying me?
- How was I received?

- How were the first two or three years of my life?
- What do I feel about my body? Is it safe to be in it?
- Do I really want to be here?

If you feel that your sense of being earthed or rooted could do with strengthening, spend more time in nature, but don't just wander through the park or woods with your mind somewhere else. Put your back against a tree, feel your bare feet in contact with the earth, stop to examine the wondrous detail. It's all about connection. Dancing and drumming help the root centre release insecurities. Yes, we live in a material world, but we don't have to OWN everything, or label it either. A lesser spotted flycatcher is a stunning bird if you look at its detail rather than trying to find it in your bird book. As you observe nature in all its abundance, begin to think of your own. Think what you have, rather than what you haven't got. Deep insecurities, bringing about anxiety, panic attacks, hyperventilation and diarrhoea are all signs of overactive adrenals. It is SO important to get in touch with this chakra and its contents, and to feel safe and interconnected – as indeed we are. Connection with, rather than denial of, our bodies will ultimately give us freedom from them, but we are not going anywhere until we have arrived.

The SACRAL or WATER/SEXUAL Chakra: Colour – Orange

Movement never lies.
It is a barometer telling the state of the soul's weather.
Martha Graham

Position on the body:	Just below the navel/ the sacrum.
Relates to:	Reproductive and urinary systems.
Body speaks through:	Cystitis, prostatitis, nephritis, menstrual difficulties and sexual dysfunction. Problems in the reproductive system.
Thoughts that affect:	I dare not be intimate. It's wrong to enjoy

myself too much. I can't cope with change. Sex is everything - or – sex is 'wrong'/scary/overwhelming. I'm not creative. I mustn't have children.

Feelings that affect: Discomfort about change. Repression of sexuality. Guilt around pleasurable sensations. Memories of sexual abuse. Fear of getting close to someone. Denial of creativity and magic – in its widest sense.

Past life themes: Lifetimes when sexuality ended in terminal disaster: persecution, betrayal, guilt. Lives as religious celibates in denial of sexuality. Lives when creativity, following your dream, led to despair or death, or when your sexual drive led you to acts that were deeply regretted Lives where there were illegal abortions, unwanted children, death in childbirth or loss of children.

Having arrived here on Earth, and being aware only of our link to our mother or whoever takes care of us, the next thing that happens is that we realise we are not alone. There are others in our immediate environment. Our Sacral chakra begins to open with awareness of the first people with whom we form what is known as our 'primary relationships'. This is where we learn about relating to one another. How they behave toward us, and each other, becomes our understanding of 'relationship'. For many people this is not an encouraging thought. 'Inner Child' therapy will often take you back to the years when this chakra flower was opening – 18 months to 6 or 7 years old – the time when how you perceived the world was defined by those around you. When we go back into our past – like turning the pages of an old photo album – we find the moments when some frightening experience froze the soul in that time frame. These moments are when the soul - our essence - just found it too much to cope with, and in order not to feel totally overwhelmed, split off or shut down. That little person who froze in that moment, however, will be pulling strings, whispering through our unconscious minds, in an attempt to avoid a repeat of the situation. We may have had a very powerful parent who made it difficult for us to establish our own boundaries. Feeling vulnerable and unsafe, we get 'sucked in' to their energy field and have difficulty in establishing our own sense of self. This subject, because it is so important, will be looked at again in more depth in the following chapter on Inner Children.

It is in the years when the Sacral chakra is opening that we discover that there is a part of our anatomy that gives us lovely feelings – entirely natural for a little person who experiences life totally through their senses. Our parents, however, might have had a different view. What they felt and expressed about their own sexuality would have had a direct effect on how we view our own. Or if we have been subjected to abuse in this area and at this time in our little lives, other difficult and painful information will have been stored around sexuality. Yet another faulty recording that may have been installed at this time might be saying 'It's dirty. Don't do that it's naughty – (or even worse) it's disgusting'. These days it seems that sex has come out of the closet and its potent energy is used by marketing moguls for selling everything from shampoo, jeans, cars and coffee to furniture and food. What happened to its value as a sacred act? Perhaps we might re-name this centre the Sacred Chakra?

Another crucial aspect of the Sacral chakra is to do with creativity (apart from making babies), and the development of your imagination. When we are small we spend a great deal of time in our imaginary world. We talk to our teddies, all of which have their own personalities, and we begin to draw and build things. Stories hold us spell-bound as we live the tales of witches and princes, treasure and adventure. Our imaginations are fertile and unfettered. We make up endless games that have no sense of outcomes or goals – we truly live in the moment. We may even have an 'imaginary' friend who is a very real presence. We are in touch with magic at this time in our lives. Unfortunately this sense of magic can easily get lost for children when the world seems to have become more dangerous and threatening. We trust those around us and are open to them. If this trust is betrayed we develop the belief that it is not safe to trust another; it is not safe to open up; it's not safe to be intimate.

Going to school soon changes the focus from the creative use of our imaginations to the left brain skills that are valued so highly in our contemporary culture. Over-dosing on TV and computers just shrivels the growth and expression of children's collective imagination. They no longer invent their own stories, because it is done for them. No more fairies at the bottom of the garden – you'll find them on Sky.

So our feelings about sexuality, our relationships with others and our creative imagination are formed during this early period of our lives, along with the flowering of the Sacral chakra. If all or any of these aspects of our life are squashed out of us, the balance will need to be redressed. The soul communicates through this chakra that every significant relationship in our lives holds a key to open the door to some aspect of ourselves that is hidden. When our buttons get pushed, it is important not to look so intently at who is pushing them, but what effect this has on us, and why. Here is the soul asking us to take responsibility for what happens to us in a wider context, so that we may be led back to our relationship with the Divine Source that is like the eternal sky behind the dramas of our passing clouds.

Can we relate to another without fear of being overwhelmed, or without needing to possess them? Do we need to get love and nurturing from someone else, because we did not get it from our mothers or fathers? Do we find partners who are like our absent parents, in our search to find balance?

Pause for a moment and ask yourself these questions:

- What were my parents' attitudes to intimacy and pleasure?
- How do I feel about my own sexuality?
- If I take myself back to the age of three, four or five, what did I love

doing?
- How do I express my creativity now?
- How do I manage change?
- What has been the most important relationship in the whole of my life? Why?

Creativity, by the way, does not mean painting like Leonardo da Vinci. It means allowing yourself to do things for the sheer joy of doing them – not because they will earn money, fill in time or are things you 'ought' to do. If you feel your Sacral chakra could do with some help to open its petals in order to become part of your orchestra, there are plenty of opportunities. Belly dancing (if you are a woman), or salsa will get that area moving and feeling. Enrol on a local 5 Rhythms experience – it's all about movement - or any kind of creative class you feel drawn to. Using your non-dominant hand to draw or write is particularly powerful. Allow yourself to indulge your senses, leaving guilt outside the door. Beautiful scents, luxurious baths, oils, massage and delicious sensuality. This chakra is about relationship! And since charity begins at home, be kind and gentle with the body that serves you so well. What would it like to do, if you threw the rulebook away?

The SOLAR PLEXUS Chakra: Colour – Yellow

Learning too soon our limitations,
we never learn our powers.
Mignon McLaughlin: The Neurotic's Notebook

Position on the body:	Solar plexus.
Relates to:	Digestive system, pancreas, liver, the ego.
Body Speaks through:	Ulcers, eating disorders, diabetes, hypertension, disorders of the stomach, pancreas, gall bladder, liver.
Thoughts that affect:	I've got no drive; I can't do it. He/she

makes me feel small. I am better than her/him. I'll do what they tell me. I'm always right. I'll show them who's in control.

Feelings that affect: Fear. Shame and guilt. Rage and aggression. Arrogance. Low self-worth. Powerful/powerless.

Past life themes: Use and abuse of power over others – master/slave dramas. Lifetimes when it was not safe to be yourself, when you had to bend yourself out of shape, be invisible, or face the consequences. Lives as victims, or alternatively, power freaks. Being controlled by others, or controlling them yourself.

This chakra is sometimes referred to as the 'emotional mind'. Just about everyone, unless they are emotionally dead, will be aware of their Solar Plexus chakra. It is where we experience 'butterflies', gut feelings and reactions, and it can be knocked for six by an emotional shock. It is where we give out, and also give in, in the energy stakes. We form strong invisible cords or bondings to others through this chakra because it's a power centre, and sources of power always attract a need for control and authority over them, whether they are personal or global. Control is the key word here. As you remember that you are a soul having a human experience, this energy vortex becomes a source of supply for self-empowerment.

The Root chakra is about our relationship to the Earth and our will to survive, the Sacral is about our relationship to others and our ability to create. The Solar Plexus is about our relationship with our selves (with a small 's' as opposed to the capital 'S' of the Higher Self). It is the next flower on the chakra stem to begin to open – around the age of 7 or 8 years old. At this age we begin to get a sense of our own presence here, we become self-conscious. The ego begins to develop, which can be a double-edged sword. Self-expression and independence are essential for the personality to find its feet and place in the world, and it's often a difficult time for parents who try to find the balance between allowing the right degree of freedom combined with protection in order to prevent inexperience leading to disaster. If your parents and teachers do all the choosing or rather controlling of your views and behaviour during this phase of development, in later life you may become a rebel or alternatively like a jelly that is poured into the mould someone else has decided should be the shape of what you become.

The upper age of the opening of the solar plexus chakra – around 12 years – marks the onset of puberty, another major time of change. But like all the chakras, the healthy opening of each one depends on the health and state of the one that opened before it. This chakra is about ego development. Egos have had a bad press, but at this point we need our egos to help us forge our personality. This is what will take us out into the world and if we don't develop a sense of who we are, we remain victims or caretakers of others. Or we need other people to continually tell us who we are, because we don't know ourselves. Later on this centre will need to relinquish its position as the charioteer, and hand over to guidance from the level of the soul – often a difficult transition – but at the age of 8 to 12 most of us are not yet concerned with these things. The challenge of the Solar Plexus is not to fall into the polarities of bully or victim, master or slave, but to find a balance or equality. We need to establish who on Earth we are before we can realise who we are in Heaven's Name.

This chakra is called the 'emotional mind' because what we think has a great effect on our feelings and emotions. A thought about something that irritates you, if given space, can develop into a full-blown rage. Rage has a huge energy that can make people feel powerful and in control of others. Often underneath this is someone who feels small and vulnerable. On the other hand, if you always feel 'less than' everybody else, you will find yourself doing anything for a quiet life, at the expense of your own wishes. Emotional and mental stress affects the functioning of this chakra and your body will inform you with ulcers, digestive disorders, comfort eating.

Perhaps you'd like to reflect on the following questions, which are related to this power-house of yours …

- What situations make me feel threatened?
- Do I give away power to avoid confrontation?
- Am I afraid of my own power?
- Do I need to get my own way?
- What would happen if I lost control?
- How do I respond to emotions?

The Solar Plexus is perhaps the centre that needs the most protection and awareness of what is happening there. One way to do this is to close your eyes and focus your attention on that area of your body. Using your breath, breathe out any tension or anxiety you may be feeling, and then imagine that centre, like a flower, is gently closing. Now in your mind's eye imagine a disc in front of that area which is marked with an equal-armed cross. This provides emergency first aid, but it might be an idea to investigate the history of these reactions, so that you can bring them into conscious understanding and then move on from them.

The HEART Chakra: Colour – Green/Rose Pink

You, yourself, as much as anybody in the entire universe,
deserve your love and affection.
Buddha

Position on the body:	Centre of the chest, to the right of your physical heart.
Relates to:	Cardiovascular and autoimmune system.
Body speaks through:	Heart and circulatory problems, cancer, AIDS, ME and allergies.
Thoughts that affect:	Love is difficult. I can't love myself. I

	love too much. No-one loves me. I can't forgive them/myself. I feel vulnerable. I might get hurt. I haven't the heart for it.
Feelings that affect:	Love. Grief. Courage. Compassion. Empathy. Yearning. Bitterness. Joy. Forgiveness. 'Illegal' love.
Past Life themes:	Times when the heart was broken by grief, or pain, resulting in 'It's not safe to love'. Times when vulnerability and openness led to an overwhelming experience (betrayal, loss separation, unrequited love). A lifetime where you left your body taking with you a deep impression that 'I will never forgive them/myself because of what they/I have done'. Or "I'll never love again …"

After we have coped with survival (Root), become aware of others (Sacral) and developed our own 'I'dentity (Solar Plexus), the opening of the flower of the Heart chakra is next on the list and may first be experienced around the age of 12 as having a crush on someone. These feelings are the first stirrings of love – feelings of connection with another person in a particular way. It's something we feel here, in our chest, which means we have arrived at the heart, the centre of the system in more ways than one. When we 'come from the heart' we can rise above the issues of security, sexuality and personal power – they will fall away in the face of a force so powerful that they cease to exist in their old forms. That force is love. Not any old love, but the kind that has no strings attached, no conditions, no scripts and hidden agendas. A rare commodity these days.

Love? In Sanskrit there are over 60 different words to describe the different faces of love. In the West we have only one that we use to describe everything from hot buttered toast to God. But whatever word you use to describe it, the true feeling of Heart Love is one that is extended to another without any need for acknowledgement or the expectation of something in return. But charity begins at home and until we can begin to love ourselves, we can never truly love another. "Love thy neighbour as thyself", said Jesus. We remember the part about loving our neighbours, but somehow the last two words escape our attention. Perhaps that is because loving yourself conjures up images of preening in front of mirrors and strutting around saying, "I am the greatest". Those are peacock postures that belong to the ego and personality – they have nothing to do with Heart Love. This love is a generating force; it radiates; it expands and it changes the rate of vibration of our whole aura, and it's in urgent need of polishing at this moment in our history. It also holds the key to our most important portal – connection with our soul.

If you look at the chakra 'map' you will notice that it is bang in the centre of the 3 lower centres, and the 3 upper ones. It is the interface between upper and lower, between Heaven and Earth. It has a foot in both camps so to speak and provides us with clues to both these 'worlds' or states of being. In the meantime you might like to pause for a moment and ask yourself these questions ....

- Who gave me love without strings attached?
- If I feel closed and defended, what do I need? What am I afraid of?
- Is forgiveness of myself or another needed?
- Can I remember joy?
- What stops me from telling someone that I love them when I'm uncertain of their response?
- What makes my heart sing?

The answers to opening the Heart (and soul) will not be found in the mind, nor by words on a page. Allowing your Heart to be 'touched' will strengthen your connection to its source of wisdom. This connection will always give you the sense of 'coming home'. Remember the old adage 'Home is where the Heart is'? - a drop of perennial wisdom coming down through the ages.

When a world finishes and time runs out,
the sleepers awaken.
They discover the meaning of love,
the depth of their eternal nature.
They find meaning in every second.
For many people in our world, the time has come to remember.
Samuel Sagan

The THROAT Chakra: Colour – Turquoise/Aquamarine

Talking is like playing on the harp;
There is as much in laying the hands on the strings to stop their vibration
As in twanging them to bring out their music.
Oliver Wendell Holmes

Position on the body:	Neck, throat, mouth, nose and ears.
Relates to:	Upper respiratory tract, thyroid, mouth and organs of speech. Auditory and nasal systems.
Body speaks through:	Problems in neck, throat, mouth and gums. Sinuses, nasal problems. Ears and auditory problems. Over/under active thyroid.
Thoughts that affect:	Mustn't say anything. Better keep quiet/fill the silence with words. Don't trust myself. What will they think if I say that? Can't express myself.
Feelings that affect:	Fear. Worthlessness. Trust. Speechless.
Past life themes:	Lives when opening your mouth resulted in disaster. Lives as preachers or someone with a 'message' who died for broadcasting their beliefs. Lives involved

with secrets and lies and their
consequences.

The throat chakra, unsurprisingly, is all about communication – honest communication. Our voices say a lot about who we are and the state of the other chakras in the orchestra. 'In the beginning was the Word and the Word was with God and the Word was God' are the opening verses of the Gospel of St John. Every word has a sound; in fact every thing has its own 'note'.

Some scientists are beginning to believe that sound created the basic pattern that enabled the universe to come into being. Sound is vibration, an invisible energy, which creates form. Perhaps everything then was created from a certain sound which created that particular form.

Each of us has a unique fingerprint, DNA structure and individual sound. The Throat chakra is concerned with the expression of that note and how it is communicated. It also has a direct link with the second – the Sacral – centre, which deals with relationships. The Sacral is about your relationships with other people in this physical dimension whereas the Throat is about a different relationship – between your personality/ego self and your soul. This centre gets out of kilter when the personality consistently speaks from its own point of view which is at variance with that of the soul. This chakra is also about trust. Can you trust your Self to speak up and speak out? When you are on the receiving end of cutting comments, or torrents of verbal lava, what happens? What happens to your voice? 'Open your mouth' says your soul, and trust me to speak the truth, not the truth of the solar plexus with all its issues around power and control, but the truth of your soul. Or in the words of Mark Twain:

If you speak the truth, you don't have to remember anything.

This chakra is also linked to your hearing – the receptive end of any dialogue. Problems with hearing might be because there is something, an inner voice, that you are preferring not to listen to. It's not always easy to speak up, and it's not what you say of course, but the way that you say it that really carries the message. Blurting things out or shouting at someone will probably not have the desired effect. The throat looks like a bottleneck on the body, and can literally create a 'bottleneck' in the communication highway between head, heart and the other three members of the chakra family. So if there isn't freeflow through this chakra, body will try to assist by physically expressing its discomfort at the situation. Continual bouts of bronchitis, laryngitis, coughs, colds, sinusitis will be the symptoms of communication problems which are being experienced by body and soul. Don't keep quiet about being 'choked' by something. Spit it out! Cough it up!

As the old Arabian proverb reminds us, "What comes from the Heart is heard by the Heart". Words spoken or deeds done from a place of truth can only result in benefit for all.

Pause for a moment and ask yourself these questions …

- Do I always say what I mean and mean what I say?
- Do I feel uncomfortable with silence?
- If I let people know who I really am, will I be rejected, or accepted?
- If I say what I feel, will I hurt others? What does that mean to me?
- Are the views that I voice my own?

If you feel that you are not expressing your true Self or what you really would like the world to hear, there are several ways of freeing your voice, one of which is to have a go at toning or chanting. Becoming familiar with the sounds you are able to make will give your Throat chakra the confidence to express itself in other areas of your life. Like an auric workout, freeing your voice will clear the airwaves and allow you to become more in tune with your own individual note. There are plenty of workshops available on freeing your voice, notably Chloe Goodchild in the UK and Jonathan Goldman in the US.

The BROW Chakra or THIRD EYE: Colour – Indigo Blue

It's not what you look at that matters, it's what you see.
Henri David Thoreau

Position on the body:	Above and between the eyebrows.
Relates to:	Mind, brain, eyes.
Body speaks through:	Tension headaches, migraine, visual problems.
Thoughts that affect:	It's only my imagination. I don't trust my intuition. Logic is the only way to sort things out. Dreams are rubbish.
Feelings that affect:	Confusion. Clarity of vision. Information overload.
Past life themes:	Lifetimes as witches, magicians and seers when the use of insight, intuition and inner vision ended in death or persecution. Abuse or development of magical powers.

This chakra is linked to the pituitary gland, which is the conductor of the endocrine orchestra as the Third Eye is the command centre of the chakra system. Here we find the managing director or overseer. Being the balance point between the left and right functions of the brain, from here it's possible to 'see' in all directions. The Third Eye looks outwards and inwards, seeing what the soul needs to observe and thus having an overview of situations. This chakra is concerned with seeing of a very different nature from that of your physical eyes, in other words insight, inner vision and in-tuition.

Living life purely from the level of personality/ego, we struggle with the issues of insecurity, lack of confidence, the need to be needed, feelings of isolation, being unloved, loss of control and other problems that are the concerns of the ego. The first step in redressing this imbalance is to acknowledge that we are not paying attention to the soul's vision. Yes, the overseer needs to hear what the workforce has to say, but not to let it run the company.

As we begin to realise that there is more to us than we thought there was, our consciousness and awareness expands. As this happens, we discover new ways of using our minds. The Third Eye is sometimes referred to as the Gateway to the Void because the next vibrational step up is the Crown chakra and our connection to All That Is. It is the home of our imagination and channel for our dreams and other communications from our souls. This eye that you can't see is the vital tool for experiencing and exploring the inner passageways of the Self. This chakra will also be affected by others who might play mind games with you (or you with them), thereby disempowering your own ability to 'see' for yourself.

Pause for a moment and ask yourself these questions ....

- Do I trust my intuition?
- Do I pay attention to my dreams? What inner visions do I have?
- Do I respect my insights?
- How balanced is my view of life?

To encourage your Third Eye to play a more active part in the scheme of things give yourself time and space for meditation and contemplation. Pay attention to your dreams, and catch them in a journal kept beside your bed before they evaporate. More on dreams and their interpretation later in the book. In the meantime, you can try this rather bizarre-sounding exercise.

Place a copper coin – about one inch in diameter – on the point above and between your eyebrows which is the position of the Third Eye. You will recognise it, as it is the anatomical indentation in the middle of the forehead. The coin, when pressed onto the spot will create a vacuum, and stay in position for as long as your forehead muscles are relaxed. Not only does this help you locate the position of your Third Eye, but it has to be the world's most inexpensive biofeedback device for releasing tension headaches. The copper of the coin also has something to do with its effectiveness, since it is an excellent conductor of heat and electricity and, according to old folk lore, its magical qualities were on a par with those of quartz crystal.

The CROWN Chakra: Colour – Amethyst/Silver/White Gold

There are joys which long to be ours.
God sends ten thousands truths, which come about us like birds seeking inlet;
but we are shut up to them, and so they bring us nothing, but sit and sing awhile upon the roof, and then fly away.
Henry Ward Beecher

Position on the body:	Top of the head.
Relates to:	Top of the skull.
Body speaks through:	Depression, epilepsy, nerve/brain and mental disorders.
Thoughts that affect:	Life is pointless. There is no higher power – I don't believe in anything. I AM All That Is.
Feelings that affect:	Despair. Desolation. Isolation. Pointlessness. Connection and sense of purpose.
Past Life Themes:	Lifetimes when you felt your god had deserted you. Lives when religious fervour had an adverse affect on you. Lives as martyrs, saints or holy people – or destroyers of such people.

The Sanskrit name for this chakra is '*Sahasrara*', meaning 'thousand-fold' which no doubt is why one of its other names is the lotus with a thousand petals. There are quite an array of colours associated with this chakra - violet, amethyst, silver, white and gold – indicating its high frequency vibration. So we have now traversed the spectrum of the rainbow from red to violet, from earth to heaven, from matter to spirit.

At a physical level, this chakra is linked to the pineal gland, which is a light detector. The Crown chakra is where the individual light of the soul is linked with the Divine, the Source, the Infinite. To use a more mundane metaphor, it is through the crown that we communicate with the Upstairs Management and a source of guidance and connection from the highest level – all we have to do to receive this is to ask, and then remain open without expectation.

Saints and holy people are depicted with a light or halo round their heads – this is the expanded Crown chakra, shining like a beacon, beaming out the fact that body and soul are one – this being is in the world but also not of it. It is through the Crown chakra that we experience the highest states of meditation, that take us into a place beyond words – an experience of no-thingness beyond mind, body and emotions. But it's important to remember that working only with the higher centres, without knowledge of the others, is like using a power tool that is not earthed. The full power of the soul, the spirit, floods through this vortex down into and through all the other chakras, filling the whole being with light. All sense of an individual self expands into the knowing experience of boundlessness. This state is referred to as 'enlightenment'. With this awareness, no task has to be undertaken using the limited strength of the little ego alone, and surrender does not feel like a threat.

Total despair is demonstrated when someone places their hands over the top of their heads. They feel as if they have lost connection with life itself. It's as if their hands are expressing their sense of being 'cut off' from the Source. Blessings are conferred here and perhaps the pointed hats of bishops and witches, and the domed headdresses of the pharaohs were intended as personal 'lightening' conductors. Spiritual awakening is about liberation, and the quest for what is really real. It's about experience, not dogma. The thousandfold mysteries of the Crown chakra beckon like a lighthouse in the darkness, unfailingly drawing us Home.

Just pause for a moment and ask yourself these questions:

- Who am I?
- What am I doing here?
- Am I alone?
- What do I truly know?

Your experience of the Crown chakra and its multidimensional nature cannot be forced, it won't happen by trying. In fact the words to hold onto through all your experiments in expansion are 'allow' and 'surrender'. These are not states that we (or rather our egos) feel comfortable with but 'letting go' (another favourite) is the first step in sending your arrow of intention out into the field of pure potential. This acts as an invitation for something infinitely larger than your little self to step in. When I'm approaching some ego-scaring situation, I remind myself of that Indiana Jones film when he has nowhere to go but to step off into the void in order to achieve his goal. As he does this – whew – a crystal bridge appears. Try it.

> Come to the edge.
> We might fall.
> Come to the edge.
> It's too high!
> COME TO THE EDGE!
> And they came
> and he pushed
> and they flew ………………
Christopher Logue on Apollinaire

Soul Focus
Your chakras are the spectrum through which your soul addresses its karmic agendas. They offer the potential to connect Heaven and Earth through the conduit of your physical body.

REMINDERS ....

- Become aware of which chakra is responding to what and who.
- Whilst most of the action may be going on in the middle, pay attention to both ends of the spectrum – the Root and the Crown – in order to find real balance.
- Notice which colours you like or dislike - how does that relate to the issues of the chakra of that colour?
- Different sound levels affect each chakra. Drums and stomping will assist your Root chakra, whilst Mozart and Gregorian chant connect to the Crown.

Resources:

Eastern Body, Western Mind: **Anodea Judith** (Celestial Arts)
Chakras and their Archetypes: **Ambika Waters** (The Crossing Press)
Anatomy of the Spirit: **Caroline Myss** (Bantam Books)
Working with Your Chakras: **Ruth White** (Piatkus)
Harry Oldfield's Invisible Universe: **Jane and Grant Solomon** (available from Oldfield Systems www.electrocrystal.com/) www.oldfieldmicro.com/

chapter 5

inner children & shadowlands

Little Prisoners of the Past

Our birth is but a sleep and a forgetting,
The soul that rises with us, our life's star,
Hath had elsewhere its setting
And cometh from afar:
Not in entire forgetfulness,
And not in utter nakedness,
But trailing clouds of glory do we come
From God, who is our home.
Heaven lies about us in our infancy!
Shades of the prison-house begin to close
Upon the growing boy.
William Wordswoth: Intimations of Immortality from
Recollections of Early Childhood (1803)

You may possibly be wondering what on earth inner children have got to do with bodies and souls. In fact what on earth *are* inner children? If you are not familiar with the term, hopefully by the end of this chapter you will have met a member of your family that you haven't seen for a while, someone who influences you in all the areas of your life that are difficult. Someone who, whilst only small, is also a source of joy and laughter and who can put you in touch with the nature of your soul.

The figure of Jesus, the Christ, appears as a Master, teacher, healer and a bright punctuation mark on the timeline of humanity's chronicled earthly experience, but many of his illuminated teachings have been bypassed and subverted into rules for dominance and division. In 1945 the United States dropped atomic bombs on Nagasaki and Hiroshima - in the name of peace! Curiously, within a year or so of that time two of the most important discoveries were made in the field of sacred literature – the Dead Sea Scrolls and the Nag Hammadi library. It was almost as if the seeds of disaster were counterbalanced by revelations of truth. The Nag Hammadi library is a collection of papyrus fragments written by members of an early Christian Coptic sect about 200 years after the time of Jesus and found in a jar in a cave at the edge of the desert in Egypt. This small group were the last of the Gnostics, who holed up in the Egyptian temple of Hathor at Dendera. Before they were rootled out and exterminated, they placed the few remaining fragments of their wisdom and knowledge in a jar and hid it in a desert cave on the other side of the Nile from Nag Hammadi where it would remain for nearly 2,000 years. These Gnostics maintained that their belief sustained the true teachings of Jesus, as opposed to what was being enforced as Orthodox Christianity by the Christian fathers. One of the key tenets of Gnosticism, as already mentioned earlier, is the belief that the path to spirituality is not in wor-shiping an external god, but in finding that divinity within yourself. Jesus was not the first to teach this path. It is the ageless perennial wisdom that had been taught in the Mystery schools for centuries which fountained briefly to the surface then, that we might drink and remember. But the fountain was soon sealed, and we were left with a travesty of those teach-ings that were meant to inspire and remind everyone that "All these things you can do, and more". Jesus spoke also about children, as the words recorded by Matthew in chapter 18 of the New Testament relate:

And He said, "I tell you the Truth.
Unless you change and become like little children,
you will never enter the Kingdom."

You might like to compare that with the Nag Hammadi library version, apparently recorded directly from Jesus by the apostle Thomas. It informs us that:

> Jesus said: The man old in days will not hesitate
> To ask a little child of seven days
> about the Place of Life,
> and he will live,
> for many who are first shall become last
> and they shall be a single One.

What did he mean when he said those words? He was certainly not suggesting that we all become childish in order to regain our sense of wholeness, or Holiness, but perhaps that we need to regain some of the childlike qualities and innate knowledge that we left behind when we began to move into adulthood.

If you have ever looked into a baby's eyes, you will have noticed its gaze of frank innocence. There is a total absence of fear, and it is almost as if it is looking right into you. It will hold its observation for as long as it is interested. What is it looking at and taking in? Is it able to remember where it just arrived from?

The research work of Dr Ian Stevenson has proved that in some cases, this is so. He is the highly respected Research Professor of Psychiatry at the University of Virginia, now in his eighties, who has meticulously documented investigations into children's claims that they have lived before. His scrupulous credentials and painstaking world-wide investigations provide irrefutable evidence of reincarnation. For over 40 years he has investigated the phobias, birthmarks and other physical anomalies in children who speak about places, people and lives that they could not possibly have knowledge of. For instance a boy in Turkey who was born with a severely malformed area on the right side of his face, which included his ear, reported that he had been shot at point blank range in this area in his last life, and had died six days later in hospital. Cases of children who felt they were the wrong gender spoke of previous lives as the opposite sex from which they had been born this time, others said they were with the 'wrong' parents. He reports that children as young as two years old will offer information about how it was 'when they were big' and talk in detail about where they lived and the others around them, sometimes even speaking languages they have never heard in this life. This memory seems to be available up to about the age of five, after which time it sinks down into the unconscious mind. Some of the statements a child may make who seems to be remembering a past incarnation are "You're not my mummy/daddy", " I've got another mummy/daddy", "When I was big I used to have ... blue eyes/ live in a white house/had a car", "I have a wife/husband/children" or "I died ... in an accident/after a fall/in a fight". This could be disconcerting for a parent being confronted with these sorts of statements from a small child. Dr Stevenson offers help for parents in such situations at his website, given at the end of this section.

No one knows exactly when the soul is fully engaged with the body it's going to inhabit. Some say it may not be until a couple of days after birth. If you remember from the section on the chakras, only the Crown and the Root are open at birth – the Crown as the entry point, and the Root in order to 'earth' the soul. If the soul has made its commitment to this body and these circumstances, it will engage with the foetus in the womb – whilst still aware of where it came from – and begin to be receptive to the earthly frequencies. These first impressions then, will be the wave-forms of feeling coming through the mother that is housing it. It will become increasingly aware of her feelings, her moods and the energy of her interactions with others. We, as the soul-child, will have experienced peace in her moments of relaxation, especially if she has played calming music, and we will have felt tension if she has been angry, sad, guilty. Remember that each feeling and emotion has its own waveform, which permeates the entire being, and at this time in our lives we are right in the middle of what our mothers' are experiencing. As Sue Gerhardt, a psycho-analytic psychotherapist and co-founder of the Oxford Parent Infant Project, points out in her book 'Why Love Matters', the picture emerging in modern science is that our genes provide us with the raw ingredients for our mind – each of us having slightly different ingredients – but it is the cooking, particularly in infancy, which matters. In other words, to cite Dr Lipton's research once again, it's our *environment* that acts as a trigger for the expression of genetic inheritance. Metaphysically speaking then, it is our early life experiences that activate the soul's theme for this particular episode on Earth. The parents we have will trigger the contents of our contracts in their roles as our initial custodians for this experience, whether they were loving, absent or abusive. Many of us born during a war emerged virtually wearing a tin hat and ready to run from the level of fear we had already experienced before we had even arrived. Dr Tian Dayton, in her book *The Quiet Voice of Soul* puts it beautifully when she says "Metaphorically, the child carries in its heart a suitcase for its life, packed by its mother".

Even if there hadn't been much space between your last life and this one, which Dr Stevenson's research would suggest, your soul will have had some connection with Home base, that place of Love without conditions, a place of beauty and fine vibration, unity and peace. It is much harder for a soul to arrive into a divided and often hostile world, than it is to leave at death to return Home. Imagine the effects on a new born baby/soul of the old methods of childbirth. Arc lights, peering faces, metal instruments, turned upside-down and slapped on the back to make it take its first breath. Enough to make anyone think twice about whether this was a good idea. Thank heavens for the return to more natural methods, such as water birthing, and mothers delivering in a squatting position instead of with their legs up in stirrups.

The newborn, innocent and vulnerable soul-child is totally dependent on others for its survival. Physical survival, whilst obviously fundamental, is secondary to the importance of nurture and love. Through love, the soul-child retains its sense of connection. It has just come from a place where Love is the force that holds everything together. The expression of anything other than love from its earthly custodians is assumed to be due to some failure of its own. No child is born a murderer, an abuser, a granny-basher. These traits are the results of what happens to innocence and the shutting down of feeling. Dr Alexander Lowen, a pioneer in the field of mind/body oriented psychotherapy, maintains that the feelings of guilt and unworthiness implanted in the first three years of life are almost universal.

Here then is the fundamental wound we all struggle with – a sense of separation – and of being 'disconnected'. A baby continually looks for and into its mother's eyes (the windows of her soul), for that connection. The relationship between parents and their babies and children influences both the biochemistry and structure of their brains. Sue Gerhardt explains "The most frequent behaviours of the parental figures, both mother and father, will be etched in the baby's neural pathways as guides to relating. These repeated experiences turn into learning, and in terms of the pathways involved in emotion, this consists primarily of learning what to expect from others in close relationships." All this is going on when the first and second chakras are opening. Much later on in life we may find ourselves looking for lost connections through music or nature, or through sex, drugs and alcohol – anything that takes away the pain of isolation and loneliness if that was what we felt when we were little.

But the source of connection that so many seem to have lost or are unable to establish is kept alive in the heart of this little child. The one who was with you at birth and who remembers his or her place of origin. The one who looked wide-eyed and wondering at the world and was fascinated by all there was around. Absorbed in watching a beetle, rain on a windowpane, daubing mud or splashing in a puddle. Like an open hand, a soft ball of wax – ready to receive the imprints of experience on Earth.

For most however, the early years were not all fun and games. The world can soon become frightening because we have little influence on what makes its mark on us. Being so open and receptive, and relying on our sixth sense to inform us of our relationship with 'out there', we experience everything through the membrane of our static-free auric fields. Since our intellects have not developed – our left brain begins its work after the right side is already functional - we rely totally on our sensory perceptions.

We may already have experienced feelings in the prenatal stage that made us feel unsafe, and after arrival here it can get worse. There may be actual physical abuse, or shocks of a different nature. One parent leaving – either through divorce, death or illness can create a state of emergency for a little person, a situation for which the child feels responsible. I always thought, for example, that it was my fault that my father never returned from the war and I was responsible for my mother's seemingly endless grief, which I found paralysing. The shocks that hit the Divine Child might seem insignificant to an adult but, as Elizabeth Kubler-Ross said in one of her powerful seminars on Life, Death and Transition, "All grief weighs the same". At that moment of shock the feelings that really needed to be expressed are stuffed away, locked up – or fly off like the raven in Grimm's Fairy Tale into the forest of the unconscious mind. A child left unattended for long periods, the one hearing parents shouting, the one sensing that 'something is wrong' but not knowing what, the unpredictability of an alcoholic parent or even being told that Father Christmas or their 'imaginary friends' do not exist can create what is called 'soul loss' in shamanic practice. These moments have a profound impact on a child who has not yet developed the ability for verbal communication.

This means that we walk on down the time-line of our lives not totally whole. It is the reason why most people are not fully 'present'. Aspects of ourselves remain frozen in that moment of shock or trauma, but still whisper from the forest "It's not safe!" And it is these whispers – sometimes commands – that trigger the same confusion, fear or pain whenever we encounter a situation that re-minds the Child of that time-held moment and all that it was perceived to mean. The soul requires the personality to turn and rescue this small person from these frozen moments or it will, on its behalf, continue to call, whisper or scream from wherever it is hidden until – if we don't pay attention – we will be driven into depression, breakdown or a dark night of the soul.

Just **STOP** for a moment …… in threatening or painful situations, what do you do? Split off, feel numb, or go deep within? And then what do you do?

In order to receive the love and acceptance we need, we develop 'coping strategies'. Here are some of the most common contemporary 'archetypes' we take on in order to find our place in the physical world. Perhaps you will notice which ones you identify with.

THE PLEASER: I suppress my own feelings in order to make everybody else feel all right. If everyone else feels all right they will not reject me. If I make people pleased, then they will not reject me and I will feel safe. If I do what people want, they will love me.

Later in life: I rush around looking after people. I don't value myself and I often feel guilty. I can only relax when everyone else has every thing they want. O dear I must go and phone poor Sarah/my father/partner.

THE ACHIEVER: I have to try harder and harder to prove to my parents that I am good enough to be loved. I keep hearing a voice saying: "You could have done better".

Later in Life: I am often a workaholic (even an alcoholic) and overstressed. Success is a matter of life or death for me. If I haven't got it right, I've got it wrong, and I will have failed (and I won't be loved). Excuse me, I have some work I must get done.

THE REBEL: Pleasing people didn't get me love. My parents were aloof and controlling. The only way I get attention is by making a fuss, or doing something naughty. This means trouble, but at least somebody sees me.

Later in life: I like to shock, and I often get angry. It's usually when I feel I am not getting any attention, or people won't do what I want them to do. And why don't you just eff off?

THE I DON'T CARE ABOUT ANYTHING: It seems that nothing I do gets any attention, so I might as well give up – there's no point in trying because whatever I do, they don't love me. I need huge amounts of encouragement to give me confidence but it never feels as if it's enough.

Later in life: I give up very easily and often feel bored and lazy. I know you don't mean it when you tell me that I'm good at what I do. What's the point of it all?

THE RATIONALISER: I live in my head, because it's the safest place to be. There was just too much emotion around in the family and it nearly frightened me to death; it was so overwhelming. It's much safer to cut out those frightening things called feelings. OR in my family feelings weren't acknowledged. I was always told I shouldn't cry or get cross, so I don't really know much about feelings ...

Later in life: Feelings? Don't go in for them much myself. When was I last angry or sad? Now let me just think ....

THE BULLY: Nobody is really around for me, but I've learned from my mum and dad that you feel safe if you make others frightened of you. I could see that by being cruel to animals and insects, and 'weeds' at school I felt safe.

Later in life: I feel powerful when I see a look of fear on your face. It's like a fuel injection for me. Other people's feelings? Not my problem – and what's yours by the way?

THE VICTIM: Oh dear! Nobody loves me. I get attention when I cry and tell mummy that someone has hurt me or I don't feel well. If I cry enough, I'll get some attention.

Later in life: It's all the fault of the government, or is it the NHS? Or perhaps it was my mum – or the weather. I can't take responsibility for my own life, because if I do, then no one will look after me. What? Of course it's someone else's fault that things don't go right in my life.

THE RESCUER: I learned that doing things for mum or dad made them give me love. They used to call me 'goody goody' and 'teacher's pet' when I went to school.

Later in life: I like victims, because I can look after their problems and don't have to pay attention to my own. I'm different from a Pleaser, because I make sure that people are dependent on me. It makes me feel in control and needed. Gotta go – a client has just called me ...

THE MANIPULATOR: The only way I can get attention is by sulking and crying. I have such a big hole in me that I feel I will never get enough love to fill it. Sometimes I get attention by refusing to eat or put on my clothes.

Later in life: I really don't know what I want apart from your attention and I will get it by fair means or foul. You're not really listening, are you?

THE DREAMER: I spend a lot of my time daydreaming. I feel comfortable doing that because I find life here harsh and a bit difficult. I prefer being in my own little world.

Later in life: I often forget to keep appointments and lose my keys. People say I'm absent-minded – what was that you were saying? Sorry, my mind was somewhere else.

THE NARCISSIST: I was such a beautiful child. Everybody adored me. I was daddy's little princess/mummy's beautiful boy. I always got my way because I learned how to manipulate people.

Later in life: Appearance is everything. I often choose friends who are much less attractive than I am, so there's no competition. Yes, I am scared of getting old, because what will happen when I lose my looks?

THE HURT CHILD: I am almost certain to be in you somewhere. Nobody really listened to me because they were too busy, or didn't understand, or were too tired, or liked my brother better than me. I've built a wall around myself, because it feels safer then.

Later in life: I sometimes feel depressed and isolated. It's difficult to let people in, so I can be sarcastic, a bit rude or hide behind my 'cheerful' mask. I often make light of what I am really feeling, so people don't know what's going on inside. You can't be too careful about the people you trust, you know.

Reconnection to your inner child is not asking you to become childish again, but to regain some of the qualities you had when a child that were squashed down, blocked off and buried, and never allowed expression. Those feelings that flew away to hide somewhere because they were unacceptable or would have been overwhelming – and then what might have happened? These buried feelings stand between us and our expansion into soulfulness. When you meet up with your inner child – and it may turn out to be a tribe of children, all of different ages – it feels as if some part of you that has been absent returns home. We are our own best parents now. We, as adults, are the best people to understand the needs of those parts of us that got left behind and frozen in an ice cube of time.

Meeting with your own inner child is like finding the missing pieces of a jigsaw. There is a powerful sense of being 'more' than you were, as one by one these little children's energy is repatriated to where it belongs. If you have photos of yourself as a child, have a good look at them, and see how present you are in them. If you come across one or two where there is clearly something going on 'behind the scenes', then connect to that little person, talk to them as if they were in the room with you, use your sixth sense to tune in and find out what this child needs from you now. This is not about blaming your parents – after all you chose them. And most parents do the best they can with what they have. They're carrying all their inner children too – and there was probably no one around to help them understand why they became emotionally disabled as adults.

Inner child work in therapy has proved to be an extremely potent and dynamic way of releasing patterns from the past and helps us to get in touch with the shadowy, unexpressed side of our selves but for those on a spiritual journey, it has to go so much deeper than that. .

Soul Focus

The soul dances, sings and makes magic through the innocence of a child.

REMINDERS ....

- Take some quiet time and go back in your mind to the point at which you were born. Then move forward allowing the subconscious right brain to float up images, or a sense of 'land-mark' moments. Start with the first seven-year period and see what you can remember about your childhood. If you have no recollection, it doesn't mean you have wiped it all out, but the question to ask is *if* you could remember, how might you have got the love and attention you needed if it wasn't freely available. Do you still look for love in this way?

- When you have reclaimed one of your 'lost' inner children make sure they know they are home (no, it isn't a silly game), by being aware of their presence until you feel they have become part of you again.
- Stop to watch a squirrel, feed the birds and observe children playing. Whose voice is telling you it's silly to kick the leaves and stamp in a puddle?
- Don't take life so seriously! Children are not concerned with outcomes and goals (unless it's an ice cream). They do what they're doing just for the joy of doing it, absorbed in the journey rather than focused on the destination.

Resources:

Homecoming: **John Bradshaw** (Piatkus)

The Inner World of Childhood: **Frances Wickes** (Coventure)

Children Who Remember Past Lives: **Ian Stevenson** (Mc Farland & Company)

http://www.healthsystem.virginia.edu/internet/personalitystudies/

Why Love Matters: **Sue Gerhardt** (Routledge)

Children's Past Lives: **Carol Bowman** (Bantam USA) www.child-pastlives.org

Recovery of Your Inner Child: **Lucia Capacchione** (Simon & Schuster)

Before we proceed further on our spiritual excavations, we will dare to take a peek at something else we may not be conscious of – the shadow-lands of our selves.

Illuminating the Darkness

It is the universal statement of a star,
the message Orion

has carried
in winter
throughout the ages:
It is the dark
which illuminates.
Lyn Dalebont (Out of the Flames)

There is a tendency amongst surfers of the New Age Wave to believe that Love and Light will prevail against all odds, and in one sense this is true, but in order for this to become so and to find the balance that takes us to realisation, we first need to acknowledge the presence of its dark opposite. We deny our shadow at our peril, since its content contains so much of us which, if repressed or unexpressed, can become an uncontrollable volcano, searching for fissures in our façade to let out its steam. Or we will find partners who will act out this other side of ourselves. As wise and visionary Carl Jung states:

One does not become enlightened by imagining figures of light,
But by making the darkness conscious.

It's only when the sun is directly overhead that it casts no shadow. Only when we are completely aligned with our Source, in a state of balance, will our shadow disappear. Until such time, our shadow dances around us, catching our attention and daring us to peer into the dark side of our nature. Since we are not sure of what might lurk in the deep dark aspects of ourselves, we prefer not to look in this direction but to keep the cellar door locked in case some overwhelming monster might unleash itself into our lives. We have just looked at our childhood histories and seen how the presence of the past affects our now and therefore our future. Yesterday has a hand in creating today and defining tomorrow until we become conscious of what and who is pulling the strings behind the scenes.

We run from our shadow, and avoid looking it in the eye through the escape routes already mentioned before – workaholism, all the other aholisms, mind-numbing (mindless) television, Prozac, sex, food or mood-altering chemicals. We may become ill, or we may sink into depression and resort to prescriptions which prevent the waves of despair from totally flooding our being. Or we might lock its contents in a box and throw away the key.

We all have a shadow, and until we are aware of at least some of its content, a major part of our energy will be unavailable to us. Our subconscious mind requires energy to keep it locked away from painful scrutiny. Robert Bly, the gifted contemporary poet and thinker, describes the shadow thus:

We spend our life until we're thirty deciding what parts of ourselves to stuff into the invisible bag we drag behind us, and we spend the rest of our lives trying to get them out again.

As children we enter the world innocent, vulnerable and spontaneous balls of energy, nevertheless with the personality ingredients needed for us to address our soul's assignment. Perhaps a passive nature is required this time, since we experienced being wilful or excessively active previously. We are entrusted to the care of others to teach us about this human experience. But we have work to do so, as mentioned before, it's more than likely that one or more from your soul family will appear as part of your human family in order to 'activate' the theme. The feelings that they bring up in you may be too much to cope with, too painful to realise, so they get pushed down into the unconscious shadow cellar of your self and locked away.

"Don't do that – it's dirty" and sexual feelings get put in the bag.

"If you don't stop crying, I'll smack you" and tears get stuffed into the bag.

"You mustn't hurt your sister" and aggression joins the others, along with shame, rage, powerlessness, creativity (don't make a mess), chaos, laughter and a host of other feelings that we *perceived* to be unacceptable or inappropriate.

Our chakras, like little time bombs, are encoded with the information that will need to come to the surface in this incarnation, but it needs to be 'activated'. If we haven't learned to feel safe in our bodies, free with our creative expression and confident with our personality, then by the time we are teenagers, we're already dragging a sack of potatoes. Now we need approval of our peers, and more 'unacceptable' traits go into our bag. It takes strength and determination to hold on to one's true nature in the face of the cultural and tribal pressures that most of us have to deal with at this time in our lives. We are sculpted, shaped and shaved so that by the time we are in our twenties, there is more of us in the bag than out of it.

All this goes on unconsciously, so it is as if we are living our lives on the tiny visible part of a huge iceberg, most of which is hidden in the ocean beneath us. If you are feeling threatened, or denying that this applies to you, then just spend a moment reflecting on what it was 'inappropriate' to express when you were young. There are some people who say "I had a wonderfully happy childhood – I'm very lucky", and they are. But every hero's journey worth the effort requires a hurdle, a dragon or two, some experience to enable the aspiring hero to hone his skills, to feel defeated and then find a source of strength that he didn't know existed. Perhaps a less polite way of expressing this would be to say that it's all about turning muck into manure.

And this is the purpose of the study of your shadow. Close scrutiny of our early lives will tell us what parts of us are lost in the forest, asleep in the castle or lie mute in a coffin. And the key to the door to the cellars and basements of our being will be found in identifying the situations and those involved who seemed to be responsible for the difficult experiences of our earlier years. They may not have *intended* to hurt us but that's what happened. Like Ann, whose soul is working with the theme of trust. When she was five, her elder sister told her. "Don't be silly – of course there isn't a Father Christmas. It's Dad!" From that moment on, she lost her ability to trust what people told her and disbelief became the safer option. She had 'forgotten' this incident until her relationship with her partner hit a crisis because she could not trust that he was telling her the truth. In regression therapy this moment of shock appeared from the shadows, enabling her to realise that her mistrust belonged to the little girl who felt she had been betrayed. Her fury at being deceived had been stuffed into her shadow bag. This story has its roots in her previous lives, when taking someone's word, or being untrustworthy herself, had resulted in radical consequences.

These childhood shocks will often (but not always) be linked to our past lives. Issues concerning power or the lack of it in the past will drop us into a family where we easily lose our own sense of self. Or if we are working on the theme of abandonment, for example, we may find ourselves as an adopted child in this lifetime trying to cope with the feeling that 'nobody wants me' – a feeling too painful to go into, so it gets stuffed away, but the energy of that unacceptable feeling runs like an undercurrent through that person's life and they *will* experience rejection until they have the courage to investigate its source, and free its history.

The trouble with feelings that get stuffed into the shadow bag, sent off into the forest, or frozen into an ice cube in that moment is that they may be dead, or numbed out, but they do not lie down. There comes a moment in most people's lives – and very often this comes as a crisis in mid-life – when the energy required to contain and restrain the contents of our shadow can no longer keep the lid on things and, like a pressure cooker, a head of steam builds up which may finally explode and splatter stew all over the ceiling. In this case, rabbit stew …

I will never forget Dr Elisabeth Kubler Ross, the Swiss psychiatrist who was responsible in the 1960s for raising awareness about the dying process, telling of her own shadow experience. Elisabeth was an identical twin, born of a stern Swiss psychiatrist and his wife. It was difficult for people to differentiate between the two girls, except that Elisabeth was the one who kept rabbits. She kept this little family of hers out in the stables and had come to terms with the fact that every so often her father would select one of them to go into the pot for Sunday lunch. But she had a favourite – Blacky – who she used to cover with straw so her father could not see him when he carried out his grim selection. Of course the dreaded day came when Blacky was spotted under his straw camouflage. Her father pointed at the half-seen rabbit and said 'This one, Elisabeth, today'. She then had to take her little friend along to the butcher, carry back his warm remains and then – horror of horrors – sit at the table with Blacky in the pot. No tears, no remonstrations – they were unacceptable in that family.

It was not until she was in her fifties, getting her luggage checked in at an airport, that the lid was taken off the feelings that had been held down and 'forgotten' in the shadow bag. An official pointed at one of her suitcases which he wanted opening: 'This one, please'. The official became her father in that moment and all the grief, impotence and rage of the little seven-year-old flooded her system. As she said, "I lost it then and there in the airport. I was uncontrollable and inconsolable." She explained that when she finally calmed down, she realised that it now felt as if she had put down a heavy load which she wasn't even aware that she had been carrying. The feelings held in Elisabeth's shadow were released in a rush, triggered by the memory of what a pointing finger had created for her in her childhood. Perhaps in a past life it was not a rabbit, but a loved one whom she had had to see executed, and this was the echo of that situation in the current incarnation.

The trouble is we all want to appear perfect, kind, compassionate and loving people, but unfortunately this cannot be the case whilst there are unacknowledged spectres – or even small ghosts – waiting to be released from their shadowlands. Denial of the existence of our shadows will result in persistent reminders in the form of patterns of behaviour or continually finding people in our lives who press the same old button. Sometimes the pressure in the shadow builds up to the point where something explosive takes place, and we wonder where on earth it came from, or we start to break up, in order to break through, calling it a break down. The system goes into chaos, in order to re-assemble itself, but at the time it feels as if we are in a very dark well. It's good to remember the somewhat sobering words attributed to Jesus, as recorded in *The Gospel of the*

Essenes:

> *He who calls forth that which is within him,*
> *That which is within him, shall save him.*
> *He who does not call forth that which is within him,*
> *That which is within him shall destroy him.*

The ancient Egyptians, in their wisdom, knew about the presence of the shadow, called the *Khaibit,* or animal soul. It was associated with Hathor, the feminine *neter* –or archetype - of reflective images. In their mystery schools the feelings buried in our subconscious were known as 'Obstacles to Flight', constellations of stuck energy that prevented the upward flight of consciousness. Releasing them was an initiatory process. Initiations are all about crossing the threshold from the mundane to the sacred and those who were to become privy to the eternal Mysteries had to go through a series of initiations in the temples along the Nile – each one a different test – before qualifying for the final initiation in the Great Pyramid. Here, in the so-called Pit, 345 feet into the bedrock of the plateau and 600 feet beneath the apex, initiates would have whatever fears they might still be holding amplified by crawling into a small body-sized tunnel in the pitch darkness, so that they could recognise any remaining obstacles to the flight of their soul.

Projections: the Me in You

When we deny or disown the qualities we have hidden away in the darkness they may find a means of expression through projection. Understanding the dynamic of projection is vitally important, and crucial to becoming aware of what lies hidden in our own shadows. As everything is drawn towards its counterpoint in order to find balance, you might observe that some people who seem open and without a drop of malice in them are partnered by someone who 'holds the shadow', someone who has a sense of 'darkness' around them or is just plain closed and creepy.

A projection, therefore, is a hidden quality, trait or characteristic of
our own that we react to when we experience it in another. Something
like throwing a brick at a cinema screen when we have a strong reaction
to something we see on it. We need to have a look at the film in the pro-
jector or get in touch with the director to find the source of the image.
When a person projects an unconscious quality existing within themselves on to another person, they react as if that quality belongs to the
other. At this point it might be worth stopping for a moment to draw up a
list of the main qualities you are looking for in your relationships with
others – and those you don't want. Limit it to four on each side. These are
mine – yours will be different.

Qualities I Look For	*Qualities I Don't Want*
Humour	Rigidity
Honesty	Workaholism
Sensitivity	Duplicity
Adventurousness	Volatility

Could you consider whether those qualities, on both sides, might also
belong to you? As well as the qualities you have listed, now go through
the same exercise with people. On one side the ones you admire, respect
and think the world of, and on the other the ones who you despise, drive
you mad or definitely dislike (and why).

People I Like	*People I Don't Like*
My next door neighbour (calm & strong)	Leader of a boy band (rude and irresponsible)
Billy Connolly (mad and funny)	John at work (self-obsessed)
Oprah Winfrey (making a difference)	Uncle Joe (untrustworthy)
My cousin Mary (deep and reflective)	BBC newscaster (pleased with herself)

Projections are not just limited to individuals, and this is where it gets globally dangerous. Organisations, religions, ideologies, skin colours and creeds may be the target as we see our collective shadows now acting out on the world stage. The hallmark of a projection is not so much the viewpoint, as the intensity and charge of the reaction experienced in a given situation. Road rage is a good demonstration of projection. Here's a rather simplistic example. John is a man who carries a lot of unexpressed anger. He feels taken for granted and put upon by his family and team managers at work, and feels impotent in both situations. On his way home one evening a fellow driver overtakes him and cuts in. This triggers the volcano of his unexpressed rage, which spews out in a way that's totally disproportionate to the situation, and has nothing to do with the poor unfortunate unsuspecting recipient who has all John's unexpressed frustrations thrown at him like a bucket of burning coals. Jung, in *Memories, Dreams and Reflections*, once again advises that:

Everything that is unconscious in ourselves, we discover in our neighbour, and treat him accordingly.

Is a homophobe covering up a latent potential in themselves? Is a capitalist, communist or fundamentalist of any kind shouting so loudly that he cannot see his own reflection in his adversary? Naming and blaming, finger pointing and mob violence are all examples of projection. A total inability to accept and deal with some inner frustration drives people to commit violence against others. History is littered with atrocities that have emerged from the counterbalance of love and light. Genghis Khan, Nero, Pol Pot, Hitler, the cannibal Jeffrey Dahmer, Fred and Rosemary West, the Moors murderers and other modern monsters such as Robert Mugabe and Saddam Hussein. When rage, envy, shame, blame, greed or grief, uncontrollably flood our senses, it is an overflow from the shadow. But in this shadow, at the heart of the darkness, we will find 'pure gold' as Jung stated. Our souls insist that we own our shadows, and will draw towards us more of the same until we become aware of and own what is really ours. On the other hand, or perhaps the other end of the see-saw, are those like the Dalai Lama, Mother Teresa, Nelson Mandela, Aung San Suu Kyi and all those unsung heroes and heroines quietly going about their business of helping and supporting others, and trying to redress the balance.

Once again we find a familiar story which tells us about the power of the shadow to wreak havoc when it is denied or ring-fenced out of our lives. This is the story of Jekyll and Hyde. Each of us is like Dr Jekyll, denying the existence of the dark and distorted Mr Hyde. This extraordinary tale, immortalised by Robert Louis Stevenson who wrote it in 1886, has a similarity to Mary Shelley's Frankenstein, written nearly seventy years earlier. Both are parables about the shadow side of our selves, and involve scientists who find the constraints of society so unbearable that they create an alter ego to live out their 'unacceptable passions'. Significantly, the first victim of both of these creations is a child. The story of Jekyll and Hyde (the pun is obvious) opens with two men passing a mysterious cellar door in a basement (representing the subconscious mind) where the sinister, deformed Mr Hyde apparently lives. They later discover that this door is connected in an L-shaped way (90-degree turn) to the home of Dr Jekyll. By taking a potion he has concocted, Jekyll is able to transform into Hyde and carry out his acts of depravity without guilt or remorse. He believes that the soul is made up of good and evil, and it is his quest to find a substance that, when ingested, will separate the two so that they do not have to live in bondage to each other and in constant competition. Of course, as the story reveals, it is not so simple and Mr Hyde (the shadow) begins to take over and ultimately kills himself, thus releasing both of them. The message is, as with the tale of Frankenstein, that we are not *either* our shadow self *or* the persona we present to the world, but *both* and also *neither*. How could our shadows and personalities define who we are if one is hidden and the other a mask? Behind the scenes our soul is waiting to express the All That Is.

If we could read the secret history of our enemies,
we should find in each man's life
sorrow and suffering enough to disarm all hostility.

Henry Wadsworth Longfellow

This is not about looking for trouble, or becoming attached to our wounds; it's about recognising that during our human experiences we collect the 'stuff' of earthly experiences, stuff which the soul no longer needs in order to fly free from the past. Shadows need acknowledging, need to have their hands shaken at least, so that they don't grow bigger in the dark and then have to break out in some disruptive and painful way.

We are not our biographies.

Soul Focus
Your soul casts no shadow.

REMINDERS ......

- Dark and light are the polarities of the same thing. The human experience for the soul is one of balancing dualities.
- Denial of our shadow selves is an obstacle on the flight path to Love.
- Recognising that those who push our buttons may be our shadows finding expressions 'out there' allows us to change our perspective.
- The first step in making the darkness light is to acknowledge it. Touch it gently or let it out all at once, but for Heaven's sake don't keep it locked away.
- Once it has become conscious, you can move beyond it. It doesn't need to be reinforced by continual recycling.

Resources:
The Dark Side of the Inner Child: **Stephen Wolinsky** (Bramble Books)
Owning Your Own Shadow: **Robert A Johnson** (Harper San Francisco)
How to Befriend Your Shadow: **John Monbourquette** (Darton Longman & Todd)

Meeting the Shadow: Edited by **Connie Zweig and Jeremiah Abrams** (Penguin Putnam Inc)
The Strange Case of Dr Jekyll & Mr Hyde and Other Tales: **Robert Louis Stevenson** (Oxford University Press)
Frankenstein: **Mary W Shelley** (Wordsworth Editions)

chapter 6

past lives

Haven't I Been Here Before?

I am a wonder whose origin is unknown
I have been in Asia with Noah in the Ark
I have witnessed the destruction of Sodom and Gomorrah
I have been in India when Roma was built
I am now come here to the remnant of Troia
I have been in the firmament with Mary Magdalene
I have drawn the genius from the cauldron of Keridwen
Taliesin c 534 – 599 CE

If we stopped our spiritual investigations and excavations with inner children and long shadow bags, it might just all feel a bit much, but by digging down a layer further into our historical sub-stratum we may discover some interesting fossils. No, not another can of worms. On the contrary we might at last begin to understand the famous Shakespearean quote from *As You Like It:*

All the world's a stage
And all the men and women merely players
They have their exits and their entrances;
And one man in his time plays many parts.

And all the world has been our stage. This beautiful blue dot on an outer spiral of a galaxy has had her face explored by human creatures since Heaven knows when, all acting our their dramas in her every corner, evolving their understanding of the nature of duality and what it means to be both human and spiritual.

Back at the drawing board now, and following on from looking back to those frozen moments of childhood and the shadow bag where deep and unexpressed feelings get contained, what if these never get addressed? Sean O Casey's rejoinder to Shakespeare sums it up: "All the world's a stage and most of us are desperately unrehearsed". It was only towards the end of the last century in the West that even thinking about these things became possible for most people. So, for literally ages, departing souls carried with them the scars of their incarnations, like astral barnacles. Another human body would be needed containing the ancestral DNA, cultural parentage and geographical position that would enhance the soul's opportunity to have the experiences required in order to address its astral barnacles and realise that they are part of the personality's attachment to the dramas it has been playing out on the earthly stage.

The earliest record of belief in reincarnation comes from ancient Egypt. Hindus, Buddhists, Chinese Taoists, Jews, Gnostics, Greeks, Romans, Aborigines, American Indians, Theosophists, Sufis, Zoroastrians, Rosicrucians, Freemasons and many, many more have a history of belief in reincarnation, karma and the evolution of the soul, sometimes referred to as the Eternal Return. Past civilisations accepted rebirth as naturally as they accepted the ebb and flow of the sea, the daily appearance of the sun and moon, and the cycles of the year.

Worn-out garments
Are shed by the body:
Worn-out bodies
Are shed by the dweller
Within the body.
New bodies are donned
By the dweller, like garments.
Bhagavad Gita II

However, although St Gregory of Nazaianus wrote in the 4th century CE that the "soul exchanges one man for another man, so that the life of humanity is continued always by means of the same soul", 100 years or so later a U-turn was made on the matter of reincarnation or, as it was known, the 'transmigration of souls'. In CE 553 the Second Christian Council of Constantinople, presided over by Emperor Justinian, declared that all beliefs in reincarnation were heresies. Apparently the Emperor felt that this concept, along with other Gnostic beliefs, was threatening the stability of the empire. Citizens who believed that they would have another chance to live might be less obedient and law-abiding than those who believed in a single judgement day for all.

Almost all the passages in the Bible that made reference to reincarnation were edited out at this point, and the gospels of the early Christian Gnostics went underground. If you were a Christian and wanted to contact God in those days (and until recently) you had to do it through the intercession of switchboard operators claiming to be the only ones who had a direct line to the Management – priests and clergy - most of whom had no direct experience themselves of what it was they were preaching about. This approach brought about many centuries of horrendous persecution, torture and death in the so-called 'Holy' Wars of the Inquisition and 'the Burnings' of literally millions of people who were healers, herbalists and Pagans. An extraordinary departure from the love, compassion and peaceful empowerment that had been taught by the originator of Christianity himself.

Great minds have pondered on the mysteries of birth, life and rebirth since the beginning of recorded history, and probably before that. Pythagoras, Socrates and Plato through Dante, Paracelsus, Shakespeare, Goethe and Wordsworth to Swedenborg, Emerson, Wagner, W B Yeats, Aldous Huxley, D H Lawrence, Rilke, Bertrand Russell, Somerset Maugham, Winston Churchill and Carl Jung who all freely accepted the philosophy of, 'I am here now, and have been here before'.

Today's research suggests that two-thirds of the world's population believes in past, present and future lives. Gradually psychologists, doctors, psychiatrists and therapists have documented their clinical evidence and brought what was previously considered forbidden, irrational or just plain fantasy into the mainstream of current thinking. And this was not because they went looking for it, but because it appeared spontaneously, in most cases, in front of their very eyes. This was certainly my own introduction to people's deep memories or past lives, and established my belief that this is not just another New Age phenomena – here today and gone tomorrow, if you'll excuse the pun. My experience, which felt strange at that time, was with someone who had come to be treated for something else. I was giving her a healing massage when suddenly she let out an anguished cry "I'm in Nagasaki …. My hands are melting ……. Where's my daughter….?" I might have thought this was curious and considered changing my massage techniques or given them up altogether, were it not for the fact that she called a couple of days later to report that the chronic eczema that she had suffered from on both her hands since an early age appeared to be in remission. This related directly to the release of this past trauma, held in her hands as chronic eczema. As she saw her hands melting from atomic radiation, the next thought was for her daughter. Her soul left the body with that deep impression. Three years later it took on another body, with the memory of that awful moment imprinted on her 'new' hands which demonstrated the memory with their inflamed condition.

As the years have passed, it seems that people's ability to access their past histories has become increasingly easier. For some – like the Nagasaki lady – it happens spontaneously and completely unexpectedly. It was like that for David, too. Walking in the countryside one gentle afternoon, accompanied by his dog, he glanced at a small wood that he was approaching. To his utter astonishment he saw 50 men emerge from the coppice, apparently foot soldiers intent on either capturing or killing him. He himself appeared to be one of a band of five men, equipped with rapiers and dressed all with a similar coat of arms on their chests … and then as he blinked his eyes, he was back in the 21st century with his dog approaching an apparently uninhabited wood. So vivid and lasting was the impact of this 'flashback' experience, that he searched to explore it deeper. In our session, he 'returns' to that moment and it immediately comes alive again, revealing the story behind this scenario. There are no such things as accidents, so whether this experience was an action 'replay' in the place where it had happened centuries before, or whether something else triggered it is less important than the wisdom that was to be found in re-living the whole story to find what it had to tell him in the here and now.

Here's a test
To find whether your mission on earth is finished.
If you're alive, it isn't.
Richard Bach: Messiah's Handbook

So what's this all about? Souls, as unique expressions of the Infinite Creative Mind, require earthly experience. As we come to the end of a cycle, it's as if our soul's memory banks evaluate the accounts and decide what experience is needed to balance the books (or opposites) so that at the next point of departure there will be no strings attaching us to Earth or unfinished business to require yet another body. If James Lovelock is right, in 100 years time there won't be so many opportunities to incarnate, since our numbers will be massively reduced by global change. Balancing the opposites may simply be to experience an uneventful life of peace and prosperity (for a change). Or it may be that there has been a longstanding interaction in past lives with another soul, who will be part of your 'group' that needs to be resolved with love and forgiveness. Perhaps there is unfinished business concerning passion or power, isolation or illness, wealth or poverty, betrayal or bereavement. There are as many possible scenarios as there are experiences. The people we find closest to us in this lifetime are the ones we need to connect with again in order to resolve incomplete dramas from previous lives. Any 'unfinished business' carried forward to be redressed is called *karma* (Sanskrit).

The Karmic Boomerang

The times we are in have facilitated our ability to clear our karma and move beyond it. With awareness of these matters increasing rapidly as the cosmic cycles reach an end point and the magnetics of the Earth falling, it seems as if our past histories are just below the surface of the present. We don't have to go through *all* our past lives, or even all the painful childhood memories *if* we can shift the perspective on how we perceive this seemingly very personal event called My Life. And until that happens, we will be playing out our karma, sometimes with others, sometimes on a bigger stage until either we realise that it's becoming more like a pantomime, or that we will give up acting as a career.

Karma is the law of cause and effect. Every action has a subsequent reaction. The more powerful the action, the more dramatic the response. It is the law of 'as you sow, so shall you reap', or what goes around, comes around. It's like a pendulum that swings violently in one direction, then the opposite direction, until after however many swings it takes, it returns to the point of balance in the centre. To overstate it, but to make a point for example, you may have been a Genghis Khan in one life drama. The next might have been as a grovelling slave. Then subsequent lives would be paler versions of both those until in the 21st century you may either be a bully at work, or a subservient housewife, chained to her domestic chores. This teaches us about the nature of duality, of what appear to be opposites but are in fact different sides of the same coin. It is all *relative*. Going beyond your karma then, is to find the perspective where you can see that every effect has its cause and it is we ourselves – not some force out there – who are responsible for our lives and all that goes on in them. Whatever happens, it is fine, because that is what is needed by the soul. Buddhists refer to this state as the Way of Non-attachment.

Experiences of the soul are recorded but not judged as 'good' or bad' – because it's all about experience. In order to fully understand the feeling of freedom, you need to have experienced being imprisoned – whether that is literally in jail, or in a relationship or situation that imprisons you. The feeling of emerging from a restraining and containing situation is only fully appreciated because it is *relative* to what was being felt before. In order to *fully* experience a lifetime enriched with love, you need to have felt the pain and sense of separation that comes from love-lessness. Knowing what it is like to be both with and without, takes you to the point of balance I keep on about. This point of balance is the middle of the see-saw. For example on one end you have your victim experience, and on the other is your bully or victor. Here in the middle you know that you have been both, but at the same time are neither of them. This realisation moves the perception of who you are beyond the dramas of the personality.

This perspective also removes the sense that fate is dealing you a rotten hand - you are not here to be punished and everything has a purpose and meaning in your life. It all depends on how you see it. Until this point of balance is acquired we will go on taking human bodies, time after time, until we realise what the earthly experience is really all about – understanding the qualities of opposites; and moving beyond both. Each time the soul returns Home, it assesses what it has experienced, and what further experience is needed to find the balance between the opposites which will create union. A decision will be made about what parents will be needed to bring this into focus (and these parents could be good, bad or indifferent), what culture and conditions are suitable and what personality ingredients will also suit your purpose. This all takes place in the in-between-world, known by Tibetan Buddhists as the *Bardo*.

The Bardo

As we have seen, we are made up of more than our physical body. The different levels of our personal auric field follow the ancient Hermetic principle already mentioned of "That which is Below corresponds to that which is Above, and that which is Above, corresponds to that which is Below, to accomplish the miracles of the One Thing". So down here on the Earth, we are that which is below and from understanding this, we know that this mirrors 'that which is Above'. Like a fractal. What we saw as our astral/emotional/mental body at a personal level is mirrored by the Earth (physical body) with the Bardo being the equivalent of the astral/mental plane, beyond which is the formless world of pure spirit from which everything else arises. This has been variously named the Pure Light of the Void, the Godhead, the state of non-dualism or Advaita. This is the container within which the other planes exist. Think of a dot in the centre of a series of concentric circles. The dot represents the physical plane, the densest level of vibration, just the same as our bodies might be the physical dot at the centre of our auric field. The first circle from the dot represents the Bardo, astral or intermediary plane and beyond that each ring represents a higher and finer plane of vibration, the contents of which we would be unable to grasp with our everyday logical minds. The concentric circles represent the planes that interface between physical reality and the 'miracles of the One Thing'. And as our own personal astral field contains all information about us, the Bardo contains all information about the collective body of all living organisms. Spiritualists call this plane the Spirit World, in the Celtic tradition it's known as the Middle Kingdom or the Faery World. Jung called it the Collective Unconscious, the Persian Sufis call it the *alam al-mithal* or Mythic World and the Aborigines, the Dreamtime. This is what the Upanishads have to say:

> *There are two states for man – the state in this world and the state in the next; there is also a third state, the state intermediate between these two, which can be likened to the dream [state]. While in the intermediate state a man experiences both the other states, that of this world and that in the next; and the manner whereof is as follows: when he dies he lives only in the subtle body, on which are left the impressions [samskaras] of his past deeds and of those impressions is he aware, illumined as they are by the light of the Transcendent Self...*

At the point of death, your earthly vehicle and its electromagnetic field cease to function and are recycled in whatever way is either chosen or happens. But our astral/mental bodies will carry with them to the Bardo the imprints of deep thoughts and feelings that have been experienced in that lifetime. These imprints are called *samskaras* and are the thoughts and feelings which 'stamp' themselves on to the soul when something is thought or felt intensely – "I must hide", "I'm responsible for this", "They all hate me", "I'm going to drown", "I can't get out", "He's going to leave me", "They'll pay for this" etc. Dying with a powerful thought such as "She has betrayed me" as you are stabbed to death by your lover, may be carried forward into another lifetime as an unreasonable fear of trusting another in a relationship. Perhaps if you have died in poverty and starvation in a previous existence you are carrying the seemingly illogical thought that "There won't be enough. We will all die ..." Our bodies can also hold the memories of past lives, as we have seen from the work of Dr Stevenson with children, in the previous chapter.

One amongst the ranks of professionals who has done an enormous amount to give past life therapy - now called Deep Memory Process - the recognition it deserves is Dr Roger Woolger, an Oxford University graduate and Jungian analyst. His lifelong study of the perennial philosophies and mystical traditions in Christianity and Sufism together with his clinical experience have created a pioneering and broad-based approach to the entire subject of reincarnation, offering us a comprehensive introduction to the psychological and spiritual depths of regressing to our past lives. He prefers to call this work Deep Memory Process Therapy since it encompasses so much more than 'simply' past lives. It includes journeying to other realities or the Tibetan Bardo, spirit release and invocation of guides, helpers and ancestors, regression to ancestral memories and their release and healing and, significantly, regression to in utero and childhood trauma. His work has led him to say: "From nearly 20 years of taking clients and colleagues through past life experiences and continuing my own personal explorations, I have come to regard this technique as one of the most concentrated and powerful tools available to psychotherapy short of psychedelic drugs". His book *Other Lives, Other Selves* is a classic work, and I personally am extremely grateful for my training with him.

Past life regression therapy looks not only at the presence of the past in order to discover the roots of current fears, phobias, situations, family patterns, health problems and relationships, but also brings the opportunity to experience what happens after the death of that historical body.

Here the work of Dr Michael Newton has also contributed to public awareness and acceptance of the validity of accessing the memory banks to free the soul. In his practice as a counsellor and hypnotherapist specialising in behaviour modification for the treatment of psychological disorders, he was often requested to regress some of his clients. Being a self-confessed sceptic, he refused on the grounds that his work was based on a more traditional approach to regression, in other words he used his skills in order to determine the origins of disturbing memories and traumas in the childhood of this lifetime. Until, that is, he worked with a patient on pain management. This young man had suffered a lifetime of chronic pain on his right side, and in one of his sessions with Dr Newton recovered the memory of a former life in World War I when, as a soldier, he had been killed by a bayonet (in his right side) in France. This resulted in the complete release of the pain which had been the constant companion of this young man for so long. Incidentally, Dr Newton had asked his patient such specific questions that he was able to check the veracity of the story with the Imperial War Museum who thought he must be a member of the family since he had such detailed knowledge of the fallen soldier. With encouragement from his clients, he began to experiment with regressing them further back in time before their last birth on Earth. The result of his thousands of case histories was the realisation that when people find their place in the spirit world – life between lives – they are in touch with their eternal nature which is more powerful even than remembering former existences on the earthly stage. It is often this part of a session that you become aware, as the soul, of what and who you truly are beyond earthly experiences. It's at this point that you are able to understand the contracts you have drawn up with other souls from your group and what needs to be done to release karma and bring understanding to current issues in the here and now. But perhaps the most important result of this part of a session is the major shift in perspective which occurs.

A Trail of Clues

Let's have a look at what other links you might find to your past lives. You have probably tripped over several of them without realising what they really are. Broadly, anything that the logical mind cannot compartmentalise is a good place to start. Whenever you think to yourself "I don't know why, but I have always..... wanted to go to China/been drawn to people with blue eyes/hated people who wear waistcoats/felt at home in the desert/can't stand bald men/been fascinated by Victorian dramas ..." you have a clue. These clues might more accurately be described as triggers, and these triggers are like switches that flick on a memory. Sometimes these are linked to the samskaras – the complex of information carried forward – and in which case they will be powerful since your soul is drawing your attention to something that needs investigating and releasing. But there are others, less loaded with portent, that indicate we have been here before.

Hobbies, or *Passionate Interests* for example. Yes, you may have "always found stamps fascinating" but the key word is 'always'. The *games* you might have played as a child – road-making in the sand, doctors and nurses, and the obvious ones of soldiers, cowboys and Indians speak for themselves.

The *TV Programmes* that you watch, the *Books* that you read and the genre of *Film* you have preferences for (or avoid at all costs) also hold clues. If you watch the soaps, there may be characters who you're drawn to or repelled by, or certain scenarios that seem to create an over-reaction. Or you may be drawn to books or films that focus on a certain period or incident in history. Some authors of historical novels will say it's as if they actually 'tap into' the story as they write it. Sounds like websites to me. Through the mind, you send that arrow of intention, it connects to the field of information which then enables download through pens or keyboards. Some subjects, such as torture, whilst obviously difficult for many people, can spark extreme reactions in others. But it was World War

II replays that did it for Alan. He was disturbed by his uncontrollable sob-
bing which would seem to come up from the very depths of his being
every time there were clips shown of the little planes flying over the
English Channel on missions. In our session, I gently asked him to close
his eyes and remember those feelings. He broke down as I said "and
where are *you* in this scene ...?" "I'm in the second plane ... there are six
of us .... We're on our way to France – Oh my god! ... They've shot
Eddie down ...... Oh! My left wing's on fire .... I'm falling down into the
sea ... No, NO! what will happen to my family ....." It wasn't the dying
that created the samskara that he carried from that experience, but the
thought that he wouldn't be able to fulfil his responsibilities to his wife
and children. In his present life he was overly protective of his family –
"Don't know why ....." Now he did. After his session, there were no more
breakdowns when he watched WWII action replays.

Irrational *Fears*, *Phobias and Behaviour Patterns* are clues to their
hidden history. Fire, heights, water, claustrophobia or even rats - as the
last thing you see when you died of the plague, leaving your children to
fend for themselves - may provide obvious links, but the more extraordinary they are, perhaps the more likely action will be taken to unravel the
riddle. Sometimes the clues seem to be programmed into a time or age-
related moment. Hannah, for example, is a highly successful fashion
buyer and consultant who travels the world in her work. At the age of 37
she suddenly notices that she is becoming panicky when about to sign her
credit card payment slips as she checks out of the hotels she is staying in.
This problem increases in intensity until it becomes an embarrassment, so
she decides to get to the bottom of it. In her session, and using her feelings as the link, she now finds herself in a stone cell with a sack over her
head. She's a herbalist and healer, who lives with her children on the edge
of a village. One day three men on horses arrive and accuse her of witchcraft. She's taken away from her home and children and flung into this
cell and then later dragged out to stand before five others, sitting at a
table, with a piece of parchment in front of one of them. He demands that
she put her mark on this statement which declares her as a witch and

heretic, involved with practices against the church. She remonstrates, insisting that her work is only to help people. They become aggressive and say that they will bring her children in and torture them in front of her "Then we'll see about you signing this!". There follows a hugely pregnant moment …. She puts her mark on the parchment, and is led off to the gallows to be hanged. She was 37 in that life time. The panic at checkouts has now evaporated, and perhaps she also understands why she has never wanted to have children.

Less dramatic, perhaps, but equally intriguing was Jenny's story attached to her phobic fear of being in the sea. With her two little sons she was quite happy at the water's edge, and up to the point were she was still able to stand, but as soon as her feet couldn't touch the bottom, she became frantic. We use this feeling as the entry point to the history of this and now she finds herself in a dark and fathomless sea, dressed in a green gown and flailing her arms. It's night time. "What's happened?" I ask. She then tells of how she was on board a cruise ship with her fiancé; they had been dancing to the band and then have a minor argument. She flounces off to go and cool down outside on deck. It has rained and in her dancing shoes, she slips and helplessly slides under the rails and out into the dark ocean where she drowns with the agonising thought "He won't know how much I love him …" To clear this samskara (and its effect in the present) she speaks to the soul of her fiancé – part of her soul family – out of time-bound reality, and there is a reunion. Her sea phobia is released.

Jane suffered from Obsessive Compulsive Disorder. Changing her clothes countless times in any one day, she had washed her hands so much that her skin was red – not that I saw that, since she wouldn't take off her gloves or coat for our session, but sat looking so terrified that it seemed even the chair would contaminate her in some way. I asked her to close her eyes and get in touch with the feeling she has when she is attempting to get rid of the 'germs' that seemed to cover her entire body. She immediately said that she was a page boy, complete with white stockings, buckle shoes and 'blown up' shorts that were worn in those times and standing in a clearing in a small wood. There was a feeling of anxiety. "What's happening?" I asked. "There are people from the village coming towards me, and they are hostile ..." When I asked her (or rather him) why this should be 'he' replied "They hate my lord. They have some score to settle with him ...... Oh! They are taking me off to the village .... Oh no! ... they are going to throw me into the midden (an outside dump for human waste of every description) ....." At which point she starts to 'clear' invisible attachments from her body as she sits in the chair, frantically trying to clean herself .... And then stillness ... the page boy is drowned in the foul sludge. What needs to be done? The body of the page boy that was left to rot, needed to be removed from its filthy grave, taken to a stream and cleansed, and then buried in a place of peace and beauty, so that the body in the 21st century would be free from its memories.

Countries, continents and landscapes offer us clues as to the geographical locations of previous incarnations, and actually visiting them can trip the switch into past life recall. You might suddenly find yourself weeping as you pass through certain parts of France where the Cathars met their final end, or you might visit somewhere that has a very familiar feel, although you've never been there before (in this lifetime, anyway). Equally, "I don't know why, but I've always wanted to go to Siberia" may not have the chance to be explored in reality but can be accessed through the virtual realms. For those on a spiritual path in this life, there are some obvious ones – India with its ashrams, Peru, Guatemala and New Mexico with their fascinating remnants of an advanced culture – and then there's Egypt. The largest open-air museum in the world is the place where I experienced meeting my own Nemesis. I came to understand why it was that I had always been drawn to men from different cultures and nationalities; I had always been 'imported'. Here in Egypt I came face to face with my past which collided with my present and changed just about everything. Living and working there with groups of people, I was also able (when I wasn't being personally liquefied) to observe how the tombs and temples affect people, and how certain characters – the 18th dynasty heretic pharaoh Akhenaten for example – were like magnets for some, and brought all manner of stories from their unconscious archives. At least three people thought they were reincarnations of this mysterious man, so what was going on? They were touched, triggered, by Akhenaten's 'presence' which can still be experienced through the few pieces of masonry that escaped destruction. But no, they were not Akhenaten, any more than the countless people who believe they were King Arthur or Mary Magdalene for that matter. This is where the lower astral planes can deliver seductive fantasies and the acid test is "Does this really help me deal with my overdraft or catch the No. 39 to work every day?" It would probably be much more useful exploring your life as a stone mason, a goatherd or a cook, if you're looking for constructive experience with relevant meaning in the here and now.

As we have seen from Dr Stevenson's and Dr Newton's evidence, our **Bodies** will also inform us of the damage one of its predecessors may have incurred. There may be intense feelings in the form of stabbing pains, feelings 'as if ..... I am being pierced or have an arrow through me..' Intense body-held feelings (like those of Dr Newton's client) - such as a stab in the back, constriction in the throat through being choked or suffocated, or a tension in the pelvic area as a result of rape - may appear in the current lifetime as restricted breathing, odd stabbing pains, or fearfulness around sexuality. My mother-in-law was so terrified that she would not be completely dead when she was buried that she left legal instructions that her wrists should be cut after her death to ensure that this didn't happen. A clear sign of a previous lifetime when she had been buried alive.

Or they may be emotional *feelings* of rage, grief, betrayal or loss that leave with the soul and re-appear in subsequent lifetimes as inexplicable echoes of previous experience. Your feelings about people and places offer clues to past life experiences that might have been tremendous or terrifying. Always feeling threatened by those in authority may reflect an overbearing parent, but that will not be the root cause of these feelings. Perhaps you were put to death by some lord or master in the past. Or you may have been the perpetrator of heinous crimes, but died peacefully in your bed without feelings of guilt or remorse. Your soul, however, will have to sort this out in the Bardo, possibly meeting with the souls of those whom you had victimised. As a result of this you, the soul, may choose to experience the crimes you committed against others. What goes around, comes around sooner or later.

And then there is the business of *soul mates.*

Don't I know you?

I have written quite a few words on this topic in my book *Soulmates*, and elsewhere, but to summarise ... for many people, the area of relationships with others is where the soul 'action' takes place.

Each of us is working on different themes, which can broadly be categorised as health, money, status, integrity, power or different issues within relationship. Sometimes there can be a mix of some – or even all – of these things, which might seem unfortunate but remember we are in the process of clearing our old, outmoded biographies. We have been fed on the myth of meetings with the one-and-only other who will make our troubles vanish. They will appear, like a knight in shining armour, or a beautiful maiden and we will no longer feel alone. Possibly no one in these pressurised times really imagines that this will happen, but we carry the seed deep within us that it will all be all right in the end. This part of the myth is true. But the happily ever after part cannot be delivered by anyone with two legs until we fully understand the dynamics at work within ourselves. So I have redefined the meaning of the word soulmate as being someone – *anyone* – with whom we have an intense encounter. Someone whom we can't ignore, no matter how hard we try. It may be that we can move away from having their physical presence in our lives, but still they tug some invisible string inside our being, insisting that even though we can't see them, they are still around and need attention.

Encounters with soulmates bring up the most powerful feelings – not all of them pleasant. These soulmates, who feel more like a going over with a brillo pad than being touched by a soft, loving feather, come in many guises. They might take the form of your mother-in-law, your boss, even your next door neighbour, but you will know them by the degree of response they evoke in you. Of course they bring us gifts and opportunities, these members of our spiritual clan, even though it sometimes feels as if the gift has been tied with razor wire. They are in our faces to teach us something, not to encourage cosy complacency, and that teaching might take many different forms, but ultimately the lesson is from the soul asking us to see beyond the drama being played out. These encounters can include the added raising agent of sexuality or overwhelming physical/mental attraction, which draws the players together with a powerful and irresistible force, making sure they don't pass by the experience. In order to get a true perspective on what is going on, it's also helpful to remember that *someone* has to catalyse the situation. I don't imagine it was easy to take on the role of Judas Iscariot. Perhaps an abusive father offers his brutalised children the opportunity to move beyond rage and revenge, and whilst not condoning his actions, to see beyond the drama. At the level of the soul it is possible to heal the situation with love instead of hate, and to find compassion for the father's own brutalised or damaged beginnings. At this point, samskaras are cleared, karma is finished, the buck has stopped being passed on through the generations and all souls are released, including any ancestors who would also have been participants in the abuser/abused/colluder soul theme. And yes, it's true that some souls will meet a 'mate' that they feel totally connected to, like two pieces of a puzzle that fit together exactly – but it is not always within the context of a marital/sexual/partnership. And in this case your soulwork will be elsewhere.

We sometimes make reference to people as being 'old souls' or 'young souls'. When our souls first take on a physical form, perhaps we are not given much choice as to specific circumstances, conditions and personality traits. The soul has chosen to experience life on earth, contained within a dense material body, governed by the laws and principles of the planet and seemingly with a factory-installed implant stating "thou shalt not remember who thou art". If we knew (intellectually) that we were here for the purpose of growing spiritually, if we were able to remember where we came from, we would not experience our lives in the way that we do. It is by living on this physical plane that the soul grows in knowledge and stature. Life itself is the alchemical process by which we transform our dense matter into refined spiritual gold. Gradually, lifetime-by-lifetime, the soul builds up this bank of experience. After the death of the physical body a balance sheet is drawn up of the life in that particular body. It will subtract what has already been dealt with and carry forward what is unfinished on its journey of growing and balancing the experience in a world of opposites.

How can we understand the full flavour of freedom unless we have been captive? The rapist needs to know what it is like to be raped, and a victim needs to balance that paralysing experience with that of a rampant aggressor. If I have starved in this or another lifetime, I will value food and not waste it but before this happens, I may need to uncover the history of what is driving my over-eating in this lifetime. If, as a soldier, I was tortured by my enemy, I can balance the scales by being a peace activist. So through lifetimes, every facet of human event and emotion is included – doubt, fear, hate, rejection, sorrow, loss, despair, jealousy, punishment and their opposites of certainty, joy, love, connection, ecstasy, compassion, empathy, loyalty and so on. It was Edgar Cayce, the so-called Sleeping Prophet who you will find out more about in the next chapter, who said:

"The plan for the soul was a cycle of experience unlimited in scope and direction, in which the new individual would come to know creation in all its aspects, at the discretion of will. The cycle would be complete when the desire of the will was no longer different from the Will of God."

He said something else that is helpful to our understanding of these matters; when asked: "From which side of my family do I inherit most?" he replied "You have inherited most from yourself, not from your family. The family is only a river through which the soul flows." The metaphysical way of expressing Dr Lipton's research results, perhaps, when he discovered that DNA does not control our biology – our genetic inheritance is activated by signals that flow though the cell's membrane.

What about chronic **Illness**? Who on earth would choose that as an experience? It may be that the soul has clothed itself in this lifetime with a personality that chooses to repress certain thoughts and feelings. Along the way there have been opportunities to make choices about responding to what life throws at you, but they may not have been taken with awareness. Repressed, unexpressed or negative emotions and repetitive thoughts prevent the free flow of energy through the subtle anatomy, as we have already seen. Over time this leads to disease. From the soul's perspective this may be to draw attention to these thoughts and feelings, or it may be about the effect that this illness has on you or others close to you. Serious illness affects people deeply and often acts as a wake-up call from the soul. Long-term illness can often seem cruel and 'unfair' - assumptions which are made without the knowledge of what is going on behind the scenes.

Dr Simonton, who received the Humanitarian Award from the Cancer Control Society in recognition for his 30 years of ground-breaking work in oncology, has done some amazing research using visualisation techniques. He reports the most remarkable outcome from patients who have beaten cancer in this way. He says they undergo a kind of transformation. Overcoming huge obstacles produces a sense of *inner strength.* This inner strength is the soul sitting in the driving seat, since it knows that death is the transition made on its journey Home. The body/personality's fear of death from disease has been overcome. It's not surprising, if your life has been lived in a spiritual desert, that death of your earthly vehicle might be terrifying. Without the knowledge that death, for the soul, is not an end but a transition, the Everyday Self feels threatened by annihilation. But it's never too late to turn this around and it's reported that many people find the peace of the soul at the end of their lives that seemed to elude them whilst they were living.

Soul Focus

Your soul gains experience though the dramas played out on Earth.
Understanding the relationship between body and soul brings
freedom from the Eternal Return.

REMINDERS .....

- Experiences on Earth are dramas for the soul.
- Knowing that we chose our parents and life circumstances brings the soul's perspective into being.
- Look at difficult situations for their potential learning.
- Who do you have powerful connections with (comfortable and uncomfortable)?
- What experience does this bring you? Check with the chapter on the chakras to see which area it affects.
- Is there a consistent repeating pattern in your life, which presents itself in different ways?
- What clues can you recognise in this lifetime that link to a previous one?
- Do you still blame your parents for the way you are? Or anyone else, for that matter, for what happens to you?

Resources:

Other Lives, Other Selves: **Dr Roger Woolger** (Aquarian Press)
www.rogerwoolger.com
Journey of Souls: **Dr Michael Newton** (Llewellyn Publications)
Soulmates: **Sue Minns** (Hodder Mobius)
Principles of Past Life Therapy: **Judy Hall** (Findhorn Press)
Across Time & Death: A Mother's Search for Her Past Life Children: **Jenny Cockell** (Simon & Schuster)

chapter 7

the psychic world wide web

Information Superhighway

Learning sleeps and snores in libraries,
But wisdom is everywhere, wide awake, on tiptoe.
Josh Billings

Everyone at one time or another has had a so-called psychic experience. Those times when you are thinking of someone only moments before the phone rings, or a letter drops through the letter or e-mail box, and it is the very person you have had on your mind, mean that you are tuned into the psychic super highway. Or perhaps you 'pick up' things about people – you get a sense of their past, or what's happening to them at the moment; or perhaps a strong feeling of an event about to happen. Then there are those hunches that you just know you have to listen to, those intuitions that prove to be correct.

Understanding that there is another dimensional reality that stands behind the physical world opens us to the concept that there is a wireless communication highway available beyond the limitations of our five physical senses of sight, hearing, taste, touch and smell. The faculty that informs us of this is sometimes referred to as our sixth sense, the one that has the ability to perceive this other dimensional reality. This is the sense that makes your hair stand on end or your skin crawl when you are in a place that may be haunted by the imprint of some powerful, painful event, or it may be a sense that you're in some sort of imminent danger, or that you shouldn't catch that plane or train (which turns out to be involved in an accident). The sixth sense encompasses such abilities as extra sensory perception (ESP), clairvoyance, premonitions and intuition. So if it's not our noses, eyes, ears and taste buds that are doing the perceiving, what is it? Our auric field. As previously mentioned, it has its own invisible intricate network which acts like a two-way radio, transmitting and receiving, picking up invisible information and filtering it into our consciousness and emitting wave forms of energy according to the state we're in. Like Dr Lipton's cell membrane, the auric field is a super sensitive filter which interfaces with the Universal Energy Field, the ocean of information in which we exist.

Everyone is aware of the huge advances in computer technology, and has heard of the Internet unless they have been living on the moon. This mind-blowing global computer network, known as the information super highway, is appropriately named the World Wide Web. With the right equipment you can log into this network and access information on every conceivable subject. You can send information to a particular individual, research anything under the sun, or broadcast your ideas in an instant to millions. It is as if we have created externally the inner technology that we have at our disposal, but have simply forgotten – or not yet learned - how to use.

Beyond my body my veins are invisible.
Antonio Porchia (1943)

Imagine for a moment that your mind is a computer, a computer that is hard-wired with information about you according to what you have experienced and recorded on it to date – your personal database, to use computer-speak. Stored in there, as well, is all your ancestral information received by courtesy of your DNA – your genetic inheritance. By entering a certain password, you can link your own personal mind-computer to the 'psychic internet', this super information highway 'out there' in the Universal Energy Field which connects you to all other individuals, each with their own database. Of course it's possible to use your mind-computer solely for daily activities and never venture on-line, but rather a shame not to use this mammoth potential for exploration.

By linking up with this information superhighway, there is the possibility to connect not only mind to mind, but also to find historical information and future projections. This highway is not limited by the confines of time-bound reality and through it we can access collective knowledge and the highest levels of wisdom available. This infinite library is often referred to as the Akashic Records *(akasha* being another Sanskrit word, meaning 'sky', space' or 'aether'), said to have existed since the beginning of Creation. It is believed that the seers, visionaries, shamans and priests of ancient peoples around the world – Indians, Moors, Tibetans, Egyptians, Persians, Chaldeans, Greeks, Chinese, Hebrews, Christians, Druids and Mayans – had the ability to access these archives as do present day indigenous cultures such as the shamans of the rainforests, Aborigines, the Dogon of West Africa and the Kalahari Bushmen.

The ancient Indian sages of the Himalayas, for example, knew that each soul recorded every moment of every existence in a 'book' and, if one attuned oneself properly, then the book could be read or viewed – that sounds pretty much like our Internet to me. So-called primitive, pre-literate cultures that lived in harmony with nature used the information highway to communicate across great distances, to forecast the weather and locate their source of food supply. Their wise elders may have used bones, the stars or even sheep's entrails as their means of 'logging on' to foretell the future or peer into someone's past but their accuracy in accessing the information is well documented. In our 'civilised' world, reading entrails wasn't really an option, so we consulted tea leaves, crystal balls and palmists. It is not that these so-called divinatory tools have any hidden powers; they are just a means for expressing information from a level beyond the physical dimension. There are many currently popular methods of tapping into wisdom from a 'higher' level including the I Ching, Tarot cards and Runes (more on this in chapter 9), but again, the quality of advice and of guidance they produce will depend on the integrity and intent of the user. If you are psychic, it does not mean that you are necessarily spiritual, and a spiritual person is not necessarily psychic. There are enough tales of so-called 'spiritual teachers' and masters of every shape and form taking advantage of and sometimes actually abusing their pupils, followers, devotees, students – anyone in fact over whom they appear to have authority – to prove the point that not all 'spiritual teachers' have the best interests of their students at heart.

There are many advantages and some disadvantages in logging into the real Internet, and so it is with connecting to the psychic information highway. It is important to be able to access the information you want – not any old junk – so time and practice are required before you start. As opening the door to a mansion and shouting "Is anybody there?" could invite something nasty from the cellar, so it is with blindly entering the psychic internet. It is important that your intention is clear. Whatever you are doing, it is always important that your *intention* is clear. Going into a travel agent's office and asking for a ticket to 'somewhere hot' could put you in the Sahara Desert or an equatorial rain forest, so the clearer and more concise your intention is, the clearer and more concise will be the response.

There are different levels of connection with the psychic superhighway, and the results of any excursion here will indicate which level has been accessed. Some people are born with acute psychic sensitivity, others can become adept with training, some become more psychic after a blow to the head (not recommended) or sometimes after a Near Death Experience (more about these in chapter 12), which radically shifts the perspective of those who have technically 'died' and then returned to life. NDEs, however, don't always have long-lasting mind and perspective altering effects, and this can prove extremely difficult. Like having a glimpse of how life might be lived with the expanded vision from a mountaintop and then finding yourself back in a dimly lit cave again, without your spectacles. It was something like this for Hazel Courtenay, an award winning health columnist for the Sunday Times, who went through a NDE in 1998, which was witnessed by her medical doctor. This experience resulted in an expanded awareness, feelings of bliss and ecstasy and a range of paranormal or psychic abilities opening up for her. Her first book – the best-selling *Divine Intervention* – records her experiences during this period of heightened awareness, which was in fact a spiritual crisis. Psychiatrist Dr Stan Grof has called these occurrences when people 'open up' in a rapid and seemingly uncontrolled way 'spiritual emergence-ys'. They are not easy to handle at the time - or subsequently – when it feels as if you have gone from 0 to 1,000 miles per hour, and then back again to zero. However, Hazel's second book, *The Evidence for the Sixth Sense*, puts it into context and is a valuable and supportive guide for the ever increasing numbers of people who are, and will be, experiencing these states.

Before having a look at the categories of those who already surf this web, it's important to have some sort of map of this uncharted territory. You might remember that beyond the boundaries of your skin are the astral, mental and spiritual fields. The astral and mental 'fields' of our aura are where emotions and thoughts register and are held. So imagine now that you are a miniscule voyager setting off from your physical form and travelling outwards in search of information and experience. You could arrive at the astral/emotional field and think that this is it – the source of all you need to know. Or you might travel one field further into the mental plane and think 'Ah! Now I have arrived.' But in fact your sights should be set on the next level beyond both these two – the spiritual plane - in order to access wisdom which is untainted by thoughts and emotions of the lower levels. So if you think about these different levels as operating not only individually, but also at the level of the human collective, imagine (or perhaps better not to) what the astral and mental planes might contain: every single thing that has ever been felt or thought by everyone. In other words it's possible to download all manner of stuff from these levels and believe that you are connecting to something spiritual. Again, this is why your *intention* is crucial. It will work like an arrow that travels through the astral planes to its destination beyond them. I'm going to risk boring you by labouring this point, as it's so important.

In early ancient Egypt, their knowledge included wisdom and magic which had not been interfered with by the power and control issues introduced by the priesthood that took place further down the line. They knew then that after death the soul returned to its place of origin – its stellar home. The Journey of Return entailed travelling through a region between Earth and the fixed circumpolar star that was the soul's first destination. This region was said to be governed by Seth, brother of Osiris and Lord of Darkness, who had all manner of enticements to keep the soul from returning to the Light of the Home Star. He could and would offer the soul an array of temptations - the use of different powers, riches, magical abilities (similar to the story of Jesus' temptation by Satan in the wilderness). This plane between Here and There reminds us of the astral plane historically referred to by alchemists and in the late 19th and early 20th century popularised through Theosophy. It is the world of emotion and of illusion, the first level beyond the physical but denser than the mental (as with the auric field). It is full of every thing imaginable – but none of it has substance. Unless your intention is clear and of the highest quality, you will – and many do – pull something out of the astral plane and believe it to be spiritual. The astral plane is where we can easily find – and possibly buy at extortionate prices – new age candyfloss. It's the fairground that bedazzles, entrances, seduces and distracts. It is not the real McCoy. Anything that inflates the ego or personality, creates the feeling of right/wrong, better/worse, higher/lower belongs to this level and is referred to as 'astral glamour'. Many teachers and gurus have come undone here, and unfortunately there are mediums and clairvoyants whose source of information is also from this level. The acid test of any information or instruction you receive is its quality and relevance (so what?), together with your own sense of whether this is a truth for you (Aha!). This is where your sixth sense comes into its own.

Ultimately everything is energy. In ancient China this energy was described as two fundamentally opposing, but complementary forces, which were to be found in all things in the universe. They were named Yin and Yang by the philosophers and metaphysicians; Yin signifying the qualities of receptivity, passivity, negativity (as in batteries), darkness, internal. It is connected to the left hand, the feminine, the moon, water and all things that are hidden. Yang on the other hand is active, transmitting, positive, light and external. It is our right (shaking, sword-holding, writing) hand, the masculine, daylight, fire, the sun. Something like Right on and Left behind. Some people are better able to be transmitters than receivers, which means in terms of the psychic superhighway that they are more suited to healing (transmitting) than clairvoyance or mediumship (receiving). And very broadly speaking, men are often more suited to healing (which is active) and women to clairvoyance (which is passive).

You may experience receiving information through your sixth sense in one of several ways.

Clairsentience: *sensation, kinesthetic or body response*

Our physical bodies respond very quickly to different levels of psychic energy. The chapter on the auric field covered the way in which we 'feel' atmospheres or vibrations that are emanating from people or places. Healers often report sensations of heat or tingling in their hands when they are bringing through healing energy to their clients. They may also become aware of sensations in their own bodies which will be directly related to what their client is presenting them with. Diviners and dowsers rely on their bodies to access information. Holding a question in their mind that requires a yes/no response, they use a tool such as a pendulum or dowsing rod to amplify the slight muscle twitches that give them the information they require.

Closely allied to bodily responses are the 'gut reactions' experienced by those who are sensitive to the moods of others. This sensitivity can be a double-edged sword if it's not managed, and whilst it may be extremely useful as a starting point for further psychic development, you certainly do not want to be open to all the super-charged images that are delivered to us every day through the media. Many counsellors and therapists use their clairsentience to enable them to be aware of the fluctuations and nuances in their clients' emotions, and to better understand what is going on behind the words. As a lie detector is able to pick up the flickering energy of an untruth, using our clairsentient ability we can also detect whether people really mean what they are saying. But tuning into what others are feeling can be draining and confusing if you are not clear about the boundary of where you end and they begin. It's important to remember that these feelings belong to the other person – not you. Just let them pass through you, being aware of your response. The need to be centred and grounded yourself in any of this work can never be overemphasised. This kind of 'tuning in' is sometimes called psychic empathy.

Clairaudience: *thinking and listening*

Our brains constitute 2% of our body weight, use 20% of the energy we manufacture and have created quite a bit of controversy around their capabilities. Perceived wisdom, based on early scientific findings is that we only use an astonishing 7-10% of its capacity. The human brain contains 10 billion neurons whose function seems to be fairly clear, but there are also 120 billion glial cells in this mind box between our ears, the primary function for which science has yet to identify. One thing is for sure – we have no idea about our brains' potential. As Sir John Eccles, Australian Neurology Nobel Laureate says "How can you calculate a percentage of infinity?" Perhaps what it does is as yet unquantifiable. Another 'As above, so below ....', since scientific thought at the moment is that our universe is made up of in excess of 90% dark matter, the function of which is uncertain. Perhaps our own 'dark matter' is interacting with the psychic superhighway, spending time with the dream maker, or doing things that we as yet have no concept of.

Your mind may be used as a medium for extra-sensory exploration in two ways. The first involves 'hearing' an inner voice that gives you information. For some people, inner auditory messages have been a very powerful source of insight and wisdom. Socrates and Joan of Arc, for example, were guided through their lives by a voice that told them what to do. Auditory messages like this usually take the form of a voice speaking inside your head, as though communicating through a telephone, and will of course have a totally different quality to the messages you might send yourself on a moment-by-moment basis "Don't forget to lock the door" or "must go and see aunt Agatha". The voice may become apparent in response to a specific question, or perhaps something that goes on repeating itself in your head until you have to pay it attention. If you want to explore the possibilities of clairaudience, you will need a calm and static free mind and body.

The other way this faculty can be explored is through *automatic writing.* In this instance the information is channelled through the arm and pen on to paper. There are all sorts of astonishing evidences of this method of linking to the superhighway, one example being the books written by Neale Donald Walsch. When in his forties and fed up with his life on many levels, he sat one night on the edge of despair and shouted "If there's anyone there, what on earth is this all about?" To his astonishment he then began to write an answer. This was the beginning of an amazing question and answer dialogue with an intelligence from a non-physical level that resulted in his books which are international bestsellers called *Conversations with God.*

Clairvoyance: *visual images, 'seeing', inner knowing*

This way of connecting to the invisible world is perhaps closest to the spiritual Self. It works through visual imagery and inner knowing. The Third Eye or Brow chakra is the energy centre connected with intuition and inner vision – in-sight in fact. This imaging in the mind's eye is not the same as visualisation, with which many people have difficulty. It's using your mind's eye to perceive, or 'get a sense' of something. There are very few people who have inner sight which has a technicolour or high resolution quality to it. So don't be put off because you are not getting this. A visualisation involves the mind. If I suggested that you closed your eyes and visualised yourself meeting a pink unicorn that had healing powers, your left brain would either totally veto complying with such a suggestion, or it could produce an image that would be pure fantasy. We have to start somewhere, however, and in order to put the left brain's judgement in the passenger rather than the driving seat, skilful use of language often does the trick. When people come for a past life regression, they often say "How do I know I will not be making it up?" By relaxing the body and guiding their awareness beyond time-bound reality, it's as if the left brain knows it's in unfamiliar territory, so it gets out of the way of what may be unfolding. Once engaged with the 'story', it is as if an energy flows through the conduit of the right brain, the link to the personal 'website' that is waiting to be accessed.

There is another form of insight that has become popularised in recent years. It's called Remote Viewing. Interestingly, knowledge of this age-old use of the psychic superhighway is brought to us through research supported by none other than the US Government's intelligence department. It was given the label of 'Scientific Remote Viewing' (SRV) to ensure that no-one linked it with flaky New Age practices, but of course what it is in reality is psychic reconnaissance – a skill used by indigenous peoples, shamans and clairvoyants throughout the ages. It involves sending one's consciousness, like an arrow, to 'see' a remote location and 'bring back' useful information about the site. It has even been alleged that this is how Sadddam Hussein was found in his 'spider hole' by the US military. You can have a go at this for yourself in a very simple way. There's no reason why you shouldn't have this ability apart from your own doubts that you do. Approach it as if you're turning on your computer, going online and then focusing on what it is you want the search engine to find. You can ask someone to choose a picture or draw something and then put it in an envelope and seal it. This can then be put in another room or in the same room as you. Then follow these steps …

Remote Viewing Exercise

Sit quietly, still your thoughts by just observing the rhythm of your breathing, and get relaxed

When you're ready, close your eyes

Focus your consciousness on the envelope

Wait, with the screen of your mind blank, until either an image appears or you get a sense of something

Write it down or draw it, and then open the envelope

When you gain a bit of confidence, you can test-drive your skill further afield by 'visiting' a location that is not known to you, but to a friend. Draw what you 'see' and then check it with your friend.

The psychic superhighways and World Wide Web have been covertly used by governments for some time as a means of transmitting intelligence and mind control, among other things. Hitler was particularly interesting in this aspect of the occult, but the Russians are possibly the most advanced in their research into this area, if the authors of *Psychic Discoveries: The Iron Curtain Lifted* are to be believed. The Russians have developed the use of telepathy, remote influencing (sinister thought), eyeless sight, healing with thought, psycho kinesis (moving objects with the power of the mind) and psychic warfare (even more sinister).

Since time began, people have consulted oracles. Kings and rulers had their own or a court metaphysician/seer/astrologer/magus on tap to give guidance in making important decisions based on the information these advisers access from other dimensions. Now we live in the age of the quick-fix and more and more people are being drawn towards consulting a psychic to find answers. So let's see who is already getting what from where.

Auric Readers and Psychometrists

Reading another person's aura is possibly the first step in accessing information about someone else from the invisible superhighway. As we have seen, your aura is a fluctuating halo of colour that surrounds you, the colours representing the state of your mind and feelings. Perhaps you have had a 'reading' with a fairground clairvoyant, or someone with a crystal ball at a village fete, just for a laugh. You may have been told something like "I can see a spot of bother around money", or "Has somebody in your family recently died?" which could mean that she has sensed or seen in your auric field tension in the Root chakra area, or signs of sadness around the Heart. "I think you're having difficulty saying something to someone" would mean she has observed a block in your Throat energy, "But never mind – the horizon's looking rosy. I can see a holiday around the corner" means she has interpreted the softer colours round your head to mean that something positive is in your mental field. This is a parody of what may happen of course, but it will give you an idea that auric readings will tell you only what you already know about yourself, nothing predictive, no deep spiritual advice. So if you come away with the thought that 'this was fantastic, she seemed to know a lot about me', then she did a good job at interpreting what she saw represented in your aura.

Someone who uses *psychometry* as a tool for tapping into information held in the invisible storage system will use an object. This can be a useful and powerful tool in experienced hands, so to speak. Let's say your cat has been missing for a couple of days. You go to consult someone in desperation to find his whereabouts. You take a collar that belongs to your cat, or something that he sleeps on. The psychometrist will hold this article, and 'tune in' to the vibrations of your cat. "Ah. I can see him" would hopefully be the first response. "He's got himself shut in something that looks like a green shed." You say you don't know of any green sheds. The psychometrist focuses in more deeply ... "He's a marmalade cat, isn't he? .... I sense that this shed is on what looks like an allotment .... Doesn't feel as if it's far from your home ..." Used in this way, psychometry can be extremely helpful.

I have a great friend whose mother disappeared on a walking holiday in the Himalayas. Two years after this desperate event, she took a photo and a ring of her mother's to a medium at the College of Psychic Studies (CPS) in London who is an excellent psychometrist (he does identification work for the police). With the photo and ring in his hands, and knowing absolutely nothing about the circumstances, he described a scene in the Himalayas, saying he saw that this person had lost her way and had tried to take a short cut to where she thought she would meet up with the others she was walking with. She had tripped whilst crossing a stream in a rough valley, fallen and hit her head on a rock. Unconscious, she had actually drowned. This of course could never be proved, but the circumstances he described perfectly fitted the terrain and what could have happened, and certainly brought a degree of peace to the mind of my friend. Psychometry is something you can easily try for yourself as a first step in exploring your ability to access the psychic superhighway. Ask a friend to choose an object that they have – one with a bit of history – for you to practise with. Sit quietly, holding it in your hand, clear your mind and wait to see what might appear in the way of images, thoughts or feelings. Or you may 'hear' with your inner ear. It's very important not to make a value judgement at this stage, because you have literally no idea. Whatever appears first, is what you follow.

Mediums, Sensitives, Clairvoyants, Psychics

All these titles mean approximately the same thing. 'Sensitive' is a new addition to the list of names given to those who have the ability to 'tune in' to their clients in order to access information for them from a level that is beyond conscious awareness. As with everything else, the quality of your 'reading' – as a session with a sensitive is often called – will depend on their integrity and the level at which they receive information. The least spectacular level of this is the one we've just looked at under auric readings – someone who might use what's known as 'shotgunning'. In other words you are offered a whole range of information about yourself, some of which might approximate the truth, some of which is so general it could apply to anyone. But the effect is something like a shotgun which sprays out a spattering of projectiles hoping that one or more will hit the target. The other possibility is that you will receive something that could change your life for ever. In all the readings that I had whilst working at the College of Psychic Studies, one such session stands out like a beacon. This was with Julie Soskin who now runs her own teaching school, and I can honestly say that 100 years of therapy might not have achieved what happened to me in that one hour I spent with her.

My father was killed in the Second World War when I was three months old, and my mother's grief and fear became my own through the very milk that sustained me. As I grew up, she spoke about their relationship and my father's passion for her. I don't remember how old I was when I stopped expecting him to return, but I do remember her saying that I was an accident and my father would have found it difficult sharing her love with me. If I was going to be here at all, then he would have wanted a boy and not a girl. This information sank like a plumb line into the sea of my unconscious mind, but resulted in my never wanting to know anything about him. I never asked any questions or kept any photos as I *perceived* that I was superfluous to his requirements. Later, my mother would speak of the volumes of letters he had written to her, kept in an old crocodile-skin suitcase together with his few belongings that had been returned from the North African desert where he and his platoon had been blown out of existence, and would ask me if I would like to read them. This suggestion actually evoked a physical response in me – although I had no idea at the time why it caused a constriction in my sacral and throat areas. And although I wanted nothing to do with him, I realise now that I searched for his face in all the men that I met.

Fast forward to the late 1980s - my mother now in care, and my marriage of 20 years on the rocks. I had been working at the College of Psychic Studies for only about two weeks and part of my job, as administrator, was to get a feel of how the different mediums worked, in order to advise which would be suitable for those seeking guidance. I have an appointment with Julie Soskin and enter the room where she is working. Hardly had I sat down when she says "Your father's here."

My heart sinks. I don't want to know about my father, but my life's purpose, my spiritual journey.

"Well," she says, "he's been waiting to see you." Then follows a description of what he looks like – or rather what he looked like – tall, with dark brown hair, and about the age of 28 or 29, and the comment that he has been on the 'other side' for quite some time.

"I can see planes, desert sands, and confusion," she says. "Three fatal wounds. His death was without suffering." Then comes the heart-stopper.

"He says he's deeply sorry that for all your life you have felt that he never loved you, since nothing could be further from the truth. He asks me to remind you of the little red dress you had, and your first two-wheeler bike, as he had a hand in these things."

This was certain proof, if I needed it. How could anyone know about the only red dress I have ever owned, and the joy at my first two-wheeler?

After I had finished crying over this – about two weeks – I decided to open the crocodile-skin case of letters. Words cannot describe that event. His wallet, watch, a pressed flower from an Oxford Ball, some of my mother's auburn hair powdered with desert sand ... and hundreds of fading letters still in their envelopes all arranged in chronological rows. Time did something strange at that point, as I seemed to enter a kind of warp, sifting through the contents of the envelopes to discover – after all these years – that I was not unwanted, but on the contrary, eagerly expected and how much he was looking forward to coming home to be with his new little family.

This demonstrates the ability of some mediums to contact and communicate with those who have died, and this contact can have enormous healing potential, as well as bringing tremendous solace to the bereaved. It's important to remember, however, that just because someone has died, it doesn't necessarily mean they have automatically acquired universal wisdom. The presence or contact with the spirit of the deceased should be validated through specific information about them that only you could possibly know, like my red dress. This kind of mediumship is known as 'evidential' – in other words, evidence of the survival beyond death. It emerged from the Spiritualist Church, a religious movement that was popular from around the 1840s to the 1920s and the central tenet of which was the belief that the spirits of the dead can be contacted by mediums. You will still find many Spiritualist Churches dotted around the world, although orthodox Christianity will have nothing to do with it. Whilst working at CPS, my born-again Christian cousin informed me that she was praying for me every day, since I was now involved with the work of the Devil. Is this the 21st century? Even the fact that CPS was founded by an Anglican clergyman, the Rev William Stainton Moses, MA, and its early members included many eminent scientists including: Dr Alfred Russel Wallace (co-discoverer with Darwin of the principles of evolution), Sir Oliver Lodge, Sir Arthur Conan Doyle and Sir William Crookes, wouldn't make even a dent in her (or others') biased judgement.

Channellers and Trance Mediums

All sorts of people seem to be channelling all sorts of other (invisible) people these days and unfortunately quite a lot of it seems to be downloaded from the astral plane. Channelling means that you literally become a channel for the words of a (hopefully) wise, discarnate being who needs a human voice box to express what they want to say either to another, or to make statements and impart knowledge about the way things are going for us down here on Earth. Perhaps the most famous channeller of all times was the prophet Mohammed. A simple but religious merchant who, every year, would take time away from his business to meditate and contemplate in a cave near Mecca. In around 610 AD he believed that he had a visitation from the archangel Gabriel, who ordered him to "Recite". He tried to insist that he was just a simple, illiterate man but Gabriel repeated the command until a thunderstruck Mohammed reiterated the words that were 'channelled' through him to his companions and followers who memorised them and then wrote them down. These visitations apparently continued for a further 20 years and the result, of course, is the holy book of Islam, the Qur'an.

There have been many less celebrated but nonetheless notable channellers in recent history. The term 'channelling' itself is claimed to have come from one such person herself – JZ Knight who says that in 1977 she and her husband were approached in their kitchen in Tacoma,Washington by a handsome 8ft entity called Ramtha, The Enlightened One. He was/is a 35,000 year old warrior from the continent of Lemuria (believed to have existed in the Pacific) who raised an army of 2.5 million to challenge the tyrannical Atlanteans who were into all manner of power-crazed plans for the inhabitants of the earth. He led his huge army across the continents of the known world, which at that time was undergoing cataclysmic geological change. According to his teachings, he led this army for 10 years until he was betrayed and almost killed. He then apparently retreated into isolation for seven years, during which time he mastered many skills, including out-of-body experiences and clairvoyance. He rejoined his army and spent 120 days teaching them everything he knew before he simply 'ascended' in front of their very eyes. He made a promise to them, before evaporating from sight, that he would return to teach them again, and so re-appeared in 1977 to JZ Knight to re-educate us 'forgotten gods'. These are the four cornerstones of Ramtha's philosophy:

- The Statement: *You are God*
- The mandate: *Make known the Unknown*
- The concept: *Consciousness and Energy Create the nature of Reality*
- The challenge: *To Conquer Yourself*

This is taught through The Ramtha School of Enlightenment, and the many books that have been channelled through JZ Knight. The latest project to come out of this organisation is an independently made film called 'What the Bleep do we Know?'. It combines interviews with eminent modern mystics, physicists, neurologists, physicians and scholars, together with fiction and animation to help us lay people understand the uncertain world of the quantum field which is hidden behind what we consider to be our normal, waking reality. Now available on DVD, it is a further demonstration that cutting edge science is moving closer to explaining what we thought was 'magic'. And in case you have difficulty in sorting through the theories presented, Alexander Bruce has produced a helpful little book, *Beyond the Bleep,* with simple explanations and more information on the personalities and teachings of these luminaries such as Doctors Candace Pert, Fred Alan Wolf, and Amit Goswami who appear in the film, as well as references for anyone seeking more information on the topics presented in the film

There are many other channellers who have brought through profound information. I have listed my favourites at the end of this chapter, but investigating for yourself is the recommended procedure. Use your own sixth sense to test whether there is wisdom for you in what is being channelled. But it does not all have this substance:

You are the template, the prototype of a new and universal species,
Part solar, part material, both temporal and eternal,
The species that will span the gulf between the visible and invisible,
Bringing new worlds into form.
Through you a new and unprecedented cycle of creation will occur.
Ken Carey: The Third Millennium

Trance mediumship is the 'old' name for channelling, and seems not to be so popular amongst sensitives as it was about 40 years ago. Consulting a trance medium does, however, take away the sneaking suspicion that the medium's personality might be filtering into the 'reading' - because it seems as if they have left the room somehow, and a completely different character is sitting in front of you. It can be a bit disconcerting when you first encounter trance mediumship. What it would be like to meet a 35,000 year old Lemurian warrior in my kitchen goes beyond my abilities to imagine.

I remember the first time I had a session with Mary Absolem who channelled an 'entity' called The Mandarin. A beautifully groomed and well-spoken woman in her late 50s, Mary greeted me and explained what would happen – that she would take several deep breaths, and then 'vacate' her body in order that The Mandarin could communicate with me. I was to ask 'him' any questions I might have and know that she would have no recollection of what our conversation entailed. With that she took her three deep breaths, and her head fell forward onto her chest. For an awful fleeting moment I thought she had passed out. Then her hands moved up, in a very Chinese way, and she/he addressed me in a totally different voice from the one I had heard a few minutes earlier. The questions that I had ready on my list to ask were about life in general and direction in particular, and the advice I received was most definitely helpful and constructive. After 45 minutes, The Mandarin drew our meeting to a close, withdrew and within a few moments Mary Absolem was there again sitting in front of me, looking as though she had just woken up from a deep sleep.

The subject of trance mediumship cannot be left without mention of Edgar Cayce (1877 –1945), considered to be the greatest psychic in recent times. He produced over 14,000 documented clairvoyant-telepathic readings for more than 6,000 people over a span of 43 years. These readings covered everything from medical diagnoses and remedies to business advice, past life information, prehistory and cosmology of the universe. He was a simple, quiet man with a strong Christian belief who would go into a trance-state from which the readings were given and about which he had no subsequent recollection. He astonished even himself when giving information on people's past lives since, as a practising Christian, this was at variance with his beliefs. He lost his voice at the age of 23 through a bout of serious laryngitis and had to live at home. About a year later, a travelling stage hypnotist who had come to the area, heard about his condition and offered to attempt a cure. Incredibly, Cayce's voice returned whilst in hypnotic trance, but vanished again on awakening. In a further session, Cayce was asked to describe the nature of his condition and cure. In trance, he did this, as if he were plural ….. "We are suffering from psychological paralysis …" the cure for which, according to 'himselves' was to increase the blood flow to his voice box. The hypnotist suggested that he do this. Cayce's face became flushed with blood and his chest area became bright red. After 20 minutes and still in a trance 'we' said his treatment was over. On awakening, his voice returned to normal.

This was not a man who sought fame and fortune, but one who struggled over whether his psychic abilities were spiritually legitimate. Quiet and unassuming, he considered his healing readings as the most important part of his work, and far preferred them to the prophetic and pre-historical information that made him a celebrity. Many consider him responsible for re-igniting the controversy about the existence of Atlantis, since he produced much information about this, and a now-fabled Hall of Records that was to be found at the end of the century (2000CE) in the vicinity of the Sphinx on the Giza Plateau in Egypt (more about this in chapter 10). There is not enough space here to single out the instances of the astonishing diagnostic and healing readings he effected, or the holes in his prophecies. But one thing is certain, and that is his intention to improve the lives of human beings through his work.

Fortunately for mediums and sensitives working these days, the Witchcraft Act, under which they could be liable for persecution was repealed in 1951. This was due to the case of Helen Duncan (1897 –1956 CE), a Scottish medium, who was the last person to be convicted under this Act. Helen Duncan was a frail woman, with six children and an invalid husband, but clearly had a powerful mediumistic gift in contacting the spirits of those no longer on Earth. In 1941 – in the middle of WWII - she held a séance in Portsmouth during which a sailor materialised. Through Helen Duncan, he told the assembled group that his ship, HMS Barham, had recently been sunk, and he wanted to contact his mother who was anxious about him. The Editor of Psychic News at that time, Maurice Barbanell, was present and innocently phoned the British Admiralty to enquire whether this information was true, and if so why had the sailor's mother not been informed about the loss of her son. Military intelligence were furious when they received this call, because for security reasons and public morale, they had withheld news of the sinking of the ship and classified it as top secret. It was believed by the Admiralty that a woman of this mediumistic calibre could put national security at risk, so she was arrested on charges of fraudulent mediumship, tried by a kangaroo court and sent to prison for nine months. According to a BBC programme about her life (aired in 2001), Winston Churchill visited her in prison and was appalled at what happened. He promised to repeal the Witchcraft Act, and this he did, after which Spiritualism became a legal religion in the United Kingdom.

When or if you decide to consult a psychic, medium, sensitive or channeller of information from any level whatever, first consider what it is you are going to consult them about. Thinking about this before your meeting will also help the medium to be more focused when you arrive. Some people become addicted to consulting others about their destinies, and can't even make relatively simple decisions about their lives without checking the stars or with their favourite psychic. It is definitely not healthy – a sort of nanny-state spirituality – to abdicate responsibility for the choices you make in your own life, and besides which it is not always 'allowed' for us to have answers in advance. Nor should a medium tell you that you were, for example, a witch who was burned at the stake in a previous life, and that's why you have a fear of fire, or are afraid to speak about your beliefs in front of others. That may (or may not) be the case, but it's not helpful, and just leaves you with more questions. But if the timing is right, your intention is clear and the medium has integrity, you should receive useful and supportive help.

One more word on the psychic information superhighway, and this is about protection. As we have anti-virus protection on our computers to protect us from unwelcome invaders, so it is with the psychic superhighway, specially if we are new to the invisible world wide web.

As Judy Hall, author of *The Art of Psychic Protection,* says "Above all else, psychic protection is about being fully grounded in your body. If you only have a toehold on the earth, you will never be fully secure". We live in an environment that is not only physically contaminated, but also psychically polluted by clouds of negative energy accumulated over the centuries, so it makes sense to take some simple precautions. We put on a raincoat and take an umbrella when going out into the rain, so our subtle body also needs some protection from exposure to potentially harmful conditions. These do not have to take the form of time-consuming rituals. The simple safety precaution of visualising a protective (white) coat around you works well.

Carlos Castaneda refers to our personal space both visible and invisible, as a 'luminous egg of energy'. He says that it is important to pay attention to what happens to this egg of ours, as the contents can drain away without our being conscious of it happening. We can waste our energy, or it may be leeched away without our realising, leaving us feeling drained and depleted. We have already looked at this in the chapter on the aura. There are many books on psychic protection, psychic self-defence and psychic attack. Don't be put off by the titles, or let fear of what you might encounter prevent you from exploring. This is why getting the basics in place is so important. Understanding your own energy field, making sure you are 'grounded' on earth and connected to the highest point of Light, your soul star (remember the Egyptians), ensures that you are centred and collected enough to set off.

Any psychic work should be preceded by 'opening up' the chakras and concluded by 'closing down' – just as you would with your computer. In chapter 2 there is an exercise on bringing expanded awareness back into focus for life in our everyday reality. After exploring the psychic superhighway it's important to be more rigorous in closing down your bio-computer – your energy field – and is a form of spiritual hygiene. It ensures that you are clear of any astral spam and that your chakras are not wide open to receive all transmissions. Follow these instructions, and once you have become familiar with them, just a thought will produce the effect.

Closing Down to Maintenance Level

- Sit in a chair with your feet on the ground.
- Close your eyes.
- Imagine your chakras like open flowers (front and back) within your auric field.
- Starting with the crown, gently imagine or sense each chakra closing to a level that feels right for everyday life.
- Pay particular attention to the solar plexus, if you are sensitive to others' energies, which can have extra protection by imagining a golden disc in front of it.
- Finally, be aware of your connection to the Earth through the soles of your feet and to your soul star as a point of light above

your Crown.
- Then imagine the energy of these two points coming together in your Heart, creating a central axis for your being.
- Now you are balanced, and aligned, grounded and guided.

The psychic super information highway has always been available to us, but because orthodox religion took a dim view of people making their own connections to other dimensions, and that included the Divine, we now have to free ourselves from centuries of conditioning which tried to make us believe that this was evil or 'weird'. Ramtha's right. We have forgotten our Divinity.

Soul Focus
Right use of psychic energy expands the soul's experience
and connects us with other levels of being.

REMINDERS .....
- Be aware of the information you 'pick'up from others and how that process works.
- Before you experiment or explore, never forget the arrow of your intention, and align your intent to the Highest Good.
- In the time you allocate for meditation, you might like to hold your focus specifically on the Third Eye, breathing into and out from it, to build its 'muscle', since this is the chakra most likely to be involved with surfing the psychic internet.
- Be discerning about what you perceive/receive, see or hear.
- Always remember to 'close down' when you have finished any interaction with the psychic superhighway.

168

Resources:

Evidence for the Sixth Sense: **Hazel Courtenay** (CICO Books)

Feeling Safe: **William Bloom** (Piatkus Books) www.williambloom.com

The Stormy Search for the Self: **Stanislav Grof** (J P Tarcher)

Are You Psychic?: **Julie Soskin** (Carroll & Brown Publishers)

Psychic Warrior: True Story of the CIA's Paranormal Espionage Programme: **David Morehouse** (Clairview Books)

Psi Spies: **Jim Marrs** (Alienzoo Inc)

Psychic Discoveries: The Iron Curtain Lifted: **Ostrander and Schroeder** (Marlowe & Co)

A Beginner's Guide to Creating Reality: **Ramtha** (JZK Publishing) www.ramtha/com

What the Bleep do we Know? **DVD**

Beyond the Bleep: **Alexander Bruce** (Disinformation Company) Both the DVD and this available through www.cygnus-books.co.uk

The Pleaidian Agenda: **Barbara Hand Clow** (Bear & Co) www.hand-clow2012.com

Earth: **Barbara Marciniak** (Bear & Co) www.pleiadians.com

The Nature of Personal Reality: **Jane Roberts** (Prentice Hall Press)

The Third Millennium: Living in the Post historic World: **Ken Carey** (Harper Collins)

See Also:
www.crimsoncircle.com

chapter 8

is anybody there?

Angels, Spirit Guides and Invisible Helpers

Millions of spiritual creatures walk the earth
Unseen, both when we wake and when we sleep.
John Milton: Paradise Lost

Angels

Who are these winged creatures that recently seem to have invaded the Western world? Will they really find you a parking place in a busy street? Do we all have a Guardian Angel who watches over us? Why don't they communicate more often?

The angelic realms are certainly experiencing a comeback – but perhaps they have never really been away. It was simply that angelology went out with the incoming, increasingly mechanistic and rational worldview that needed to reduce the universe and everything in it to a machine. Such things as angels were relegated to the libraries of classical religious art and thinking, as the chasm between science and mysticism widened, and astronomy and astrology become divorced from each other in the seventeenth century.

However, with the startling revelations of modern physics and cosmology, it is being discovered by intelligent minds such as Matthew Fox (a visionary theologian) and Rupert Sheldrake (who has already been mentioned in connection with his research into morphogenetic fields), that not only are angels fact rather than fantasy, but they are also far greater and more powerful beings than we ever realised. Belief in them can revolutionise our lives and effect profound changes, both individually and collectively. The key here being 'belief in them', as will be explained.

Throughout recorded history there have been many references to the presence of winged heavenly beings, referred to as messengers, bringers of light, help and guidance – sometimes referred to as the *Elohim*, or Shining Ones. If you look closely at all the names of the angels (even the word itself) they end with 'el', meaning 'shining'. Are they like a stream of consciousness acting as an intermediary presence between our human selves and a force that would be too overwhelmingly powerful for us to interpret in a meaningful way? Are they intercessionaries, emissaries of light, bringing information and guidance to us in a form that we can understand? Their ability to shape-shift means that the way in which they were seen and depicted through the centuries has changed *according to the belief system of the time*. The role of angel as guardian or protector can possibly be traced back to the images of supernatural, winged creatures found in ancient Mesopotamia and Sumeria. Again, unearthly winged beings appear in Babylonian, Persian, Egyptian and Greek religious iconography. These original light-bearers then became the angels we are now familiar with, through the three major world religions of Judaism, Christianity and Islam. It was after all the archangel Gabriel who delivered the news to Mary that she was to be the mother of Jesus, and to Mohammed in his retreat that he needed to "Recite" the words of God that were to be given him. Images of winged beings which were created much earlier than these three major religions are still to be found on the walls of tombs and temples in dynastic Egypt, on Sumerian artefacts and formed an important part in the pre-Christian religions of Mithras and Zoroastra.

There is an implicate order expressed in everything in the known universe. Our own planet exists within a solar system that exists within our galaxy, which in turn belongs to a group of galaxies, each with its own solar systems, planets and stars, and so on into infinity – the universe as a hologram in fact – a concept which is difficult to grasp with our finite minds, but touched in the words of the visionary poet, William Blake:

To see a world in a Grain of Sand,
and a Heaven in a Wild Flower,
hold Infinity in the palm of your hand,
and eternity in an hour.

Which is a poetic way of describing the Hermetic Principle of 'as above, so below'. Just think for a moment about your own body and how like a universe it is. Millions of cells like small planets with electrons and neutrons orbiting the nuclei. Bodies within bodies. We organise ourselves into groups or clusters on a larger body, the Earth, which also forms part of an even larger body, our solar system. The pattern is repeated up and down the scales of magnitude. Nothing exists in isolation. We are all part of an enfolded and unfolding creation. Who can say whether a brain cell is more important than a toenail cell? A lump of granite more meaningful than a goose?

As we begin to realise what we have done to the planet we currently call our home, we can see that by separating ourselves from the knowledge that everything and everyone has a place in this 'multiverse' we have interfered with its organic evolution and created a terminal illness for ourselves. This arrogant, exclusive attitude has taken us to the edge of extinction, to a point where things have become so extreme, we are forced to take another look at the world we have created. As the Essene Gospel of Peace prophesies ...

And one day the eyes of your spirit shall open,
and you shall know all things.

No wonder then, that 35,000-year-old Lemurians are appearing in kitchens and so many people are having angel experiences as well as spiritual emergencies. As the scales fall from our eyes, we can look out to the heavens and accept that we need help and that we do not have all the answers. What – or rather who – ever angels are, they certainly seem to have responded to our appeal.

A so-called 'angel experience' is definitely something that brings a smile to the face of those who have had them. When angels have appeared to people in the scriptures, they don't just arrive and frighten them out of their wits. They herald their presence with the words "Be not afraid", as they did to the Virgin Mary and the shepherds watching their flocks at the time of the birth of Jesus. Angels have often appeared to people as 'mysterious strangers' arriving in times of distress, knowing exactly what help is needed and then vanishing. No one knows who they were or where they came from. They sometimes appear in human form but there may be something about them, retrospectively, that makes you aware that they are 'different'.

"Be not afraid to have strangers in your house, for some thereby have entertained angels unawares" the readers of the book of Hebrews in the Bible's New Testament are asked. Entertaining strangers in our house is not something most people would feel inclined to do in these suspicion-filled and fear-full times.

It seems as if there are many ways and forms that angels make their presence felt in human lives and always for the benefit of those to whom they come. Whether these are truly angels of the original Elohim is debatable, as research into the accessible history of who and what these beings were reveals something somewhat different from our contemporary conception of what angels are. But actually it's all about what you *believe,* as I have inferred before. It doesn't really matter if they are angels or something else, as this story of 5-year-old Tommy, as told to me by his mother, indicates.

In hospital for an operation, and undergoing surgery, Tommy has a Near Death Experience (NDE) in which his body is technically 'dead' for a few minutes. He then returns to life, recovers from the operation and is taken home, where his mum asks him what he remembers of his experience. "I went through this tunnel of light, it was lovely, and then I was met at the end by Zadakiel ....." His delighted mother then says " Oh! how wonderful, Tom – an angel!". " No, no, not an angel" replies Tommy "it was Zadakiel from Star Wars ...". So the being that met Tommy at the end of the tunnel that was taking his soul to where it belonged, was 'someone' whom he felt safe with and trusted, someone more powerful than he, but someone he recognised. If it had been his mother having a near-death- experience she would no doubt have reported meeting someone different at the end of the tunnel, since a character from Star Wars wouldn't have the same meaning for her.

So perhaps there is a wonderfully benevolent body of 'overseers' who have the ability to materialise into our dense physical reality in whatever form is appropriate, to give help in moments of distress, moments when we've lost our way and need some guidance. Everybody in the world would trust an angel, wouldn't they?

What is certain is that the more we believe in angels, the more we keep on dialling their number as it were, and strengthening that connection, the more active they become in our lives. And far from being a bunch of bare-bottomed cherubs flitting about looking coy, perhaps they are representatives of an enormously powerful force that has made itself available to help, guard and guide us humans back to the recognition of who we truly are. The more we believe in something, the more likely it is to manifest. If you don't believe in angels – you'll probably never encounter one. The placebo effect has proved that believing in a curative brings about healing, even though the content of the 'curative' has no healing properties. Energy follows thought, and the thought is the arrow that is fired into the quantum realms, astral plane, akashic record or information superhighway which collapses its target into the physical world. Be careful what you think!

Spirit Guides

If you have ever consulted a psychic or medium, you may have noticed that they refer to their 'guide' or spirit helper. As mentioned earlier, it makes sense if you are entering or accessing unfamiliar territory that you have someone with you who is familiar with the terrain, or one who seems to be the gatekeeper of the fields of information you need to be able to access on behalf of those who come to you for guidance. These spirit guides are sometimes referred to as 'discarnates', meaning that they have once been on the earth in human form (unlike angels) and are now on the other side of the veil that separates the physical and spiritual worlds. These guides are those souls who have volunteered for service to mankind and, because they have been human themselves, offer a different kind of support from the kind that the angels seem to be giving. A guide could be a more evolved aspect of your soul group, who will act as a go-between for communication and transfer of experience from you down here in the front-line, as it were, and the rest of the group of which you are a representative. They may be teachers dedicated to raising our level of awareness (here comes the Lemurian again), or beings from our own or other star systems, or – as in cultures that use shamanic practices – they may appear in the form of a 'power animal' or wise ancestor.

Whoever or whatever they are, they will be the appropriate guide for the level of work or exploration that you are involved with. Stephen Turoff, for example, is a well-known British psychic surgeon who accomplishes a lot of his powerful healing work through the guidance of a doctor who lived in the 19th century. It might, of course, be one of his own dramatis personae popping in from a previous lifetime. Sometimes a spirit guide may actually take over the physical body of their channel – but only with their agreement – in order to bring information through, with the consciousness of the channel being set aside, as we saw in the last chapter.

If you are aware of a spirit guide being with you, it's important not to become too attached to them as they appear to change for some people during their lifetime, according to needs and development, and whilst they are here to help, they are not here to take away your responsibilities, or ability to be independent enough to make your own decisions about life. Ultimately the work of the soul is about collecting experience and recognising that trials and tribulations are presented not as a form of punishment but to draw our attention to something, in order to change or challenge our perception of what we think is 'real'. It may be that in some instances we use the term spirit guide when we are in fact in touch with a wiser aspect of ourselves that we have become disconnected from. This could be especially true if we have become used to receiving instruction and wisdom from an external source and are not as familiar with our inner world as a more introspective person would be.

Many mediums who work with guides also have the ability to perceive the guide of the person consulting them, and whilst it might be reassuring for you to think that you have a wise monk at your elbow, it would have much more value if you were able to connect and communicate with this entity yourself, and then you would *know*.

Guides are cross-cultural and take many forms, but there does seem to have been a plethora of Native American Indians, Chinese philosophers and Tibetan monks in the recent past. I have often wondered why there never seem to be any Druids.

For some reason spirit guides are more often male than female (as with angels). Is this because we are still emerging from over 2,000 years of patriarchal authority, during which time much feminine wisdom was suppressed? However, the guides offering themselves for service appear to have changed of late and a new wave of helpful beings has entered the third dimension to give us assistance it seems. These are called Ascended Masters and are so popular that they even have their own website, where you can put in your details, press a button and 'your' ascended master will reveal himself (yes, most of them male again) to you. The names of some of them may be unfamiliar – Count St Germain, Sanat Kumar, Serapis Bey, Hilarion – even St Francis of Assisi is also considered to be part of this Great White Brotherhood who have signed up to help us towards mastery and ascension. The first maxim in all healing work and guiding others is to "Do no harm", with the corollary one would hope of not making anything more complicated than it need be. Since I have no direct experience of any of these Ascended Masters, I am not in a position to make a comment, although I might just pass a reminder about astral glamour and what is emerging from 'www.theastralplanes.net.' There are Ascended Masters and ascended masters. The genuine articles were once in human form. They became masters of the earthly experience and 'ascended' lock, stock and body to the next dimension. Each agreed to volunteer for service to those of us struggling on the same path. Sorry, but I think it's unlikely you'll find the real thing on the internet.

Sometimes a guide may appear in the form of someone you knew or knew of, and again it is important to remember that just because someone has died, it does not necessarily mean that they have automatically acquired wisdom. This reminds me of a story about a woman who complained that the guidance she had received through a medium from her deceased husband, Fred, had led her down the road to ruin. His instructions came through a clairvoyant, and she followed them to the letter. As a result of taking Fred's advice, she found herself living in a place which didn't suit her, miles away from the rest of her family and tied down with an enormous mortgage. Now she was furious with the medium, who bore the brunt of her anger and frustration. Fred could, of course, have been trying to teach her the need for discernment and to make decisions without him.

Ruth White has been communicating with her guide, *Gildas* – a 14th century French monk – for over 40 years and has written several books containing his wisdom. In her book *Working with Guides and Angels,* Gildas is asked to explain the being and function of guides. This is part of what he says:

"The original spark or soul comes from the Source. In order to become like the Source and also to ensure that the Source is not static, the soul takes on incarnation and journeys through many lifetimes in search of evolution. Gradually an overseeing, observing self emerges and then each time incarnation takes place only a part of the whole becomes personified in order to undergo the further experience which the essence requires in its search for wholeness.

When the soul thread is sufficiently evolved, the wheel of rebirth is no longer its main concern or focus. There is an opportunity to continue on the path of evolution by being of service in different ways. Guides and communicators have agreed to aid the collective journey by sharing the less finite view and wider perspective seen from other planes of being. This is why we seek individuals on earth with whom to communicate. Our aim is to help in making the experience of incarnation less blinkered or limited in vision.

Guides cross the interface between planes in order to communicate. They have different concerns or aims in making their contact with incarnate human beings. For some, the main focus will be healing, for others teaching, whilst yet others will seek to inspire the artist, poet, architect, musician or writer.

Even the Great Masters or Ascended Ones seek more direct and constant contact with the earth plane during the times you are now experiencing. You, and therefore we, are at a dangerous but exciting point in the evolution of consciousness.

Our beings on these planes are more diffuse than are yours on earth. We take on a personality so that we can have more understandable, direct and tender contact with you – but we no longer endure the limitations of personality as you do.

A great and golden opportunity lies ahead. We communicate in order that in spite of the chaotic or even violent experiences you have, you should not lose hope or faith about the future. We bring positive hope for the potential of humankind to live together in light, love and optimum health."

What could be clearer than that? Do you feel you are ready to meet a guide? Before you begin to make moves in this direction, it is important to feel that you have a strong sense of your own independent discerning self. Otherwise there would be a risk of your becoming too reliant on your guide for advice on the day-to-day running of your life. Guides are not here to make decisions for us, or to replace our own, possibly dormant, ability for discernment. Guides appear to those who have developed a strong sense of self regarding who and what they are, and not to those who are continually looking to others to both define and support them.

If you establish contact with a guide, in whatever form, it is also important to remember that you are in control of the situation. Any guide that insists on interfering in your daily life, or asks you to communicate at three in the morning needs investigation. You want to be connected to a guide with the highest integrity in order to trust and value the communication.

It's not a good idea to fire off the question "Is anybody there?" when opening up your satellite dish for reception to all stations. As already explained, there are all manner of channels you can tune into that cannot possibly give you what you might seek from a guide. As with everything else, intention and maintaining a sense that you are in a sacred area will ensure that you connect to the highest source of guidance available. In order to make the connection to your wise being or guide, it is important that you yourself are coming from a place of inner peace and awareness. Creating your own inner sanctuary provides you with a place for contemplation and reflection, and a means for your guide to come forward. If they don't appear immediately – or at all – don't despair. Firstly we have to ask for this guidance and then let go of any expectation of what might happen. As soon as we try too hard to do any work with the invisible realms, the left brain engages, creates tension and the free flow of energy blocks. The more relaxed you are, and free from expectation, the more likely you are to be surprised by what might happen. Guides come in many shapes and sizes, sometimes appearing as a field of colour or energy rather than a recognisable form. The main thing to note is the *quality* of the experience.

I spent years wondering why a guide never appeared to me, having given them ample opportunity I thought. Did no one out there want to be my guide? Was I not 'advanced' enough to merit a supernatural mentor? It took me some time to realise that I might not be aware of a personalised guide but, my goodness, I am guided by something. I have no idea even of what that something is, but I do know when it directs my path.

Advanced Beings (ABs)
One last word on the subject of guidance, and that concerns the matter of

extra terrestrial presence on our planet, and I am not talking about green men in saucers.

The focus of this book is understanding the human experience from a spiritual perspective and if we take even a small peek at the development of our self-consciousness there are some large gaps in continuity and apparently inexplicable quantum leaps in our history.

Since World War II, thousands, if not millions of people have reported seeing UFOs, and an untold number of others have reported actual encounters with Extraterrestrials (ETs). Thousands of these reports have been thoroughly investigated by government agencies, scientists, private investigators and health care professionals. This has gone some way to removing the whole subject from its 1960s image of oddball UFO spotters in woolly hats – with minds to match - and equipped with strange sky-watching apparatus. Probably for the vast majority though, this topic is still laden with doubt and suspicion and belongs in the box marked Loony Fringe. Or perhaps we just don't want to know, and if we did, so what? It's certainly something that is laden with conspiracy theories about government cover-ups, disinformation, military secrets and ridicule. Worth remembering here that if you want to marginalize anything out of importance in people's minds, making fun of it is an effective method. Feeling humiliated by others in the tribe is not a comfortable human experience.

I'd like to tickle your curiosity on this subject in the hope that you will investigate further even though direct experience in this particular instance would seem to have more to do with chance and destiny than design. But are today's reports of ET contacts and 'abductions' so very different from the human contacts with gods and angels described in the ancient sacred texts of Judaism, Christianity and Islam?

Practically every tradition in the world has gods – under local names – who descended from the sky or heavens in astonishing gravity-defying machines. These gods had magic powers, introduced agricultural and farming methods, domesticated animals and brought with them seeds of new species of plants and trees. These traditional 'myths' point to a family of gods who – like all families – had their own internal conflicts and power struggles but they were definitely different from the everyday human inhabitants of the Earth at that time. Cross-culturally the legends speak of these sky-gods as intervening in human lives, creating a 'new' breed by having sexual intercourse with 'the daughters of men' or implanting genetically engineered sperm in human wombs.

Perhaps we can fast-forward into 21st century science laboratories for a moment, and zoom in on the investigative work being carried out on DNA and our genetic ancestry. As a matter of astonishing interest, there are 125 billion miles of DNA in each of our bodies. Some biologists describe DNA as an "ancient high biotechnology" containing "over a hundred trillion times as much information by volume as our most sophisticated information storage devices." DNA is only 10 atoms wide and as such constitutes a sort of ultimate technology, Jeremy Narby informs us, and what's more it is organic and so miniaturised that it approaches the limits of material existence. With that in mind, we go to the work of Professor Paul Davies, of the Macquarie University in Sydney, Australia who published an article in the New Scientist in August 2004 in which he argued that non-coding sequences in human DNA – known as 'junk' DNA – may in fact be extraterrestrial information or messages. He explains that:

> *DNA, the molecule that contains the script of life, encodes its data in a four-letter alphabet. This would be an ideal medium for storing a cosmic calling card. In many organisms, humans included, genes make up only a tiny fraction of their DNA. Much of the rest seems to be biological gobbledygook, often called "junk DNA". There is plenty of room there for ExtraTerrestrials to etch a molecular message without damaging any vital genetic functions.*

Perhaps it's important to point out that 97% of our DNA is so-called 'junk'. 97% of 125 billion miles of database seems rather a lot of information hanging around doing nothing. But perhaps it is like the Hall of Records – a mystery waiting to be discovered, after which our entire history will have to be rewritten.

Zecharia Sitchin, biblical scholar and historian, has distinguished himself through revelations brought about by his ability to read ancient Sumerian clay tablets. His interpretations have led to the publishing of a series of books under the heading *The Earth Chronicles* in which he puts forward the theory – based on his findings - that there is another planet in our solar system. This planet was called Niburu by the Sumerians (Marduk in Babylonian cosmology) and is/was the home of a technically advanced extraterrestrial race called the Annunaki – or the Nephilim of the Bible. Niburu/Marduk has a long elliptical orbit which passes close to Earth roughly every 3,600 years. He claims that the Annunaki first hopped off their planet onto Earth about 450,000 years ago, looking for minerals, especially gold, and, by genetic manipulation of the primitive hominoid inhabitants, ultimately created Homo sapiens. Then there's the work of anthropologist Dr Arthur Horn. He used to teach the Theory of Evolution to his students – now he argues against it. He has identified a number of gaps in the 'Darwinian-anthropological version of primate and human evolution' and suggests that these are the most likely places where extraterrestrials intervened. He believes the quantum leaps and missing links that appear in our evolution were the moments when tinkering with human DNA occurred. First, the appearance of advanced primates 40 million years ago, then the appearance of the first biological family in Africa (Australopithecines or Hominidae) four million years ago. Thirdly the development of Homo habilis (handy man) about two and a half million years ago; then the development of Homo erectus around 1.8 million years ago and finally the development of Homo sapiens [knowing man] around 300,000 years ago.

In the *Dictionary of World Mythology* another leading scholar of ancient civilisations, Arthur Cotterell, writes this:

The civilisations of the first planters – the cities of the Nile, the Euphrates-Tigris Valley, and the Indus – evolved mythologies connected with a priesthood. The Sumerians even looked upon themselves as the property of their gods; they were workers on the divine estate.

He also quotes the social anthropologist Bronislaw Malinowski as saying "The myth in a primitive society ... is not mere tale told but a reality lived".

Apart from the Sumerian cuneiform texts and cylinder seals, the earliest recorded encounters between Advanced Beings and humans form the basis of the Book of Genesis - the initial book of the Pentateuch of the Hebrew Torah - known to Christians as the Old Testament. They have also been recorded in the Book of Enoch, which now forms part of the Canon of Scripture of the Ethiopian Orthodox Church.

> *The Shining Ones said, 'Let us*
> *make Man in our image*
> *in the likeness of ourselves'*
> **Genesis 1:26**

The common name for god is in the plural in Hebrew – it is *Elohim*. The word *EL* is a very ancient word with a long etymological history that has revealing common origins with many other ancient words in other languages for example:

The Sumerian	EL	meant *brightness* or *shining*
The Babylonian	ELLU	meant *the bright one*
The old Welsh	ELLYL	meant *a shining being*
The Old Irish	AILLIL	meant *shining*
The old Cornish	EL	meant *an angel*
The English	ELF	meant *a shining being*
The Inca	ILLA	meant *brightness or shining*

Christian and Barbara Joy O'Brien: The Shining Ones

But nowhere have we found (as yet) anything to tell us who exactly these

Shining Ones were, who apparently made mankind in their image and like-ness. That they were very tall, had huge eyes and were visitors here is recorded along with descriptions of the garden they created in Ehdin (pre-viously known as Kharsag) – a place in the mountains of southern Lebanon near Mount Hermon and not far from mysterious Baalbek. Here they introduced new species of plants, hydro-electric power and taught the human inhabitants (known as Lowlanders) the agricultural sciences and animal husbandry. At some point Kharsag/Edin was destroyed by tempest, fire and flooding, and they moved into the Mesopotamian Valley. This is estimated to be around 5,500 BCE. About three thousand years later they de-centralised, taking their knowledge to other parts of the globe, includ-ing Greece, Norway, the British Isles, Brittany and Mesoamerica, civilis-ing the local population and installing megalithic structures.

But where did they come from – was it really Planet X? Why did they come and do what they did and then leave? Is it their departure that is responsible for so many religious beliefs about 'a return' – the Second Coming of Christ or the appearance of a Messiah? Were these the 'gods' the Aztecs were expecting when the conquistador Cortes landed in Mexico in 1518 and then slaughtered them all?

These Elohim may have been shining ones, but they were more than abstract concepts of gods. They were flesh and blood characters that descended to Earth exhibiting awesome powers (for those days) and fully engaging with the human inhabitants.

In the meantime, arguments and discussions about which god said what to whom, which one is right and indeed whether there is a god at all continue like a fierce game of tennis. Darwin vs God, Science vs Religion, Evolution vs Creationism – what shall we believe? Blind faith is not an option. We must each return to the basic litmus tests of where we find that Aha! knowing response that comes from the heart's wisdom. Of course our souls can find expression within religious structure, but belief systems must always be examined. Humans have communicated with gods, angels, departed humans and light beings for literally ages. Sane people have heard inner voices directing the course of their lives and sometimes history. We are definitely not alone.

You will make your own mind up about the variety of 'outside' help that might be available, if you choose to ask. But whatever or whoever you choose, remember that any teacher, guide or therapist worthy of the name, will always work towards making themselves obsolete. Like teaching a child to read or write, once they understand, then they must do it for themselves rather than become parrots of their teachers.

Soul Focus
The journey of the soul does not have to be made alone.
Guidance is available for every step of the way.

REMINDERS .....

- Not everyone can 'see' or is aware of a personal guide, but guidance and support is always there if you *ask*.
- If a personal guide hasn't presented themselves, take yourself to an inner place of sanctity and peace. Ask, and then wait, and let go of expectation.
- Check the *quality* of your guide or teacher. Accept nothing except that which 'does no harm', encourages connection rather than division, and expands the understanding of you, your Self.

Resources:

The Physics of Angels: **Matthew Fox & Rupert Sheldrake** (Harper Collins)
An Angel in Your Pocket: **Rosemary Ellen Guiley** (Thorsons)
Working with Guides and Angels: **Ruth White** (Piatkus)
The Shining Ones: **Christian & Joy O'Brian** (Dianthus Publishing Ltd)
The Earth Chronicles: **Zecharia Sitchen** (various publishers)
Humanity's Extra Terrestrial Origins: **(Arthur D Horn)** (A & L Horn)
Gods, Genes & Consciousness: **Paul von Ward**
www.exopolitics.com

chapter 9

divine-ing tools

Cosmic Weather Forecasting

And God said,
Let there be lights in the firmament of heaven
To divide the day from the night; and let them be
For signs, and for seasons, and for days, and years.
Genesis 1:14

There's no need to despair if a personal guide fails to make an appearance. It doesn't mean that no-one's looking after you or you're not 'advanced' enough to have a supernatural being who has chosen you personally to guide you and others through life. Nor does it count if someone else tells you that they see a Tibetan monk or anyone else standing behind you. This is all about direct experience, *your own* direct experience which is the only way to personal knowing. And whatever you do, don't try and invent one. Not 'having' a guide has the definite advantage of training your own inner guidance in a way that those who have guides may not. Besides, there are other tools through and with which you can tap into the different levels of the Astral Plane, Intermediate World, Bardo, Spirit World or whatever name you want to use to describe that which lies between physical reality and the Pure Light of the Void. There are many levels to all worlds, and this one is no exception.

Information – as with the Internet – may be accessed from the astral planes on whatever subject you care to mention ranging from whether you should move house to what your soul's purpose might be. So on one end of the scale we have divination – enquiry of the Divine for guidance – and on the other we have 'fortune-telling' for advice on daily matters.

Divination, as Wikipedia informs us, "is a universal cultural phenomenon which anthropologists have observed as being present in many religions and cultures in all ages up to the present day". In this chapter we will have a look at the different tools available which help navigate the human experience; tools that inform us of what's happening in the bigger picture, which we are unable to access with our limited powers of perception.

Divination is literally the attempt to ascertain information by interpretation of omens, or a *supernatural* agency. In other words, it is using a source of information beyond the conscious mind to help us understand either what *has* happened, what *is* happening or the possibilities of what *will* happen in general or in particular. This search for interpretation and forecasting has gone mainstream, as we can see from daily horoscopes in the popular press, the popularity of Tarot readings, and psychic hotlines - none of which can be counted on for their reliability. Living in a world which seems so acutely uncertain for millions of people in different ways, and being out of touch with their own ability to 'read the signs', people are frantically searching for some kind of reassurance perhaps to help them believe that there is an order behind what appears to be a world in meltdown. Divining in all its many and various forms is another way of accessing the psychic super information highway, but involves a tool, a map of the heavens, an intermediary 'device'.

Across the world people use very different and quite extraordinary means to the same end. In ancient Mesopotamia after ritually sacrificing an animal, its organs and entrails would be 'divined' for anomalies (curious understanding of divine) which would signify or foretell future events. This was called *extispicy*. We may be familiar with having palms read here in the West, but there is also sole-of-the foot reading, called *podomancy,* shape-of-the-head reading, called *phrenology*, face-reading in China, *numerology, cartomancy* and countless others. Bags full of bones are cast in indigenous cultures and read in the same way that we might peer at the tea leaves in a cup, that is until the ubiquitous tea bag took over from the friendly teapot. There is such an astonishing array of devices that have been used throughout the ages, that we must draw the conclusion that *any-*

thing can be used.

> *You simply need to know how to connect everything in the universe with everything else – until finally the only things left to connect are You and God.*
> **Lon Milo DuQuette**

Pendulum Swings

Divination involves first asking a question, and the most basic response we could expect to any question would be a Yes or No, which limits the question somewhat. This is all that is required, however, from a divinatory practice called dowsing. Most people have heard of water divining – or water witching – which has existed in various forms for literally thousands of years, because humans have needed to know where there were sources of this vital source of life. More recently it has come to be called divining, since it appeared that some unseen force jerked the forked hazel twig that was traditionally held by the diviner when they walked over or got near to a source of water. But this form of dowsing can be used for more than just locating water. Things that have got lost - for instance: keys, dogs or people – may be found, and without having to search for a forked hazel twig. It is also an extremely useful and valuable tool for locating what is called *geopathic stress* - the cause not only of what's become known as 'sick building syndrome', but more seriously has been proven to be a common factor in serious and chronic illnesses and numerous minor complaints including depression and other nervous conditions. According to the Dulwich Health Society – an organisation founded by Rolf Gordon after his son died from cancer as a direct result of geopathic stress - thousands of medical doctors and therapists now confirm that geopathic stress must be cleared from the environment of the patient before treatment can be 100% successful. Geopathic stress itself does not cause illness, but lowers your immune system so that there is less chance of fighting invaders. It also prevents your body from properly absorbing vitamins, minerals and vital trace elements from food and supplements, often resulting in allergies and a lowered resistance to environmental pollution. What is it then, this invisible invader of personal space? It is an energy created by the Earth's vibrations rising up through the Earth and then getting distorted by weak electromagnetic fields created by subterranean running water, such as pipes, drains or streams, certain mineral concentrations, fault lines and underground cavities. When this vibration is distorted it becomes abnormally high and harmful to living organisms. Have a look at the website at the end of this chapter for more information, and also information on how to dowse yourself and your home for the presence of geopathic stress which will be found in Rolf Gordon's book *Are You Sleeping in a Safe Place?*

First of all you need an instrument (until you can do it intuitively). You can use a pendulum to dowse, or a device called L-rods – so called because of their shape – or even a stick. The most commonly used is the pendulum, which you can find in most New Age stores or from a large selection available through the British Society of Dowsers. They may be made of wood, crystal, brass or stainless steel, but can be any object you already own, such as a ring, pendant or a heavy button which you dangle from a piece of thick thread. Easy to make and to try for yourself.

How does dowsing work? When you dowse, unconscious muscle movements are magnified and expressed through the dowsing tool. This movement is the body's reaction to a message received from the UEF in response to your intention. It travels via your unconscious mind – thereby short circuiting literal-mind interference. Since energy follows thought or intention, before you start to use your pendulum or rods it is important to clear your mind of everything except the question to which you want a 'yes' or 'no' answer. Phrase the question clearly in your head and then watch the response via the pendulum. Since you can only get a 'yes' or 'no' response from a pendulum, you should only ask questions that can be answered in this way. It is also unwise to ask emotionally charged questions such as "Should I emigrate to Australia?" or "Will I marry this person?". It would be difficult to keep some feeling from such questions, which would interfere with the objectivity and clarity required to receive an unbiased response from the pendulum.

Once you have become more confident, and can stop your mind from interfering with the procedure it will become easier and easier, and you can start to ask more interesting questions. Dowsing can be used to determine which foods agree with your body, and which are best to avoid. For instance, you may be very partial to cheese, but it may not agree with your body. To find out, hold your pendulum over a piece of cheese and then clear your mind of all thoughts apart from "Is this good for me?" If you want help in finding lost articles, first ask the question "Are my keys in the house?"; "Are they in the washing machine?"; "Are they in the bedroom?" and so on until you locate them. Practise makes perfect but in the meantime you need to find out how your pendulum swings when it is saying 'yes' or 'no'. So buy or make yourself a pendulum. The thread should be about 10 inches long. Hold it between your thumb and first or second finger, allowing it to dangle about 6 inches below, and then do the following exercise to find out what movement it will make and how to interpret its response to your questions.

How does your Pendulum speak to you?

Sit comfortably. Make sure your arm holding the pendulum is not tense.

Breathe and relax.

Hold it over your right knee.

Ask in your mind the question "Is this my right knee?" (I know this sounds silly, but do it anyway.)

Possibly the pendulum will begin to move in a clockwise direction (most people's 'yes' or positive response) – but your 'yes' may be a forward/backward swinging movement. Let the pendulum tell you.

Now you need to find out what your 'no' or negative response is. Hold the pendulum over your *left* knee and this time ask. "Is this my right knee?" and see what happens.

Using a pendulum is a good way to hone your divinatory skills, and will give you confidence to try something more adventurous. However, please don't become a dowsing bore, who hangs their pendulum over every plate of food that appears in front of them, or can't buy anything in the supermarket without 'checking'.

Dowsing is a basic body-oriented divinatory tool, whose history has been linked mainly with earthly matters, such as searching for water, gold, tin and other substances hidden underground. As we move into the more subtle realms of divination there is something important that needs to be understood, and that is the interpretation of 'signs'. You can look at a crystal ball and see only a crystal ball, or a collection of tea leaves and see only the end of your cuppa so what happens that turns the mundane into the magical? Well it's all about the right mind. Remember how the left hemisphere of our brain sees the world through a literal analytical lens? This absolutely will not work in the area of divining; in fact if you can't get out of your head, so to speak, there is little point in trying more subtle forms of divination, so just stay with the dowsing until something else starts to open up. The language of the soul, speaking through the right hemisphere, is the language of metaphor, pun, image and *symbol*.

The language of words is not enough. The spirit speaks in pictures
And let whoever would listen hark to the cards!
In their mirror the past and present lie as one,
And from that story told, the future takes its form.
Who would read a picture book may know as a child the secrets of the ages.
Shapes and patterns, colours and signs whisper their message.
The wise gaze deep and listen from within.
Jonathan Cainer and Carl Rider: The Psychic Explorer

Chinese Chops

There are plenty of symbols – 64 to be exact – in one of the oldest books in human history, the Chinese I Ching or Classic Book of Changes which dates back to nearly 4000 BCE. This ancient and most extraordinary oracle was consulted by casting not bones, but a bunch of yarrow stalks six times. From the order in which they fell the querent ('the one who queries') constructed a six-line hexagram which then led him to one of the 64 hexagrams – 'chops' - found in the book, each one providing a judgement, a commentary, an image and interpretation of each of the 6 lines.

The fundamental wisdom of this serious oracle is based on the understanding of the dynamic of Yin and Yang being opposite sides of the same coin, the primal opposing but complementary forces found in all things in the universe as mentioned in the previous chapter. Its wisdom guides us to find balance through opposites and to accept change as being the waveform moving through the universe which brings about progression. Nothing is static, but constantly changing, a fact now being validated by frontier scientists. You don't need to throw a handful of yarrow sticks to access this ancient understanding of the Way Things Are – it works just as well and is much easier with three coins, as long as it's clear which is heads and which is tails. The answer may seem enigmatic at first glance, but you can be sure there will be wisdom to help you hold your balance. Thomas Crum, author and aikido instructor, provides just the right metaphor when he advises us that

Instead of seeing the rug being pulled from under us,
We can learn to dance on a shifting carpet.

All the 64 hexagrams represent a stage on life's continuum. Positives and negatives are all part of the process, completely natural expressions of what is unfolding. The I Ching stresses the importance not only of balance, but proper timing and understanding of one's place in the continuum at this moment in the Eternal Now. Don't expect direct answers from the enigmatic I Ching, and take time to reflect on the meaning of the oracle's response to your question.

Here are a few rules that are best observed if you are taking this whole thing seriously, and which apply not only to the I Ching, but any and every oracle or divining 'tool' from whom you require guidance or advice.

Rules for the Querent

- Consulting an oracle or using some other form of divination links you to a source of information beyond your conscious mind. In order that the quality of the information delivered comes with integrity and wisdom that you can trust, it is your responsibility as the querent to ask considered questions that come from a genuine need for guidance. Otherwise you may find yourself getting ticked off by the oracle. Certainly the I Ching does not tolerate idle curiosity.

- Spend a little time on formulating your query and do this in such a way that, unlike dowsing, it requires more than a yes/no response. The clearer the question the clearer the answer. So rather than ask, for example, "How long will this situation continue?" better to frame it as "What is this situation teaching me?" because the situation will continue or repeat until you, the soul, have got the message.

- Never ask the same question twice, just because you don't like what the oracle has said the first time. You may ask a second question, however, asking for a finer tuning on the first response.

- The less emotionally involved with the question you are, the clearer will be the answer. Sometimes, therefore, it's useful to get a friend to ask the question on your behalf.

- If your conditioning is so strong that it regards all this as some sort of mumbo jumbo, then it might help to imagine that you are consulting a wiser aspect of your Self (which you are). If you could imagine your Higher Self as a wise archetype – what sort of being would you trust? Direct your question to that being.

- The question is more important than the answer. This may sound a curious piece of advice, but, as already stressed, woolly questions get woolly answers. Fire your question like an arrow, holding it in the whole of your being as you take aim and send it through the clouds of mental and emotional static as if it were able to reach a star.

Stars in your Skies

Stars, of course, are where humankind has directed their gaze in order to forecast and understand events down here on earth for literally ages. Again the Hermetic Principle of "As above, so below ...." has been applied in virtually every culture of the world since humans became self-conscious. In fact astrology, which is what this is about, was believed to be one of the ways that god communicated to his physical creation until Sir Isaac Newton's discoveries and theories blew this away around 300 years ago. Jung called it 'the psychology of antiquity'. Now quantum physics has spun the wheel again and everything is being seen as inter-connected and interchangeable as the ancients knew and understood. The wonder of astrology, similar to the I Ching, is that it tells us about what IS, where we are as particles on a wave of the Great Sea, and what that Great Sea is up to itself. So it will tell us about the *weather* we can expect to experience, based on the position of celestial co-ordinates and their interaction with each other and each of us as individuals within the Great Sea. Not only will it tell us, for example, that the actions of the powerful planet Mars will make the 'climate' more likely for war or peace but it will also inform us on our own personal weather system, when there are likely to be storms or moments of peace and tranquillity. What astrology will not tell us is whether we are going to leave our partners, win the lottery, move to Madagascar or die of cancer.

How on earth does what happens in the heavens give us any idea of what 'weather' we might expect? Because of this interconnectedness. Since the emergence of what's known as the theory of chaos, we know that the flap of a butterfly's wings in Brazil can set off (or prevent) a tornado in Tokyo. How then could we possibly think that the movements of large bodies in the tiny part of the Great Sea in which we live would not affect particles bobbing about in the same part of that wave? We know for certain how the movement of the moon shifts not only vast quantities of ocean backwards and forwards but affects fertility cycles on Earth, makes wolves howl and mad people madder. The sun, our own star, is responsible for our very existence and is the kingpin as it were in each of our individual natal charts as well as defining which of the 12 Signs we have arrived in. Solar flares and sunspot activity have enormous impact on life on earth. We take for granted the exquisite balance in which everything is held, but what a mystery it all is. In the words of Sir Martin Rees, the Astronomer Royal:

There appear to be a large number of very fortunate coincidences which allow the existence of we human beings. There is the expansion rate of the universe, which is precariously balanced between being too fast for the formation of galaxies, etc., and too slow such that the cosmos collapses. In short it is just right, to a very high degree of accuracy.

Who am I to disagree with the Astronomer Royal, but I certainly wouldn't agree that everything hangs together due to 'very fortunate coincidences'. It's not an accident, it's a design.

Your natal chart, in the unlikely event of your not already knowing this, is a map of what exactly was going on in the Great Celestial Sea at the moment you popped out of the relative safety of your mother's womb to begin your current earthly experience. So in effect it is a diagram of the heavens as seen from a given place on the earth at a given moment. But just knowing that you are a Capricorn or a Scorpio will give you as much information about yourself as saying you are a cake. These huge generalisations have one thing right; you are a cake and not a biscuit or a pie, but what other ingredients have been added to the recipe? At the particular time and place of your birth the planets, sun and moon were in a completely unique position in the sky. No other person in the world will ever share exactly the same birth chart as you, not even an identical twin. Your natal chart is like a single frame on an infinite reel which is recording the movements of the Great Ocean for that second. It is a split nanosecond, but a defining one for each of us.

That moment will have been ordered by the soul because at that moment in time and space all the ingredients required for this particular journey will be 'active'. The soul, for example, may need the communication skills of a Gemini in this lifetime or to bring inner or outer balance as a Libran. But a Gemini may have to come to terms with fears of impermanence and the Libran with accepting that life is not all pleasant and beautiful. At this moment of your physical appearance, the Sun will be in one of the twelve 30 degree arcs that it passes through during the course of a year, giving us the Signs of the Zodiac. So although that moment of your birth might appear to be static - something that will remain the same throughout your lifetime - in fact the way the planets continually move around the sun unfolds the chart's potential.

The planets moving around in the heavens will not tell us *what* is going to happen any more than our sun sign tells us *who* we are. A birth chart is like opening a packet of seeds that shows you the possibilities and potential contained within you and the sort of conditions you are likely to experience during the planting and growing of the seeds, if you choose to plant them. So here is your own unique blueprint in all its splendour, like your DNA and fingerprint, which shows all the possibilities and potential available in your specific packet. All the seeds may not necessarily flower, but by having a good look you can get an idea of your potential.

Your sun sign, then, is a celestial symbol for the light that shines into your life. The symbol for the sun is a circle with a dot in the centre indicating that it is the centre of our own particular solar system as well, in this case, as yours, and around which everything else revolves. It also represents the Circle of Spirit with the individual creative spark at its centre. In your chart it represents what is at the heart of you and, because it symbolises the active or Yang side of your personality, provides the drive for you to realise the positive attributes of your sign.

The moon, on the other hand, will be placed in a different sign at the time of your birth and stands for the Yin or hidden, emotional aspects of your personality. While the sun pushes us to strive for differentiation, the moon wants to have its emotional needs met and to merge with another. Your sun sign speaks of your active, decision-making abilities, while the moon tells of your basic instinctive needs, your deep emotions that wax and wane, fluctuating with the tides of life.

The placement of each of the planets in your birth chart will then expand the portrait of your personality, adding subtle ingredients to the basic recipe which creates your own unique expression of your soul's human form. Mercury, for example, is the smallest and fastest planet in our solar system and where it is placed in your chart gives a clue about your ability to comprehend and communicate, your need to understand things and also whether you will recognise the interconnectedness of everything, or just be a bank full of data.

We may have all heard that men come from Mars and women from Venus, but the placement of these two planets in our charts will give us clues about our own masculine and feminine attributes. You may be living in a woman's body, but you need to understand the masculine aspect of yourself, as a man needs to understand and accept his femininity without feeling he's compromising his maleness. The ancient astrological glyphs for these two planets are now used as biological symbols for male and female. As the sun and moon represent father and mother, here we have Mars as the conqueror and Venus the lover. Their positioning in your chart is particularly interesting in that they reveal what we might look for in an 'opposite number' – or rather those qualities that we require ourselves, so need to have them reflected back in order for us to own them in ourselves.

Where the other planets are placed in our own individual charts will be in the various zodiacal signs and will help us identify which of the four types, relating to the four elements, we fall into. In order to understand this more fully, you need your chart in front of you, and even then to a newcomer it can look like a confusing spider's web of lines and weird symbols. Once you get the hang of it, you will see which planets are in which houses (signs) when you were born. So although your sun may be in the watery sign of Cancer, you may have a preponderance of planets in the earth or air signs, which will temper the effect of the wateriness – symbolising emotions – of your personality.

These are extremely basic astrological facts which haven't even begun to touch the depth of this ancient divinatory tool. Because it is an art as well as a science and can be overwhelming to the uninitiated, it is important to find an astrologer whose interpretations of your natal chart clarify rather than confuse. Astro-speak can leave the head spinning. "Aha! well, Mars is sitting right there in your 12th house. No wonder things are tricky" might make you feel as if you are a victim of circumstance; a pawn in someone else's game which is not what is at the core of astrology. As Lyn Birkbeck informs us in his breathtakingly comprehensive work *The Instant Astrologer,* astrology is:

- A key to freedom
- Something that reveals us to be part of a far greater and all-encompassing, totally interconnecting reality
- The Law of Correspondence or 'As above so below'. A practical guide to everyday living
- A body of wisdom which allows us to see the macrocosm through

the microcosm
* A tool for gaining self-knowledge
* A mystery. Astrology is the Science of Life, but practising it is an art

These days there are many different approaches to the interpretation of charts which have branched out from the more traditional Predictive Astrology. There is Computer Astrology which gives you pages of description as interpreted from factors given to a computer for analysis. Sometimes helpful, but somewhat clinical and lacking context. Then there's the Dabbling Astrologer who probably does a bit of everything – cards, crystals, healing, clairvoyance and so on, but who won't supply theoretical concepts. Most useful is the Psychological Astrologer who emerged in the last century at the time when the lid blew off many things and we started to investigate our selves. As Lyn Birkbeck says "The case for Psychological Astrology is a strong one because it is saying that it is useless and fanciful to predict what lies ahead upon the road of life if you have no knowledge of the vehicle that's travelling down it – you".

Designer Divining

And talking of vehicles, another heavyweight has emerged relatively recently into the age-old search for the meaning of life, the universe and our own individual place in it. The very nature of its 'arrival' should be enough to make us sit up and take notice.

In 1987 there was an extraordinary event in the sky which, for the first time in recorded history, was seen with the naked eye. From a mountain-top in Chile people actually witnessed a supernova – the death of a star – taking place, creating an explosion so enormous that it can hardly be imagined. With its dying breath, this blue supergiant – now known by science as 1987A – flooded the universe including Earth with a neutrino stream of subatomic information. Recent discoveries in the field of astrophysics reveal that stellar matter from distant galaxies is actually passing through our bodies. Thus the death of a star carries profound seeding implications for the whole of humanity.

Something on a different scale but obviously related, also happened in 1987 at around the same time. Living on Ibiza, a small island in the Mediterranean, was a man whose name is now RaUruHu. Coming from a very well-educated and wealthy Canadian background he was more a scientist than a mystic – in fact he didn't even know what his birth sign was – until January 1987. It was on returning home one evening that he encountered an intelligence which brought him to his knees. It said to him "Are you ready to work?" and since declining was not an option, for the next eight days and nights he transcribed what has come into being as the Human Design System. "The Human Design System" says Ra "is not in the world because of me. It is in the world because everybody was seeded with that information in those eight days; the whole planet. We were all receptive to the neutrino stream that poured through."

Human Design is a synthesis of four ancient cosmologies, three of which we have already explored – the Hindu chakra system, astrology and the I Ching – and the Judaic Kabbalah. These ancient wisdoms are synthesised with the latest scientific discoveries in the field of genetics. At the heart of the Human Design System lies the exact mathematical correlation between the I Ching and the human genetic code. 64 hexagrams in one and 64 codons - the chemical groupings in our DNA - in the other. Whilst all human beings share the same basic genetic code, each of us is unique.

The discovery of the molecular structure of DNA showed us that there is a fundamental universal pattern underlying all life and from which everything is an expression. Human Design works on the theory that there is a direct link between the timing of our birth and the way in which our genes are imprinted. Using computer technology, your birth data is passed through a universal matrix or 'hexagram wheel' resulting in sequences of numbers which are then translated into a biochemical map of the body, known as a bodygraph – your own unique human design. From this bodygraph a trained Human Design analyst will tell you what the basic genetic patterns in your life are, including physical and psychological health, relationships, identity and awareness. Actually what you learn about is what it's really like to be you. It's as if you suddenly discover that you are driving a tractor not a Porsche (or the other way round) and there's a tremendous sense of freedom. This begins to melt the layers and layers of conditioning; the motorways of life that the tractor couldn't cope with or the muddy fields that the Porsche got bogged down in. Understanding your design reminds you that you can live in your own unique vehicle without compromise or fear. We are ruled by our chemistry, without even being aware of it. Part of your chart's interpretation will include an understanding of the 'Not-Self', which is what you are most attracted to in life, what you long for and how you can be conditioned away from your true nature – showing you your potential for wisdom or confusion.

A few years ago, Richard Rudd, who set up the Human Design system in the UK, took it 'beyond itself'. Definitely not a systems person, his one-off workshops are astonishing voyages of discovery. Just to enter his website (www.genekeys.co.uk) is like visiting a magical labyrinth.

This is simply a brief summary of a profound tool so if you are interested, check out the websites at the end of the chapter.

Life is Just a Pack of Cards

There is yet another age-old, tried and tested, user-friendly form of divination at hand, and these are cards. Most people can probably find a pack somewhere about the place, although sadly these days there seems to be little time for games of Hearts or Pontoon, now replaced by Internet gambling. These game-playing cards have been traditionally used by fortune-tellers to give us a take on health, wealth and relationships but recently have been superseded in this department by their distant relative – the Tarot deck. The Tarot was tarred and feathered as 'the work of the devil' by religious leaders, a testimony to the fact of its abilities to connect the querent to a higher level of intelligence than those who were in charge of telling us what and how to believe might have wished. This old form of divination, whose roots and connection to our everyday cards still remain uncertain, has come out of the closet where it had been hiding from religious persecution for a few hundred years, and not only branched out but blossomed into myriads of flowers, so you can pick the one that appeals. There is the Celtic Tarot, the Witch Tarot, the Inner Child, the Cat People, the Aquarian, the Animal Totem and – really - the Silicon Valley Tarot, to name just a few. For those wishing to stay with the original archetypes, then look for the Rider Waite deck or the Tarot of Marseilles.

Whatever your choice, the Tarot can show you, through the images on the cards, what archetypal forces are involved in any situation and how you personally stand in such a situation. So the meaning that the Emperor, The World or the Tower will convey to one who uses the original form may be just as significant as what The Hacker, Stock Options and Double Latte convey to the reader of the Silicon Valley deck. It all depends on what kind of world you live in.

There are some particular packs that I have found very helpful in navigating choppy waters or to get an insight into feelings of stuckness or being switched off. At the level of soul, you need look no further than the beautiful and powerful *Soul Cards* produced by Deborah Koff-Chapin. Without an interpretive book to accompany it, the card you choose really has to be 'felt' in order to understand its significance. Then there is an old favourite and always spot on with its practical advice, *The Osho Zen Tarot* published by St Martin's Press. A final mention goes to the Nordic or Viking Runes which are very simple and precise in their directions. A bag full of little stone-like tablets marked with geometric glyphs point your attention towards a force at work in your subconscious which is influencing you at present. Same old story, different presentation.

The Runes are an instrument for learning the will of the Divine in our lives.
Or, more simply put, they are a means of listening to that part of ourselves that knows everything we need to know for our lives now.
Ralph Blum: The Book of Runes

The only way to find out what works for you is to experiment. Whatever or whichever you choose as your favoured means of divine-ing, the principles for using them are the same. Integrity, intention and clear focus will bring information from the highest or deepest source, and supply you with the signposts you need.

Soul Focus

Oracles and divinatory tools are devices that pronounce on What Is. Their usefulness for the soul's journey is as a compass not a crutch.

REMINDERS ….

- A divinatory tool has no power of its own but, like a computer, may be used as a means of tuning in to the information highway.
- These tools can help us tap into and understand the forces at work in the Great Sea of Potential that is influencing us in this moment.
- Treating divination as a sacred act, like going into a church, temple or somewhere holy, will bring the insights you are seeking.
- It's the quality of the question that counts. Keep it clear and simple.
- Ultimately, we have all the knowledge we need within us.

Resources

Are You Sleeping in a Safe Place? **Rolf Gordon** (Available through: www.dulwichhealth.co.uk)

The Book of Ordinary Oracles: **Lon Milo DuQuette** (Weiser Books)

The Watkins Astrological Handbook (Watkins) formerly *Do-It-Yourself Astrology* (Element) : **Lyn Birkbeck**

The Astrological Oracle: **Lyn Birkbeck** (Thorsons)

Divine Astrology: **Lyn Birkbeck** (O Books) www.lynbirkbeck.com

Astrology for Beginners: **Geoffrey Cornelius, Maggie Hyde & Chris Webster** (Icon)

The Book of Runes: **Ralph Blum** (Connections)

www.humandesign-uk.com
www.genekeys.co.uk

chapter 10

what's the use
of ancient wisdom?

To begin at the beginning... Crystal Connections

*The soul passes from form to form, and the mansions of her pilgrimage
are manifold. Thou puttest off thy bodies as raiment, and as vesture
thou dost fold them up. Thou art from old, O soul of man, yea thou
art from everlasting.*
Hermes Trismegistus: Egyptian Hermetic Fragments

To begin at the beginning .....
What relevance does the ancient past hold for contemporary explorers of
consciousness and soul seekers in a techno world where today's news is
tomorrow's wrapping for fish and chips? What has this to do with bodies
and souls?

The history of just about everything is written by winners, the ones in
power, and their victories and triumphs then become recorded as the 'official' version of what's what, thus allowing them to chronicle events in the
way they wish them to be perceived. This version is then handed down to
future generations, becomes part of the educational curriculum, and is
accepted as being a true record of events. If we are to believe science and
history, we, in the twenty-first century, are the most advanced and highly
evolved human beings ever to inhabit the planet. This is an assumption
and it may not be so. What has happened, however, is that our advances
in science and technology have enabled us to discover that our ancient
forbears understood much more than they have been credited with. But
their knowledge was not used to create a soul-less society, rather to
enhance their human abilities to keep in touch with the true nature of their

spiritual selves as expressed through their individual souls.

In the last chapter we investigated some ancient – and one very modern – means of finding clues as to the nature of our existence as a nano dot in this vast universe. Looking for answers to fundamental questions may always have been on the minds of conscious humans but it seems to be increasingly urgent to find some authentic answers. Previously we have taken our religions' word as law as far as the meanings of life are concerned, but now there are many of us for whom dogma and doggerel seem to have crushed the spirit. Huge rents are appearing in the shrouds that have bound and gagged living truths; revelations are emerging from excavations and translations; something wonderful is coming alive. Whatever we think about Dan Brown's *Da Vinci Code,* it has stirred up the pot and given people the incentive to investigate rather than just accept what we are fed by others with definitely dodgy agendas. It's curious though, that now all embargos have been removed, we are turning to *ancient* oracles for guidance, almost as if we are retracing our steps to see where it was that we dropped a stitch, or somehow took a wrong turning as we hurtled full tilt into the 21st century and towards what we now know as a very uncertain future on this one-and-only garden in our solar system. Is this because most people perceive history as a straight line, appearing from the mists of an unknown time and moving like an arrow towards another question mark in the future?

We have made the mistake of seeing this forward movement as signifying a progression, an advance, for humankind in every respect. In many ways this might be so, but what a price we will pay for forgetting our mysteries, disregarding our dreams and losing the ability to use the doorways into and out from our minds. Single-mindedly cultivating the capabilities of the left hemispheres of our brains has resulted in our soul-less perspective separating us from the magic of the natural world with all her kingdoms. Now we have become intellectual parasites operating outside the laws of symbiosis that govern the physical world that we, as souls, are here to experience.

The Industrial Revolution catapulted us into a materially and economically successful Western-based culture in which we saw the final divisions arise between magic, religion and science. Alchemy, herbalism and astrology were replaced by science, pharmaceuticals and space exploration, and we allowed ourselves to be turned away from our role as planetary gardeners. Now our landscapes are covered with concrete and cables and we have contaminated the very air which sustains us and all life. Even now, as the alarm bells shatter our mindless slumber, there are those in power who are insisting that economic growth must be sustained, and this will provide the financial means for us to deal with what is already upon us. Perhaps they have a Plan B in mind for themselves but for the vast majority of animate life in this garden, this is an untenable option.

As if we knew something was radically awry, we have begun to look around, and unable to find direction in the techno world we have created, we turn to the tiny remaining pockets of indigenous cultures that have only just survived the havoc we have already wreaked as we 'conquered' the Earth, leaving trails of broken societies in our wake. Suddenly the wisdom of the North American Hopi Elders, the science of the Dogon in West Africa, the shamans from the South American rainforests, the Mayan Elders, Maoris, Indian sages and Kalahari Bushmen might show us how we left something vital behind in our search for 'progress'.

The Kogi Indians have lived for four centuries in seclusion in their eyrie in the Sierra Nevada mountains of northern Columbia. Their mythology says they are the 'Elder Brother' of humanity while the people in the West and non-Amerindians are 'Younger Brother'. In 1990 their observance of an impending ecological crisis signified by changing bird migrations and the lack of snow in the highest regions of the Sierra Nevada prompted the priests or 'Mamas' of the Kogi to emerge from their isolation to inform Younger Brother that unless we change our ways, the world will end. The Mamas were educated in the dark as children, and this early sensory deprivation has made them finely attuned to the mysteries and pleasures of their mountain environment – they work with the 'Great Mother', the originator, creator, source of material and spiritual

206

sustenance. The message they delivered to the world in a film called *'From the Heart of the World: the Elder Brothers' Warning'* made by Alan Ereira for the BBC in 1992 was that

> ....*the world doesn't have to end; it could go on, but unless we stop violating the earth and nature, depleting The Great Mother of her material energy, her organs, her vitality; unless people stop working against the Great Mother, the world will not last ...*

Unfortunately we all know now that this grim prediction is becoming a reality.

How ironic that guidelines for the future may be found not in new advances in technology, but from those who have been continually sustained by the fount of Perennial Wisdom – that stream of knowledge containing the gnosis of what is, was, and always will be available for those who have eyes to see and ears to hear.

India, China, Tibet, Mesopotamia, Sumeria and Egypt – all giants in terms of spiritual knowledge – understood the nature of the soul's journey through the physical 'dream' world. They were also masters of the psychic superhighway, as Hitler knew when sending his SS henchmen to Tibet to bring back the monks who would impart their occult secrets – amongst which was how to 'fly'.

As the Kali Yuga draws to a close – thank heavens – and we are able to see how this Age of Iron and its characteristics of warfare, industrialisation, destruction, avarice, wrath, lust, unfair taxations, drunkenness and devastation have taken us to the brink of extinction, something has started to surface from that perennial underground stream. Our anthropologists have discovered for themselves the source of knowledge that shamans have been accessing for thousands of years for the benefit, mostly, of their communities. Pharmacologists and ethno-biologists have consulted indigenous Indians on the medicinal content of plants in the once massive pharmacopeia of the South American rainforests and some have made vast fortunes and built mega-industries without a dollar of compensation to the source of this knowledge. Archaeologists have dug up the past and revealed some astonishing facts, some of which have never seen the light of day, since they would confound the established views on who we are, what we are and where we came from.

Our modern technologies have revealed some things that we could not have understood without the aid of our computers, helping us re-evaluate and shift our perspective. The old sciences of archaeoastronomy and geo-mancy have been reborn. The remains of ancient cities, temples and sacred sites have revealed artefacts and information that have made us re-think our views on the capabilities of our ancestors and those who tended this garden before us. As air travel has enabled our bodies to move about the globe, it has given our souls the opportunity to remember places and landscapes we may have been familiar with in previous incarnations or ones that hold a key to unfinished business – which is what happened to me as soon as I put my foot on the ground at Cairo airport.

Half the world must have visited the most spectacular ancient legacy still available to visitors in the world – Egypt – and wondered for them-selves about the origins and motivations behind what still remains of this most sophisticated civilisation. There is still an estimated 70% of it lying under the desert sands or buried forever by urbanisation. The technology used to create what we see in Egypt defies replication even in the 21st century. How extraordinary that it is still a commonly held belief that the ancient Egyptians were a bunch of master builders who worshipped a whole range of animal-headed and other 'gods' and were obsessed with death and funerary ritual. What a truly shocking assessment of a people for whom the themes that are central to their art and architecture are rein-carnation, resurrection and the journey of the soul through the underworld – matters about which science today knows nothing. Perhaps it's because our 21st century minds have lost the ability to understand that Divine Law expresses itself in the physical world through art, architecture, the sacred sciences of dance and sound, the natural kingdoms of the Earth, and our bodies. Life itself was their religion.What appears to be an Egyptian pre-occupation with death is in fact its opposite – a preoccupation with a soul-oriented life in the deepest possible sense. How you lived your life would determine what followed, and perhaps the most relevant aspect of their wisdom and knowledge for us today, at the level of soul, is that they understood that our hearts have their own intelligence. In Egypt the heart was considered the organ of thought; 'think with your heart and feel with your mind' was the maxim that held the key to returning to the Source. At the end of a person's life, their hearts (symbolised by a pot, called *ab)* would be placed on the scales of Ma'at and weighed against the feather of truth and integrity. The heart at this point represents the life and soul of that person and if it is 'weighed down' with actions in opposition to the Spirit of Ma'at, then the monstrous creature, Ammit – the eater of the heart – will swallow the person who has betrayed their heart. The result is another incarnation; another physical form will be required until the heart will be as light as the feather. Reincarnation, therefore, was to be avoided at all costs.

We all know that the Egyptians mummified their dead, but perhaps not everyone knows that the heart was the only organ left in the body after death. The brains were extracted through the nostrils (so much for that), and the liver, lungs, stomach and intestines were placed in four *canopic* jars. The heart remained in the body cavity and had a scarab placed on it as a symbol of the transformation that would occur at the end of the soul's journey through the *duat* or underworld, on its way to reunion with its Source.

The early Egyptians – whoever they were – not only understood that the heart had its own intelligence, but were also masters of metallurgy, medicine, surgery, dentistry, music, astronomy, glass-making, sculpture, art, symbolism, mathematics, geometry, alchemy, and of course what they are universally acknowledged for – mind-boggling architectural design and construction. In order to truly understand the way these people saw the world, our 21st century minds would need to enter into their mentality and the spirit that was alive at that time. Perhaps this is not an option for us now. But since their aim, over 5,000 years ago, would seem to have a resonance with our own needs at this moment then it's worth taking a deeper look at their legacy. Although tempting to digress, the origins of who or what the original 'gods' might have been is a separate study, and fascinating for those who might be interested.

Everything had meaning for the early Egyptians. Everything was symbolic, starting with their written language – the hieroglyph – right through to the layout and dimensions of the Great Pyramid. Their temples, many of which can still be found and 'felt' along the banks of the Nile - itself a symbol of the Milky Way – were endowed with the energy, the quality, of the 'god' to whom they were consecrated. They were like generating batteries that maintained the stability of Egypt. Contained within a wall, they represented the Divine House, outside of which were the dark chaotic forces of Set, Lord of Storms. The temple was also a symbol of the body of man, the most interior space being approximately in the position of the pituitary gland, the gland that is linked to the Ajna or Third Eye chakra. This centre is where the soul and the personality come together under the impulse from the crown, the centre where the soul enters the human being. The Third Eye is where we 'see' things differently, beyond apparent duality, and it is a place of contact with the imaginal realms. Here in the *naos,* or inner sanctum of the temple, was where the essential energy, the quintessence of the 'god' was held. To reach this, you would have had to pass through a series of barriers, the outermost being the massive walls of the outer pylon, in the middle of which was a narrow entranceway. The general public never set foot beyond this outer pylon. The whole temple was sacred and accessible only to those of royal blood and the priesthood. Once through the outer pylon, you would have found yourself in a huge open courtyard, beyond which there are further pylons each of which would have had great cedar doors, closed against the incomer. Beyond the pylons and courtyards you would then come to pillared hallways, vestibules and sanctuaries, every one of which would have been protected by similar heavy wooden doors, inlaid with bronze, and which had to be swung open in order for the priests to proceed.

No threshold in Egypt could be crossed unconsciously and particularly in the temple. Every door took you closer to the holy of holies and into a world which did not belong to mortals. It was only by virtue of that which was divine in yourself that you might dare to advance toward the sanctuary where the god dwelt, enclosed in a windowless granite chamber.

There are few who have deciphered the true meaning behind what we find in Egypt, least of all Egyptologists; but the last twenty years has produced some wonderful, credible, maverick researchers, one of whom is John Anthony West who has astutely observed that:

Egyptian civilisation was not a development, it was a legacy.

Who were these early kings, priests and pharaohs who seemed suddenly to arrive and demonstrate an advanced level of intellect and understanding? Where did they come from and how did they know how to do what they did? And then where did they go? Always the burning questions for which there are no clear answers – only as many hypotheses as there are hieroglyphs. Perhaps the words of Peter Dawkins, philosopher, seer and geomancer, who gives teaching and training in the core truths of the mystery traditions, would be a good reminder at this point. In his book, *Arcadia*, he states that:

The Ancient Egyptian civilisation was carefully planned and guided from start to finish, as a statement and expression of the Ageless Wisdom. There was always, from generation to generation, an inner council of Egyptian sages – the 'prophets' or highest initiates of the lands – who knew the plan and were guardians of it, and responsible for seeing that the plan was carried out as well as possible. Collectively they were known as the Tat (Thoth) Brotherhood, meaning they were the living representatives of the Divine Word of Truth which the Egyptians called TAT. This Brotherhood was composed of immortal beings connected to the four centres of light and learning in Egypt.

Rather than get befuddled by volumes of information, the most immediate way to catch a sense of what the Egyptian Mystery is all about is to return personally to its sacred places and use your sixth sense to tune in to what is to this day still to be found there, since we are surely not going to grasp the meaning using our analytical minds.

Our ability to do this will be enhanced by the location of the sacred sites themselves. It's an 'energy' thing. The sites were set up for this very purpose – interaction with the power of the Divine – a place where humans and the heavenly may communicate - and hence the structure of the temple. Each doorway represented a stage further in moving closer to the essence of the Divine that is held enclosed in the innermost sanctum. Each doorway involved ritual and the uttering of sacred sounds, so that by the time the heart of the temple was reached, you had raised your vibrational level to a point at which no fuses would be blown when you encountered the Divine Power. Being filled with this power would raise your consciousness, expanding the mortal energy field so that if you were a priest or pharaoh who would subsequently be addressing the people outside the temple confines, you would be filled with divine, rather than human, illumination. This energy would then be 'generated' to the people – a teaching without words. The ability to expand your energy field to encompass or connect with something much greater than your human self was significantly enhanced by the sacred geometry used in creating the proportions of the place, together with the materials used to create it. Let's have a closer look at the properties of granite in particular, since this was the material of choice for power points – and not only in Egypt. Its qualities were clearly understood all those millennia ago as demonstrated by its specific use, even though this involved hauling blocks weighing hundreds of tons some 600 miles to locations such as the pyramids on the Giza Plateau, Meidum, Saqqara and the obelisks at various centres throughout Egypt.

Granite is an igneous, radioactive rock which contains silicon-quartz, a semi-conductor. When a charge passes through quartz, pressures arise and it begins to vibrate at higher frequencies. It therefore embodies the qualities common to all crystal quartz of being able to receive, transmit and store 'information'. Electrical circuits can be created within the granite itself, making it sensitive to electromagnetic fields. The hieroglyph for granite, significantly, also means 'dream, discover, imagine and conceive'. In unventilated places, such as the King's Chamber, granite can produce levels of radon; a toxic gas which, in sufficient concentrations, can induce altered states of consciousness. Wherever there is radon, there is quartz. No wonder then that it was used in the most important part of the temple, including that of the largest temple in the world – the Great Pyramid.

The so-called King's Chamber inside this massive 480 ft high monument is walled with squared dark granite blocks of immense size. The ceiling is formed from nine enormous beams of the same material, one of which weighs 70 tons. The whole chamber is built in accordance with the measurements of the sacred Golden Section ratio. There is a red granite box in the chamber. It is referred to as a 'sarcophagus', which implies that it was used as a container for a dead body or a coffin. This is an assumption based on no evidence whatsoever. It is a deduction based on the fact that indeed many ancient Egyptians were entombed in granite sarcophagi (all with heavy granite lids), in highly decorated chambers, but they are all underground, and since the first part of the after-life was believed to be a passage through the underworld, being entombed underground would set you off in the right direction. The King's Chamber is over 200 ft above ground, completely undecorated and the granite box has no lid.

Many of the Greek philosophers such as Pythagoras, Plato and Herodotus were privy to the initiations that took place in the temples and pyramids and the secrets of the Egyptian Mystery Schools – the spiritual universities of antiquity. Jesus and other luminaries are also believed to have spent time learning in Egypt. Alexander the Great consulted the oracle at Siwa Oasis in the Egyptian Desert for guidance, and Alexandria, the home of what was once the largest library in the world, was named after him. The Royal Library in Alexandria housed some 40,000 manuscripts from many nations including Assyria, Greece, Persia, India and others.

Over 100 scholars lived at the Museum attached to it, employed full time to write, research, lecture or translate copy documents.

The destruction of this vast repository of accumulated knowledge with lecture halls and study rooms was begun by none other than Julius Caesar himself (in 48BCE). Whether this was by accident or design, it is worth noting that he was also responsible for the first full-blown genocide on European soil. The Age of Kali Yuga had begun. In order to eradicate the teachings from the ancient world, further attempts to annihilate the Library took place, but the most shocking and lethal blow involved the brutal murder of Hypatia by a Christian mob. She was beautiful, intelligent and the last known Pagan teacher of the Mystery Schools. She was noted for her mastery of Platonic philosophy, mathematics and *theurgy* – literally 'god-working' – a kind of magical invocation that could be compared with advanced practices of visualisation in Tantra & Dzogchen, according to John Lamb Lash in his brilliant and heretical book *Not in His Image*. Hypatia left her work in the lecture hall of the Library one day in 415 CE, and called for her chariot, but she never completed the journey to her home. A menacing Christian mob blocked her path, pulled her from her chariot, tore off her clothes and, shouting that she was a witch and a heretic, they kicked and beat her to death. Not content with that, they pounded her body to a pulp and tore off her limbs. Finally, fired with some beast-like energy and as if to totally dismantle her being, the crazed mob scraped off the flesh from her body with razor-sharp oyster shells which had been handed to them for the job. Her death is regarded by some as the final assault on the Library although the last individual to get the blame for its destruction was the Muslim Caliph Omar, a couple of hundred years later. However, the tragedy is not about who destroyed it but that it was destroyed at all.

As it rose to power, the Roman Church ordered the Gnostic books to be rootled out and destroyed. Theodosious, who ruled between 379 and 395 CE made it his personal business to annihilate all traces of Pagan and Gnostic literature. 27,000 scrolls from the Mystery Schools were collected and burned because he was told that they contained Gnostic teachings that contradicted his – adopted – belief system. Church policy was for their historians to write only what showed their institutions in a favourable light and to destroy all conflicting accounts. This outrageous abuse and vandalism was echoed a thousand years later in America when the European invaders re-enacted the violence that had been inflicted on their own ancestors in the early Christian era. Amerindians were robbed and murdered systematically. Christian whites were not held accountable for the abuse of non-Christians. Dark Ages indeed.

To this day no-one knows what ancient Egyptian sounded like as a language and the hieroglyphs that cover every temple and tomb remained undeciphered until the discovery of the Rosetta Stone in 1799 – deciphered by Jean-Francois Champollion in 1822.

At about this time we have the first actual record of a 'Kings' Chamber' experience coming from none other than Napoleon Bonaparte. Intent on conquering Egypt – possibly connected to his links with Freemasonry – he was in Cairo in 1799, visiting the Pyramid with the Imam Muhammed as his guide. At a certain point Bonaparte asked to be left alone to spend the night in the King's Chamber, as Alexander the Great was reported to have done before him. He emerged the following morning looking very pale and reflective and when asked if he'd witnessed anything mysterious, he said that he never wanted the incident mentioned again. When he became emperor, many years later, he continued to refuse to speak about whatever it was that had happened to him, hinting only that he had received some portend of his destiny. Just before his death on St Helena he seemed on the point of speaking about his experience, but changed his mind at the last minute, and instead shook his head saying "What's the use. You would never believe me ..."

Someone who was more forthcoming on his King's Chamber experience was Dr Paul Brunton, a teacher, philosopher and man who dedicated his entire life to an inward and spiritual quest. In 1936 his book *A Search in Secret Egypt* was published in which he gives a graphic account of his detailed exploration of the Great Pyramid and his solitary overnight stay in the King's Chamber. In the all-encompassing darkness, he began to feel as if the space was peopled with unseen beings, not all of which seemed pleased at his presence in their territory. A new and different element then began to introduce itself to him, in the shape of two white-robed beings in the 'unmistakable regalia' of the High Priests of an ancient Egyptian cult. *"Why dost thou come to this place, seeking to evoke the secret powers? Are not mortal ways enough for thee?"* one of them seemed to be asking somehow within his head. Having responded with an emphatic *"They are not!"* he was then warned that *"... the way of Dream will draw thee far from the fold of reason. Some have gone upon it – and come back mad. Turn now whilst there is yet time, and follow the path appointed for mortal feet."*

He relates that what followed was a procession of scary (to say the least) different physical sensations which he was convinced were part of the process of his spirit passing to the regions beyond death. His conscious awareness moved out of his body – which he could observe lying on its back on the stone floor with its arms crossed across its breast – but to which he was still attached by a faint silvery light. He knew, he says, why the old Egyptians had given in their hieroglyphs the pictured symbol of a bird to man's soul-form. He experienced a sense of intense lightness in his duplicate body and said to himself *"This is the state of death. Now I know that I am a soul, that I can exist apart from the body..."*. He realised that his earthly body which he could observe beneath him had imprisoned the real being that was now free. Suddenly the white robed priest was beside him instructing him *"Thou hast now learned the great lesson. Man, whose soul was born out of the Undying, can never really die. Set this truth in words known to men...."* He then had some meetings and brief conversations with the so-called dead that he had once known and was told that they too live, even as the Pyramid, which has seen the death of half a world, lives on.

His ethereal companion then said some pretty interesting things.

"Know, my son, that in this ancient fane (temple) lies the lost record of the early races of man and of the Covenant which they made with

their Creator through the first of His great prophets. Know, too, that chosen men were brought here of old to be shown this Covenant that they might return to their fellows and keep the great secret alive. Take back with thee the warning that when men forsake their Creator and look on their fellows with hate, as with the princes of Atlantis in whose time this Pyramid was built, they are destroyed by the weight of their own iniquity, even as the people of Atlantis were destroyed.

It was not the Creator who sank Atlantis, but the selfishness, the cruelty, the spiritual blindness of the people who dwelt on those doomed islands. The Creator loves all; but the lives of men are governed by invisible laws, which He has set over them. Take back this warning."

After these words had been transmitted, something even stranger followed. In his astral-body-state, he was shown a passageway within the Pyramid leading to a temple-like chamber, which has as yet not been discovered. In his excitement he turned to see how he had entered this passageway only to see that where there should have been an opening, it was closed with square blocks. And at that moment he felt as if he was being whirled away by some irresistible force, and a moment later he saw his inert body lying on the stone. His wise companion then delivered his next pronouncement which holds as much, if not more, import for us now, nearly 80 years later, as it did then.

"My son," said the High Priest, "it matters not whether thou discoverest the door or not. Find but the secret passage within the mind that will lead thee to the hidden chamber within thine own soul, and thou shalt have found something worthy indeed. The mystery of the Great Pyramid is the mystery of thine own self. The secret chambers and ancient records are all contained in thine own nature. The lesson of the Pyramid is that man must turn inward, must venture to the unknown centre of his being to find his soul, even as he must venture to the unknown depths of this fane to find its profoundest secret.

Farewell!"

And with that he felt as if he was whirling into some vortex that sucked him downwards, finally melting back into his physical body, after which, unsurprisingly, he fainted. When the armed guard unlocked the iron gate soon after dawn, he was met by a dusty, weary and dishevelled figure who stumbled out of the Pyramid's dark entrance, took a deep breath and looked as if he were paying homage to the Sun god Ra for the gift of light. And in case you might be wondering whether he had taken a magic mushroom or two, the answer is no. His only preparation before entering the Pyramid was to fast for four days.

My own experience with others in the King's Chamber, when we have commissioned private time there, is not nearly so dramatic, but nevertheless astonishing. After taking ten days or so to travel from Aswan, following the path of the initiates through the remaining temples, and spending time in Luxor, the pharaonic headquarters known then as Thebes, we finally arrive at the Great Pyramid. By this time everyone is very open and in tune with the presence that is still to be found in Egypt in spite of the hordes of tourists. We start our journey in the subterranean chamber, known as the Pit, which is 360 or so feet down into the bedrock and directly under the apex of the Pyramid. From there we proceed up to the so-called Queen's Chamber, approximately half way up the Pyramid before our final ascent through the cavernous Grand Gallery and into the King's Chamber. There we begin our Heart Chanting, as we have done in the other chambers and throughout our journey, when it felt appropriate. The group maintains this continuous sound while each individual takes a turn at lying inside the red granite coffer, to experience the effect of sound, granite and sacred geometry. On one occasion this was recorded, and when played back it sounded as if we had been joined by a celestial choir, proving the point that the granite of the Great Pyramid, when activated by sound – in this case the human voice – creates a 'supernatural' experience Actually 'magical' is the word. As David Elkington in *The Name of the Gods* comments:

The technical skill of the Egyptians has always been self-evident. It's now equally evident that this was matched by a profound knowledge of harmony, proportion, geometry and design.

The intelligence that manifested all that we find so mysterious in Egypt knew that these sacred places of power create an interface between the human and the Divine. It understood that by combining the powers firstly of the place itself and then adding the amplifying ability of stone used specifically to shape a space according to the principles of sacred geometry, resulted in a 'container', an alchemical retort. Adding other ingredients such as sound, movement or ritual within this space, it was possible to transcend the mundane. Literally to bring down Heaven to Earth. Of course it was not only in Egypt that these secrets were known. There are sites all over the world that appear to have been masterminded by the same intelligence and where you will be able to find a sense of 'presence'. These places share the same defining characteristics:

- powerful Earth energies
- megalithic stones, which amplify the effects and create a
- sacred space in alignment with sun, moon or other celestial bodies

The power of sound, intrinsic in many mystical experiences, was used not only by mortals to communicate with other levels of consciousness, but also as a tool to manoeuvre and place these enormous blocks of stone into perfect positioning. The Mahatma Dhut Kuhl, in his "*A Treatise on Cosmic Fire*", channelled by Alice Bailey stated that:

The laws governing the erection of large buildings and the handling of great weights will someday be understood in terms of sound ... they were raised through the ability of the early builders to create a vacuum through sound.

In the village of Shivapur, near Poona in India, is a little mosque dedicated to the Sufi holy man Qamar Ali Dervish. Outside in the courtyard of the mosque is a stone weighing 128 pounds and, during daily prayer, 11 devotees surround the stone, repeating the holy man's name. When they reach a certain pitch, the 11 men are able to lift the stone by using one finger each. As soon as the chanting stops, the devotees jump back as the stone resumes its everyday weight and thuds back to the ground. A

Swedish aircraft industrialist, Henry Kjellson, was travelling though the Himalayas in the post-war era and witnessed a fascinating stone levitation – this time in Tibet. He describes how a group of monks hauled (by yak) stones measuring one and a half metres square up to a plateau, and placed them in a specifically designed hole, bowl-shaped at one meter in diameter and 15 centimetres deep in the centre. The hole was 100 metres away from a cliff wall, 400 metres high, on top of which was a building to be constructed. 63 metres behind the hole stood 19 musicians, and behind each of them 20 priests radiating out in lines, separated from one another in groups at five degree intervals and forming a quarter circle with the hole as its focal centre. These distances appear to have been of the utmost importance, for all were carefully measured by the monks using lengths of knotted leather. The musicians possessed a total of 13 drums of three different sizes, and alternating between them were six large trumpets. On command, the drums and trumpets were sounded, and the priests chanted in unison, together forming sharp blasts of sound at a beat of two-per-minute. After four minutes, Kjellson observed that the stones placed in the target hole began to wobble, move side to side, and then as the beats of sound increased, they suddenly soared the 400 metres in a parabolic arc to the top of the cliff. In this manner, Kjellson recorded, the monks were able to move five or six blocks an hour.

Was this how they placed over 2 million limestone blocks each weighing two and a half tons to make the Great Pyramid? Perhaps this is how the Blue Stone which is found in the British megalithic site of Stonehenge was moved from Wales and put into position. And how massive granite obelisks were transported and raised, not to mention the giant of all giants, the Trilithon at Baalbek in Lebanon. This mind-blowing giant consists of three stones weighing in at 800 tons each and so closely aligned that you can't put a needle between them. Whilst these monsters provide the foundation for the Roman Temple of Jupiter, not one emperor claimed credit for its construction. Its origins are a mystery. Zecharia Sitchin however, believes that these massive stones provided a parking place for the chariots of the gods. It is not far, after all, from the Garden in Ehdin.

Stones have a religious history, and have been connected with god or the Divine through the ages.   Today the Black Stone on the eastern corner of the 60ft square structure called the Kaaba is at the centre of the most religiously and revered site in the world – Mecca – which is visited by nearly two million Muslims every year, some of whom believe the Black Stone has supernatural powers and the ability to cleanse worshippers of their sins by absorbing them into itself. They say it was once a dazzling white, but has become blackened because of what it has absorbed over the centuries.

Crystal Connections

Our understanding that stones – or more precisely crystals – have the ability to perform any number of assignments, including healing people of 'negative' energies (although it would probably be over ambitious to expect the clearance of sin – whatever that means) has resulted in an explosion of the mineral kingdom into homes, handbags, workplaces and onto human bodies.   They have become perhaps the most popular and widely used accoutrement of the revolution in consciousness. Before crystals became a prerequisite for every New Age traveller, they had already become an invaluable tool in technological advances. As technology makes visible what was previously only open to clairvoyants and shamans, the invisible becomes visible. Kirlian photography, auric photography and equipment able to detect the chakra system and the acupuncture meridians have provided empirical evidence for those who need it. The growing knowledge regarding the use of crystals to transmute and transform electromagnetic energy has played an increasingly important role in the evolution of these new technologies.

A ruby crystal, for example, was a key component in the first laser developed in the early 1960s. From the laser came quantum leaps in medical science as well as the birth of the hologram. The holographic model provides us with a new way of appreciating the multidimensional universe, referred to these days as the 'multiverse'. Since then the possibilities of crystals storing thousands of three-dimensional images is being researched. Silicon chips make the computer world go round. The mineral kingdom has provided the tools to amplify our capacity for information access and storage that are radically and rapidly changing our world

The Earth herself is essentially crystalline in nature, giving her an ability to respond to incoming electromagnetic waves. So where her energies interact with external influences a power point is found. Being much more sensitive to their environment than modern man, our ancestors detected these places, utilised the energy and they became 'sacred spots' over time. The power available was amplified by the use of specific stone and ritual and often these places were linked to each other. Rather like a system of phone booths scattered over the landscape, or acupuncture points on the earth's energy meridians, these places were used by ancient people to dial the Divine, to make a connection with another reality. It is on these sacred earth sites that you will now find churches, which have utilised the power of the place for the same reasons. The nave, or altar, was the inner sanctum where only ordained priests were – and still are in many churches - allowed to tread. Here is the most powerful place in the building. The priest, with the aid of sound, incense and ritual would amplify his 'divinity', enabling him to dispense it to the ordinary people in the form of the Eucharist – not a lot of difference between this and ancient Egypt. These sacred sites or earthly power points where natural met supernatural are found throughout the world. Caves, shrines, sacred groves, magic mountains, sacred wells and springs all offer us the opportunity to intercourse with the Divine. It's all about *resonance*. We are walking on the face of an essentially crystalline structure and our human bodies are also largely crystalline in our organic makeup. Blood plasma, bone structure, sweat, muscle, fat, urine – anywhere where there is a water content (and we like the earth, are over 70% water) there are molecules that behave as if they were crystals, liquid crystals.

The investigation by science into crystalline structures has resulted in liquid crystal displays (LCDs) that we have now become familiar with, but possibly not aware of how they operate behind the screens of our electronic devices. They're an appropriate metaphor for understanding the importance of the human body as a device for accessing multidimensional channels. Frontier Scientists – again remembering the work of Dr Bruce Lipton - have come to recognise that many of the cellular membranes and structures within our own bodies are actually liquid crystals. It is the ability of crystal to store, transmit, amplify and receive information that interests both scientists and the explorer of expanding consciousness.

We might think that utilising crystals for communication, solar power, information storage and laser applications in industry and medicine is new to our planet, but crystal technology was known long before even ancient Egypt came into existence by the civilisation known as Atlantis.

There are many stories told about the Atlantean civilisation, and endless debates about whether or not it actually existed. Immortalised by the Greek philosopher Plato (c427-347 BCE), in his works the *Criticas* and *Timaeus,* there is a growing body of evidence to support the belief that such a civilisation did indeed exist. According to the trance readings of Edgar Cayce, the Atlanteans combined a high level of technological expertise with an understanding of spiritual laws. It appears, however, that they lost their way, became morally bankrupt and used their soul-less technologies to experiment with genetic engineering and abuse their knowledge of the life force. They were called the Sons of Belial or Baalilal. It is alleged that a cataclysmic end wiped out all record of this powerful, highly intelligent and advanced civilisation. Or did it?

It was said by Cayce that the survivors of the devastation spread and settled in Peru, Egypt, Mexico and Central, South and North America, which would explain why these cultures share a common iconography and also a common history of flood and Atlantean legends. Similarly, he said that before the inundation that wiped out this highly sophisticated culture, there were those within the civilisation who realised what was about to happen. Known as the Followers of the Law of One, they believed in the unity of all life which related to a single all-encompassing creator. They were spiritually motivated and sought to raise the spiritual and physical conditions of those around them.

The Sons of Belial, however, had made large inroads into authoritarian positions which enabled them to have control over the Atlantean energy source – giant crystals. The Atlanteans used crystal-sourced piezoelectricity as we use electricity. They also discovered the tremendous power inherent in sunlight, utilising crystals to amplify and direct solar energy that enabled them to power their transport and communication systems. Interestingly, physicist James Clerk Maxwell worked out, in 1871, that light would exert a force on any surface that it hits – like wind on a sail – and this would produce power. These huge crystals (one of which is said to be responsible to this day for the anomalous events in the Bermuda Triangle), known as the 'sun crystals', were taken over by the Sons of Belial and used for coercion, torture and punishment. They were already applying their knowledge of the life force in genetic engineering to create a mutant race of physically strong but unintelligent workers.

The Followers of the Law of One knew that this would lead to the end of their civilisation. The misuse of these powerful crystals would eventually have profound effects on the environment, so they prepared for disaster by organising three major migratory routes to leave Atlantis. Groups of individuals would go to Egypt, to Peru in South America and to the Yucatan Peninsula. These groups would take with them crystals containing records of aspects of their lives and technology, which could be preserved for humanity to access some time in the future. These survivors would also take with them the traditions and beliefs of the Law of One.

Included in the thousands of readings given by Edgar Cayce there were many concerning Egypt. He predicted that a Hall of Records would be discovered under the Great Sphinx and that the information in this underground library would be stored in crystals. He said that when this information was revealed, our history would have to be re-written. So far there have been no excavations, but an anomalous cavity has been detected by ground-sensing radar under the left paw of the Sphinx. Watch that space.

But just to finish off the tale of Atlantis for a moment. The legends suggest that Atlantis flourished from a period dating from at least 150,000 until approximately 10,000 BCE when a flood of biblical proportions overwhelmed it. The technology the Atlanteans developed was based on higher-dimensional frequencies and the life force itself, and involved the energetic applications of crystals, most specifically quartz crystal. Being the most structured of all crystal, with a very exact rate of vibration, its regular and precise oscillations form a reference by which bits of time can be measured and displayed. As in Atlantis, so in the 20th century apparently. Marcel Vogel, a senior researcher with IBM for 27 years discovered that:

> *"The crystal is a natural object whose inner structure exhibits a state of perfection and balance. When it is cut to the proper form and when the human mind enters into relationship with its structural perfection, the crystal emits a vibration that extends and amplifies the power of the user's mind. Like a laser, it radiates energy in a coherent, highly concentrated form, and this energy may be transmitted into objects or people at will.*
>
> *Although the crystal may be used for 'mind to mind' communication, its higher purpose ... is in the service of humanity for the removal of pain and suffering. With proper training, a healer can release negative thought-forms, which have taken shape as disease patterns in a patient's physical body.*
>
> *As psychics have often pointed out, when a person becomes emotionally distressed, a weakness forms in his subtle energy body and disease may soon follow. With a properly cut crystal, however, a healer can, like a surgeon cutting away a tumour, release negative*

patterns in the energy body, allowing the physical to return to a state of wholeness."
Marcel Vogel: Vibrational Medicine

Harnessing crystal power for yourself could be confusing, since there is a myriad array available of every shape, size and colour. How do you know which crystal does what? As far as choice, often there isn't one, since as you cast your eyes over a display of crystals, one in particular will seem to be drawing your attention. "I just had to buy that beautiful piece of amethyst", or "I couldn't resist that rose quartz – it was as if it was speaking to me". Perhaps this is again a demonstration of resonant frequencies. When we are drawn to a particular crystal, could it be that the crystalline structures in our bodies are moved, like a tuning fork, to come into sympathetic resonance with that crystal that's winking at us in order to restore balance? Different crystals should be used for different purposes and, like any tool, they should be cared for and looked after. They have a consciousness but they do not have a conscience. They may be used to transmit, receive and amplify a specific waveform of energy and the quality of that energy depends on the user. Like electricity, it is a power source that may be used for positive or negative results. Crystals are neutral in themselves, but they can be charged with whatever energy we put into them. This energy can then be transmitted into the atmosphere, or another person's aura, thoughts or energy body.

A crystal may be used for many different things. You may feel drawn to wearing one round your neck to help keep your electromagnetic field in balance. You may like to hold a particular crystal during meditation to amplify the effect. You may have a crystal for healing, or place them round your house because of their beauty, not realising that they give off negative ions, which create a sense of well-being. If you are a 'crystal person' then you will know how important it is to care for these gifts from the Earth. A crystal covered in dust and tucked away in a corner will not support you as a power tool. There are hundreds of books on crystals, their meanings and uses, so I will not take more of your time elaborating on something which many others know much more about. If you were not convinced of the 'value' of these age-old tools, perhaps at least you have found something here to validate your intuitive attraction and can deepen your relationship with them. There were those throughout time who considered the quartz crystal as the strongest power object of all, and from the Kivaro in South America to the tribes of Australia they considered quartz crystal as 'living' or 'live rock'. Whether their knowledge was an Atlantean legacy or whether it was something they discovered for themselves is immaterial but no medicine bag would be without one. These people were – and are – the shamans.

Soul Focus

There are gifts for the soul when in the presence of the past.
The Kingdoms of the Earth offer tools to take us beyond our
everyday selves.

REMINDERS ...

- The ancients knew a thing or two, but in order to know it for *yourself*, find some places of power - either in the natural world or religious structures – clear your mind of any expectations, and open yourself to what experience might follow.
- Sound together with sacred space, either individually or combined, plus intention enables your conscious awareness to expand beyond the Everyday Personality.
- Each crystal has its own energy or spirit. There are many different varieties, so read a book to learn more about which ones do what, or take a basic course in crystals to see if you feel a resonance with them.
- Crystals should be cleansed and re-programmed regularly to give you their full benefit.
- Crystals are powerhouses – treat them with the respect they deserve.

Resources: Ancient Wisdom

The Science of the Dogon: **Laird Scranton** (Inner Traditions)
The Traveller's Key to Ancient Egypt: **John Anthony West** (Quest Books) www.jawest.net
A Search in Secret Egypt: **Dr Paul Brunton** (Red Wheel/Weiser)
Forbidden History: Compiled by **Douglas Kenyon** (Bear & Co) www.dailygrail.com
In the Name of the Gods: **David Elkington** (Green Man Press)
Secrets of Ancient and Sacred Places: **Paul Devereux** (Brockhampton Press) www.pauldevereux.co.uk
Not in His Image: **John Lamb Lash** (Chelsea Green Publishing)
High Priests and Quantum Genes: **Michael Hayes** (Black Spring Press)
The Ancient Secrets of the Flower of Life Vols 1 & 2: **Drunvalo Melchizedeck** (Clear Light Trust)
Awakening to Zero Point: **Gregg Braden** (Radio Bookstore Press) www.greggbraden.com
Sacred Geometry: **Robert Lawlor** (Thames and Hudson Ltd)
Forbidden Archaeology The Hidden History of the Human Race: **Michael Cremo and Richard Thompson** (Bhaktivedanta Book Trust)
Fingerprints of the Gods: **Graham Hancock** (Crown Publications)
For a fuller list see my website: www.sueminns.co.uk

Resources: Crystals

The Crystal Bible: **Judy Hall** (Walking Stick Press)
The Crystal De-coder: **Sue Lilly** (Barrons)
The Book of Stones: **Robert Simmons & Naisaha Ahsian** (Heaven & Earth Publishing)

chapter 11

the shaman's way

Medicine for the Soul... The Stuff of Dreams

In going down into the secrets of his own mind,
He has descended into the secrets of all minds.
Ralph Waldo Emerson

Medicine for the Soul

The way of the shaman is another source of ancient wisdom that we seem to suddenly have re-discovered. It was always there, of course, another tributary of the underground river of Ageless Wisdom from which we had turned away. Then the seismic effect of the 1960s seemed to shake so much from where it had been hiding.

Shamanism is a world-wide phenomenon whose beginnings are hidden in the impenetrable mists of the ancient past. Probably as old as human consciousness, it predates the earliest recorded civilisations by thousands of years. Although the term itself originates from the Tungus tribe in Siberia and means 'one who sees in the dark' or has the ability to see 'with the strong eye' or 'with the heart', the practise of shamanism existed on all inhabited continents.

Romanian-born Mircea Eliade was director of the History of Religions Department at the University of Chicago for 30 years, and it is his book, published in 1951, called *Shamanism: Archaic Techniques of Ecstasy,* that has become the classic reference for anyone interested in investigating his extensive and scholarly research into the subject. As an eminent interpreter of world religions, he regarded shamanism as combining mysticism, magic and 'religion' and as a source of power that brought meaning and value – a sense of the sacred – to the lives of those touched by it. His conclusion is that shamanism underpins all the other spiritual traditions on the planet; one of its most distinctive features being the journey to other worlds in an altered state of consciousness. It was also his opinion that what is really important about shamanism is the fact that the shaman knows that we are not alone. Michael Harner is another heavyweight who has brought awareness of shamanism to a much wider and extremely receptive audience. It seems as if many of us have recognised in the shamanic way, a path we have been seeking for ages, one that is somehow familiar and one we can trust. This is because it is a path that speaks to the soul. Harner, an anthropologist, speaks with the wisdom of his own direct experience with the indigenous peoples of the Upper Amazon, Mexico, Peru, the Canadian Arctic, Samiland and western North America. Practising shamanism since 1961 his organisation, the Foundation for Shamanic Studies, offers courses and trainings in core shamanism in the US and Europe. This is how he defines it:

> *Shamanism is a path of knowledge, not of faith, and that knowledge cannot come from me or anyone else in this reality. To acquire that knowledge, including the knowledge of the reality of the spirits, it is necessary to step through the shaman's doorway and acquire empirical evidence.*

So if it's not a belief system, and not a religion, what is it? How can we step through the shaman's doorway to find out for ourselves? And what might we find on the other side? Perhaps we, ourselves, are the doorway? First of all shamanism is a direct method for expanding consciousness. The techniques it offers us for accessing energy, power, vision, healing and creativity are not complex and provide a method of experiencing revelations and spiritual realms for ourselves unrestricted by the rules and regulations of world views or organised religion. It is a path that has soul-appeal because it concerns the interconnectedness of all things at all levels. It is an inspirational tool for our times. Shamanic practices have been a constant for thousands of years, but why would they offer us an inspirational tool for these times? Because they are inclusive, all encompassing and enable *direct* experience, not second-hand, for those who practice them – and most of all because they work.

It's important to emphasise that it is highly unlikely that any of us could become shamans in the true sense of the word. Traditionally a shaman would be a healer, a miracle-doer, a medicine man, seer, priest, story-teller and magician, with the ability to access information and wisdom from 'non-ordinary' reality. Or to put it really simply, a shaman is a woman or man who changes their state of consciousness at will, in order to contact and/or travel to another reality to obtain power and knowledge. When the mission is accomplished, the shaman journeys home to use this power and knowledge to help either himself or others.

He (less often a 'she') is the wise person of the community who is consulted on all matters pertaining to the health and welfare of everyone. It has to be said that not all of them have used (and still do) their knowledge benevolently, such as the *muganga* of East Africa, voodoo priests, witch-doctors, sorcerers and practitioners of the black arts – all still very much alive and powerful in many cultures. The shamans of the West – witches, wizards, Druid seers and alchemists - were all stamped out by Christianity, the legacy of which has been an inheritance of fear and suspicion around the shamanic premise that the visible world is pervaded by invisible forces or 'spirits' that affect the lives of the living. To be a true shaman, you will have undergone a rite of passage that will have initiated you into the shaman's path. This might have been a near-death experience, a lightning strike, a serious illness or some event that involved looking death in the eye and surrendering yourself to whatever would happen next. These experiences result in a major shift in perspective and open the doorway into other worlds. In some cultures the shaman's role is an inherited position, and in others shamans are 'called' to this work, and work it is, often involving living on the edge of the community in semi-isolation in order to walk between the worlds without too many distractions from everyday life.

Shamans consider that all human problems arise from loss of power, or loss of soul – meaning here a person's vital essence. In indigenous cultures, this loss was attributed to the soul being frightened away, or straying, or being stolen. In today's world this equates with the shock to the soul of incest, abuse, loss of someone close, surgery, accident, illness, miscarriage, abortion, or war, any of which may manifest in depression, dissociation or some form of addiction in an attempt to mask the too-painful feelings. We have already seen how the soul-child can be frightened out of its wits by what it perceives as a threat to its very survival. Any event, as we discovered in chapter 5 on the Inner Children, can cause our vital essence to separate from us in order to survive the experience. This results in feelings of not really being here and engaged in life.

"Soul loss can be observed today as a psychological phenomenon in the everyday lives of the human beings around us. Loss of soul appears in the form of a sudden onset of apathy and listlessness; the joy has gone out of life, initiative is cropped, one feels empty, everything seems pointless" says Marie-Louise von Franz, founder of the Jung Institute in Zurich and interpreter of over 65,000 dreams in her practice as a psychotherapist.

You might like to ask yourself the following questions to identify whether soul loss is something you have experienced yourself, and how it impacts on your life…

- Do you have difficulty staying 'present' in your body, and ever feel as if you're somehow detached from it – 'beside yourself' so to speak?
- Do you suffer from chronic depression?
- Do you ever feel numb, apathetic, or deadened?
- Are you often ill with an assortment of minor ailments, or even serious ones?
- Were you chronically ill as a child?
- Are there gaps in your memory of your life after the age of five?
- Does it feel as if you might have blacked out significant moments of shock in your life?
- Do you struggle with addictions to anything – drink, drugs, food,

sex or gambling?

- Do you find yourself avoiding being on your own, filling your life with external distractions to avoid a sense of emptiness that always seems to be knocking on your door?
- Have you found it difficult to move on with your life after a painful separation from someone else?

Any of these symptoms would indicate to a shaman that soul loss has occurred, so a journey would be made, on your behalf, out of time-bound reality and into the worlds of non-ordinary reality, to find the missing or lost part of you.

This travelling is known as shamanic journeying and is fundamental to the shaman's work. Linking ancient with contemporary wisdom, Albert Einstein's comment that:

the significant problems we have cannot be solved at the same level of thinking with which we create them

might as well have been the shaman's approach.

As with all journeys, one or two preparations have to be made. A shaman knows that everything has its own spirit – or energy – so the journey will involve communication with whatever spirits may be encountered that might help – or hinder – his mission. Every stone, plant, bird, creature or place is alive and carrying information so first of all the *intention* of the journey (as with every exploration of this nature) is set. Then the spirits of the four directions, the sky, the earth and the spirit of the place itself will be 'called in' using the sound of a rattle. No journey is attempted without the sense that the shaman has filled up with a power and energy that is greater than his little human self. At this point the drum may be used, whose monotonous and rhythmic sound will alter the shaman's brainwaves from the waking state of beta, slowing down to alpha and then deeper into theta – the state from which the journey begins – and provide a 'track' for his journey. Other traditions will add the use of bells, rattles, sticks and chanting, or even dancing into a trance state. The assistance of the plant kingdom may also be enlisted in the form of a psychotropic (hallucinogenic) substance that is eaten, drunk or smoked. Recent advances in neurochemistry show that the human brain carries its own consciousness-altering substances, particularly in females, perhaps explaining why there are more men than women using them as rocket fuel.

His consciousness will then leave 'ordinary' reality and the journey into non-ordinary reality begins, starting in his mind from a place in nature which will facilitate entry into one of the three 'worlds' in which he might travel on his quest to find what he needs to find. This place of entry is known as the *axis mundi* – the world tree – that unites all the planes of existence. The tree will be climbed for access to the Upper World, or the roots will provide the means of access to the Lower World. Journeys may also be made in the Middle World, depending on the quest he is on. The snake and the eagle are two creatures particularly associated with the axis mundi – two snakes coiling round it to enter the upper world for wisdom reflect the shaman's role and have given us the symbol of the caduceus now used by the medical profession as a symbol of healing.

The worlds the shaman travels are similar to the worlds described by the mystics. Jesus also described these worlds to his apostles after his crucifixion, as translated from the Bruce and Askew codices, which form part of the Coptic Gnostic Library. They are also similar to reality as described by frontier science – that the universe is a hologram, we are all interconnected as indivisible parts of the same hologram, and therefore each of us contains a holographic replica of the whole. This means that *everything* has significance. Once again we trip over the Hermetic Principle of macrocosm and microcosm reflecting each other.

Shamans never travel in unfamiliar territory without a guide who knows the terrain. Guides come in many shapes and sizes. Perhaps the one we have become most familiar with in urban shamanic practice comes from the Native American Indian tradition and is the power animal. But there are also the ancestors, spirit guides, angels, birds or any other being personal to the shaman. The guide will assist the shaman on his quest to find the lost soul-part. This might be discovered as a child, in hiding or locked away somewhere, and the shaman will invite it to return with him to where it belongs, since it will be safe now. The shaman 'carries' the child and brings it back to the axis mundi and into ordinary reality where it will be 'blown' back into the waiting recipient. Once this lost energy is repatriated, so to speak, there is a sense of having recovered something that makes you feel somehow more complete and able to be present, and healing takes place.

Other work of the shaman will involve journeying for information for the community. Jeremy Narby, in his extraordinary book The Cosmic Serpent, tells us about his research as an anthropologist which revealed that shamans access an intelligence – which they say is nature's –which gives them information that has stunning correspondences with molecular biology. It also supplies them with invaluable practical information.

Working with the indigenous tribes of the Amazon rain forests, he observed that they used a substance called curare paste in their blowguns. This is a muscle-paralysing substance, made from 70 different plant species, which is boiled for 72 hours. It kills tree-born animals without poisoning their meat, but causes their muscles to relax so that they lose their grip and fall to the ground. When hit by an ordinary arrow, monkeys tend to wrap their tails round a branch and so die out of the archer's reach. Curare is effective only if injected under the skin – if it's swallowed, nothing happens. The Amazon rain forests contain half of all the plant species on Earth, so how did these people know which plants, in what combination and what preparation, were required to produce curare paste? Their answer to him was that the creator of the universe had given it to them through their shamans.

Curare has now been developed synthetically by pharmacists in laboratories and is used extensively in medical practice to anaesthetise patients. This is just one example of how the ecological knowledge of indigenous people is now widely used to heal disease. Narby also believes that shamans take their consciousness down to the molecular level and gain access to biomolecular information. In other words they have the ability to communicate with the multidimensional universe – the micro and macrocosm.

It is because of this that shamanic practice has such value for us today. Although the vast majority of us will not be and are not shamans, we can learn so much from their practices.

> *Soul loss is regarded as the gravest diagnosis in the shamanic nomenclature, being seen as a cause of illness and death. Yet it is not referred to at all in the modern Western medical books. Nevertheless, it is becoming increasingly clear that what the shaman refers to as soul loss – that is injury to the inviolate core that is the essence of the person's being – does manifest in despair, immunological damage, cancer, and a host of other very serious disorders. It seems to follow the demise of relationships with loved ones, career, or other significant attachments.*
>
> **Jeanne Achterberg:** The Wounded Healer

It may be that someone has 'lost their voice', or 'lost their heart', or some other essential aspect of personal power. All ailments, disease and emotional problems are caused by this loss of power, or soul loss. So if you are someone who has an affinity with the natural world, shamanic practice may well offer the path on which you will feel most comfortable in connecting your body to your soul. And if you are not, then I suggest you give it a go for the same reason. It's important to remember that there's no such thing as failure. There are some people who carry deep-seated beliefs that shamanism doesn't quite have the spiritual value that other practices have, power animals are just a bridge too far and too basic to be spirit helpers and somehow not holy, like spirit guides. The fact is that many of us have not been in our bodies or connected to the Earth for years, for the reasons already discussed. Journeying is a powerful way to come home to your soul and connect with our Great Mother – the Earth.

Another reminder that we will not be going anywhere until we have arrived.

A quiet word of warning. Because this has become a powerful path for many, it has given rise to what are known as 'plastic shamans' who take advantage of genuine seekers. Never put your trust in someone who you think has all the answers without checking their credibility and credentials, and don't let anyone push you into anything you don't feel comfortable with just because they tell you it's all part of your initiation or whatever. Others can show us the way, but no-one can do it for us. Listed at the end are the web addresses of authentic shamanic teaching organisations including some with whom I've studied.

When you start to think about it, any inner exploration is like a shamanic journey – any excursion into the psychic information highway, be it a past life or a guided meditation – and the same principles apply. Intention, first and foremost, followed by attention – so you observe acutely what follows rather than have a half-hearted focus - then comes acceptance of what is shown or revealed without attempting to change it; and finally reflection on its meaning and importance.

It's already been said that shamans have tools to help them travel in non-ordinary reality, and one of these is psychoactive plant substances which are either smoked or swallowed in order to assist lift-off to other realms.

We have drunk the Soma: we have become
Immortal; we have gone to the light; we have found
* the gods. What can hatred and the malice of a*
mortal do to us now, O immortal one?
Rig Veda (c. 1000 BCE)

Some of us are so 'in our heads' that journeying to the drum may still not produce a totally credible experience. Psychoactive substances have been used by people for thousands of years in order to help them understand the nature of the human experience, explore the outer reaches of their consciousness or bring information into the third dimensional reality.

These substances come predominantly from the plant kingdom and are divided into Master and Minor Plant Teachers. The seven master teachers of the plant world are datura, iboga, peyote, amanita muscaria, San Pedro cactus, Indo-Aryan soma and ayahuasca. These days there has been a phenomenal increase in the use of chemical psychedelics and mind-altering drugs – perhaps an unconscious need to experience more than what the physical world has to offer. Dr Stan Grof 's work with LSD broke new ground in a therapeutic and clinical context in the 1960s; Timothy Leary overdid it somewhat; but Terence McKenna, who died in 2000, was a writer and philosopher whose attention was drawn to psychedelics by Aldous Huxley. On a journey to the Colombian Amazon with his brother Dennis, he allowed himself to be the subject of a psychedelic experiment using the plant oo-koo-he, which he claimed produced a universal visionary religious experience. The voice that spoke to him on this journey prompted him to explore the structure of an early form of the I Ching and resulted in his book *Novelty Theory* in which he says:

> *In the Amazon and other places where visionary plants are understood and used, you are conveyed into worlds that are appallingly different from ordinary reality. Their vividness cannot be stressed enough. They are more real than real, and that's something that you sense intuitively. They establish an ontological priority. Once you get that under your belt and let it rattle around in your mind, then the compass of your life begins to spin and you realize that you are not looking in on the Other; the Other is looking in on you. This is a tremendous challenge to the intellectual structures that have carried us so far during the last thousand years. We can do tricks with atoms, there's no question about that, but these tricks immolate us. The higher-order structure of molecules, let alone organelles and that kind of thing, is intellectual incognita to us. We have no notion of how these things work or what is going on. Yet it is from those levels that the constituent modalities of reality are being laid down.*

The work of these pioneers, and others, was instrumental in convincing many that, used in the name of considered exploration rather than simply blowing your mind, psychoactive substances were and are path-finders. They are sometimes referred to as *entheogens,* the etymology of which is 'god within; god- or spirit-facilitating'. Once, when a journalist casually referred to peyote (a classic entheogen) as a drug, a Huichol Indian shaman replied, "Aspirin is a drug, peyote is sacred." Personally I have never taken anything more powerful than the odd joint offered to me by my sons after supper and whilst making me laugh a lot, there was nothing deep and meaningful about the experience. Marijuana is considered to be a Minor plant teacher, since although it has the ability to take you out of your Everyday Personality, it doesn't reach the depths of experience offered by the Masters. I first heard about the power of the teacher plant, ayahuasca, from Roger Woolger about 12 years ago, and something stirred in me then. It was as if the plant herself had planted a seed somewhere in my psyche, and although it sounded a pretty scary experience, I knew I would drink this brew (I just can't call it tea) at some point in the future.

Around 15 million people in Brazil regularly take ayahuasca as the sacred sacrament in Christian-based ceremonies of three Churches. Men, women and children swallow the concoction, and then their visionary experiences are overlaid with Christian music, prayer and movement. Ayahuasca is still illegal in most other countries around the world because of its DMT content, which is found in the leaves of the bush *psychotria viridis,* one of the component plants of ayahuasca. DMT (*dimethyltraptamine)* is not only a powerful hallucinogen, but is also a neurotransmitter found in the human brain. In our bodies, any excess is immediately metabolised and removed. In order for this not to happen when swallowing ayahuasca, the DMT-containing chacruna leaves are added to the mashed and boiled stems of the forest liana or vine, *banisteriopsis caapi.* – sometimes called 'Vine of the Soul' because of the effects of taking this brew. The unique action of the macerated vine disables the bodily function that would otherwise remove the DMT and allows it to cross the blood/brain barrier producing the effects for which it is now becoming renowned. The combination of these two plants results in a thick, dark brown liquid which tastes and smells like concentrated, fermenting, jungle swamp juice. It could never be called recreational and it is not a drug. But it is emerging from the South American rainforests to offer us radical healing for radical sickness – the separation from our souls. Why would a master plant substance used by indigenous shamans for centuries have any value for those inhabiting a different kind of jungle?

Several years after I had first heard about it, my dear friend Gary told me he had been going to South America for ayahuasca ceremonies in the jungle near Manaos and that these were facilitated by Eduardo da Luna and a remarkable lady called Silvia Polivoy. Silvia's ceremonies, or rather seminars, are not run by Amazonian ayahuasceros. Her approach is 100% psycho-spiritual. In other words they are about healing and releasing patterns and blocks from the past and opening to the vistas of the soul and spirit. Silvia now runs her seminars in Bahia, the cultural and historical heart of Brazil and works with Zoe7. She is a licensed clinical psychologist, who had a busy practice in Buenos Aires once upon a time, but felt that this approach to human problems was limited. So for a period of years she took herself off to train and work with Mexican and Peruvian shamans and came to recognise the immense value that their use of psychoactive plants and ancient traditions held for us in our modern, mad world. Through her own experiences, she realised that ayahuasca enabled the drinker to have such powerful visions that they were able to work through their psychological issues and heal – thus accessing their inner strength and own personal power. It's all about self empowerment. Her seminars focus on accessing hidden resources of inner strength and personal power that belong to the shaman that is within us all – the Soul.

My own personal reason for trekking halfway across the globe and looking fear straight in the eye was because I felt I had reached a kind of 'membrane' in my meditation, journeys and understanding of the nature of things. Stuck in other words. Others have different reasons – to get in touch with their feelings, be a more loving person, address their addictions, free their sexuality, offload their phobias, heal their illness, experience God – or any one of all the millions of issues that are obstacles for the personality in search of its soul. What I went for, with high ideas of revelations and visions, was of course not what happened. And here is the wonder of ayahuasca. It seems as if this plant medicine acts like a spiritual dyno-rod. Before any epiphanic, transcendent meeting with your soul or the Great Spirit can take place, the pathways need to be cleared.

Over the last 20 years I have done a fair bit of work on myself, and am familiar with my historical patterns. But I had also locked some things away so securely that I no longer had the key. Nothing, however, escapes the eagle eye of Lady Ayahuasca, as she snakes through the caverns of your psyche and slithers into the secret boxes of your archives. This process can involve quite a bit of purging – from both ends of the spectrum so to speak – the more 'stuff' in the passageways of the self, the more likely it is that you will have to throw it up in your early experiences. All I can say is that a bit of vomiting to free you and your soul has got to be worth it. And it's not as if you have to continue this process. In the words of Ram Dass:

when you get the message, hang up the phone.

Details of Silvia's seminars can be found on both her website and my own; addresses are under ***Resources.***

Soul Focus

The shaman's way is the natural path to connection with your soul. Their tools take the Everyday Self out of its box to reveal the astonishing qualities of both Soul and Spirit.

REMINDERS ...

- Shamans have kept alive the knowledge of the natural and supernatural worlds throughout the ages. Science is now validating much of their knowledge.

* *Every* thing has its own spirit or energy, and is interconnected in an implicate order.
* Shamans know how to navigate the different realities, and have guides and helpers in all of them.
* Their work is carried out within the three realms of Spirit, Everyday Life and Soul, which they call the Upper, Middle and Lower Worlds.
* Following the principles of Intention, Attention, Acceptance and Reflection ensures successful journeying.

Resources Shamanism:

The Way of the Shaman: **Michael Harner** (Harper SanFrancisco)
www.shamanism.org: The Foundation for Shamanic Studies
The Shamanic Way of the Bee: **Simon Buxton** (Destiny Books)
www.sacredtrust.org The Sacred Trust
Soul Retrieval: **Sandra Ingerman** (Harper Collins)
Shamanism as a Spiritual Practice for Daily Life: **Tom Cowan** (The Crossing Press)
Breaking Open the Head: **Dan Pinchbeck** (Broadway Books)
Supernatural: **Graham Hancock** (Century)
Shamanism and the Mystery Lines: **Paul Devereux** (Quantum)
The Cosmic Serpent: DNA and the Origins of Knowledge: **Jeremy Narby** (Victor Gollancz
www.shamanism.dk - **Jonathan Horwitz** (Courses, articles and shamanic tools)
www.shamanism.co.uk - **Leo Rutherford** and **Eagle's Wing**
http://www.johnperkins.org/: - **John Perkins**
www.ayahuasca-healing.net - for the work of **Silvia Polivoy** in Brazil
www.sueminns.co.uk - for my personal experience and pictures of Bahia
www.csp.org - **The Council for Spiritual Practices**

The Stuff of Dreams ....

Who looks outside, dreams;
Who looks inside, wakes.
C G Jung

A dream could be considered to be a journey, but unless it is what is
known as a 'lucid dream' (that is you are conscious of what is happening
and can move about at will within that dream), it will come unbidden and
from some place beyond waking awareness. We are not usually in control
of what happens in our dreams, which is one of the reasons why they are
so important. Shamanic journeys on the other hand, are made in full consciousness and have a specific purpose. Both dreams and journeys, understood and utilised as a source of valuable information by wise people
through the ages, have an extremely important role to play in the understanding of a longer, wider and deeper journey – the soul's final return
Home after all its earthly experiences.

Although some people insist that they never dream, it has been scien-
tifically proven that all of us have dreams. Mostly the difficulty seems to
be in trying to remember what it is that we have dreamt and interpreting
the meaning. Why would we want to? Because dreams are the means by
which the soul can communicate directly with the personality.

A dream is a theatre in which the dreamer himself is
the scene, the player, the prompter, the producer, the author,
the public and the critic

says wise old **C G Jung.**

In other words, if we are all actors, reading a particular script for a specific play called This Lifetime, it makes sense to take direction from the
producer. Because we become so engrossed in acting the part we are playing, we forget that at the end of this production we will put down our

scripts, leave the stage and go off and have a glass of wine with the others involved in this particular drama. Because we can become so closely identified with our scripts, we believe that we actually are the part we are playing. The director, the soul, can only make its presence felt when the ego in the control tower of our minds is off duty. That is when we are asleep. But even then many people will dismiss these communications as being 'only a dream' and feel that it's not worth spending time on thinking about why it appeared or what it might be about.

Science has not been able to locate where our mind is housed, but this personal mega-computer takes in enormous amounts of information on a minute-by-minute basis. A large proportion of this information is irrelevant and will never be required - faces in traffic jams, the shape of clouds, the contents of supermarket shelves. So, as with a computer, it needs to regularly clear itself of obsolete, out of date information and send it off to the recycling bin. As our liver sorts out ingested matter and de-toxifies the body, so there are hundreds of other physical and mental sifting processes going on within us without our conscious knowledge. It appears that some dreams perform this task for our minds. They are the information off-loading dreams that may just be a jumble of incomprehensible muddled images, moving very fast, like playing a video backwards at high speed, but they provide the valuable service of preventing information overload. It is a well-known fact that sleep deprivation can send people mad.

The other sort of dream – messenger dreams, the ones with something to say – are the ones we are interested in here, and they may appear to the dreamer for a variety of reasons. These are the dreams that give us clues about what makes us tick and what is going on in the submerged part of the iceberg of our mind. They are the vehicle through which our soul speaks to us.

Historically, dreams have always been taken seriously. Biblical kings, prophets and Egyptian pharaohs would have had a special person – possibly a magus or seer - on hand to reveal their meaning. Here is a spiritual paradox. If a dream is bringing a message, making a statement, revealing a truth, then why doesn't it do so in black and white? Firstly because dreams have their own particular language, a shorthand code that goes beyond the limiting use of words and invites us to perceive ourselves and the universe in a wider, deeper way. This language, as we have already seen, was used by those wise old Egyptians whose hieroglyphs all had both physical and metaphysical meanings. Take the image of an owl, for example. In the context of it being a component part of a word, it represented the letter 'M'. But an owl is also a symbol for many other things – wisdom, the ability to see in the dark, or whatever it represented to those around to read it at the time. As usual, Carl Jung, that great visionary psychologist has something to say:

A word or an image is symbolic when it implies something more than its obvious and immediate meaning. It has a wider, 'unconscious' aspect that is never precisely defined or fully explained. Nor can one hope to define or explain it. As the mind explores the symbol, it is led to ideas that lie beyond the grasp of reason.

The language of dreams, then, like hieroglyphs, is the language of symbol. Secondly, a dream stays always out of reach, until we have understood the meaning – it is a mystery asking us to solve its riddles in order to catch our attention. A symbol, as distinct from a word, is something that cannot have a precise meaning. It will depend on your own personal lens of perception. A dog appearing in a dream may bring a feeling of fear and mistrust for some people, whereas for others it will evoke a sense of faithful companionship.

It was both Freud and Jung who were responsible for restoring dreams to their rightful place as a rich source of information from you to yourself, about your Self. Freud believed that slips of the tongue and dreams revealed the repressed feelings that (often around sexuality) were submerged because they were either socially unacceptable or too frightening to deal with. Carl Jung, initially a pupil of Freud, parted company with him as he, Jung, became deeply influenced by the power of myth, mysticism, metaphysics and religious experience, from which developed the now widely accepted Jungian (or analytical), psychology. The baton of uncovering the depth and breadth of the human psyche was then carried forward by people such as Abraham Maslow and Roberto Assagioli, the founding father of Transpersonal Psychology, which places great importance on messages from the unconscious mind and dream analysis.

Within every one of us there is a deep well of fears, hopes and desires. Sometimes, even though we are able to feel them, we are still unable to express them. We may keep on repressing what we truly feel, but ultimately the soul will build up enough pressure to push information through to the surface in order to encourage growth. To quote Jung yet again:

What remains in the unconscious mind, manifests as Fate.

This may involve a life crisis of some kind, which offers the opportunity for spiritual emergence-y, or in other words, a break down to break through. Or we may sink into depression - another message from the soul, if we dare to taste it's bitter flavour without resorting to chemical blankets. At this critical time we may experience what Jung referred to as 'Big Dreams', or dreams that carry great portent and are pregnant with meaning. Such dreams come to tell us about what is happening, and to see more clearly what is going on in our deep well. When we dare to peer down into the depths, we will always find the golden coins of soul wisdom.

Apart from clutter-clearing and messenger dreams regarding a current situation, there are other kinds. Teaching, problem-solving, precognitive, prophetic or visionary, healing, past life, communications with those who have died, and no doubt others. We will look at the most commonly experienced categories here ...

Problem Solving or Guidance Dreams are those that you can programme for yourself in order to clarify a situation. Sometimes referred to as an 'incubating' dream, it means that before you go to sleep, you focus on something specific that is troubling you. Try writing it down on a piece of paper in a clear and concise way, and then put it under your pillow. Send out that arrow of intention "I need insight into what's happening at work/with my partner/why I am not moving forwards (or whatever it is that you need). I am ready to receive a dream to help me understand the situation. Thank you, Soul/Higher Self/Psyche or Wotever." Then put the thought out of your mind, handing it over and sending it off, like posting a letter to your unconscious mind. When you wake up in the morning you may remember a dream containing your answer, or perhaps the answer by itself will be in your head. Or maybe it will be later in the day that you suddenly become aware that your answer has arrived, delivered by courtesy of your unconscious mind.

Precognitive Dreams can give you a glimpse into the future and may act as a wake-up call to those people who have not yet accepted that our concept of life is not the only one. Future events have appeared to many people in dreams and can sometimes have a disturbing effect on the recipient if they involve catastrophe of some sort. Therefore it is vital to remember, especially when you are first learning to recall your dreams, that sometimes they are simply reflections of our unconscious mind, playing back to us what we may fear or desire.

Visionary Dreams are the ones that come from the highest level from which we are able to receive communication without evaporating. You can call this level whatever you want – God (somewhat emotive), the Creative Force, Source of All That Is, but a Power greater than your individual self. A visionary dream is unusual, and is more than a 'Big Dream' in that it has a different quality of awareness to it, and its strength and intensity may leave you feeling deeply affected for some time. The message may be verbal, visual or even simply a feeling that you need to translate into words. However the message is delivered, the content of it will be absolutely clear.

Teaching Dreams are believed to be a nightly occurrence in order that we can 'process' and face our daily problems. They tell us about what is actually going on in the well of our unconscious minds – things that might be causing a disturbance on the surface. Or they may give encouraging glimpses to show that growth and stability are slowly emerging from current turbulence. It's important to remember that your dreams are all about *you.* You are the writer, the producer, the actor and the director. Other people in your dream usually represent aspects of yourself. Your mother's appearance may be speaking about the mothering side of you. A child could represent one of your inner children and your boss, perhaps your inner authority figure. People dressed in black or with black skins are representatives emerging from your shadow self. In whatever way the qualities of the dramatis personae in your dreams express themselves will be the key to the meaning for you. An animal tells you about your basic instinctual nature with its many facets. Are you mouse-like or is there an inner tiger waiting to be released? Houses or buildings – structures - speak about your own structure, your own housing. Are your inner rooms cluttered? Is there work to be done in the cellar (the subconscious)? The state of your kitchen in a dream will tell you about your inner nourishment. Each room will tell you something.

Planes and trains and bicycles are not necessarily saying that you are going to Australia next week, but could be telling you that you are on the move somewhere within yourself. Or are you station-ary? What does the road or track look like? Are you having a 'rough ride' at the moment? Moving to a different plane of understanding? By now you will have got the picture.

Erica, a highly successful consultant whose life moves at tremendous speed is the sort of person who can do five things at once and plan her holiday for next year at the same time. She had just begun to awaken to the spiritual side of her nature and had started taking classes at the College of Psychic Studies in London. Her dream opened at Euston railway station ("It's where I get the train to go home"). In her dream she was carrying shopping in bags and was with a group of people that included her partner. A smallish, Asian man who had a copy of the Big Issue (a magazine published on behalf of the homeless) in his hand approached her. Together, they went into a café, leaving her partner (the masculine aspect of herself) with the baggage. She then passed through a turnstile, rather than going through the larger open space available, and felt afraid when the Asian man moved closer to her. Then he disappeared in the crowd, but she could just about see him through the people.

The explanation here would be that in this dream, she found herself in a place of transition (the station). She had got baggage (issues) with her and felt somewhat apprehensive when approached by this 'foreigner' (her soul nature), who was holding a very big issue for her and was someone (an aspect of herself) who gets lost in the crowd of other things in her life. But she was prepared to go with him to a café (place of communication where she could get to know more about this 'foreign' side of herself), although she preferred to go through a narrow turnstile rather than take the easier route through the wide entrance, which might have rushed their meeting. As this dream was so vivid, we found it useful to take it further in a session. By simply closing her eyes and returning to the station, she gave herself the opportunity to become more familiar with this 'stranger' and to talk about the Big Issue that he was holding for her to read.

Our dream makers enjoy puns. 'Too big for your boots'? 'Ironing things out'? 'Making a nonsense of something'? 'Dancing to another's tune?' 'Cooking something up'? or getting closer to 'someone' who is holding the big issue will all be presented pictorially. A dream dictionary helps to understand dream-speak, but the most important thing to remember is the whole shape of the dream, the feeling content of it all, which is particular to only you.

Just about every book you find on dreams suggests that keeping a Dream Journal is the best way of notifying your unconscious mind that you are taking dreams seriously. This way you will end up with the most informative book on dreams you could ever acquire – your own dream book. Keeping this book beside your bed, with pen ready to write means that a dream is less likely to escape. Some people recommend lying still after you have woken up until you have reeled the dream back into your conscious mind, and then write it down. The first thing to note is the general atmosphere of the dream. How did you feel when you woke up? Then note down the theme of the dream, or the narrative, catching as much of the detail as possible including the numbers of things as they too have relevance. It helps to give the dream a title like 'Man in the Hedge', 'In a Very Public Convenience' or 'Lost in the Desert'. Be sure not to make any judgements or assessments at this stage. However, you might like to note what you think was the possible trigger for this particular dream. Afterwards you can engage your rational mind to search for the meaning. If you are baffled by any of the contents, look them up in a book such as the ones listed under **Resources** at the end of the chapter.

A dream which is not interpreted
Is like a letter which is unread.
The Talmud

Soul Focus
Dreams are a way for the soul to communicate to you
without interference of the ego/personality.

REMINDERS ...
- Your dreams belong to you, and deserve attention and respect.
- The language of dreams is sign, symbol and scene.
- Characters in the dream represent aspects of your Self.
- Understanding your dreams helps you understand yourself, and casts light on current situations.
- Give yourself a pre-sleep suggestion that you will remember your dreams.

Resources
The Element Encyclopaedia of Symbols: Edited by **Udo Becker** (Element)
The Dream Dictionary: **Tony Crisp** (Bantam Doubleday)

The Inner Eye: **Joan Windsor** (Gateway Books)
The Dream Bible: **Brenda Mallon** (Godsfeld Press)
Teach Yourself to Dream: **David Fontana** (Duncan Baird Publishers)

chapter 12

ultimate journey

The Not-so-grim Reaper

Death is not extinguishing the light;
it is putting out the lamp because dawn has come.
Rabindranath Tagore

Death. It's curious how we don't talk about it – at least not our own. There seems to be an invisible embargo on the one absolute certainty in an otherwise totally unpredictable world where change is the only constant. And although we are subjected daily to information and images surrounding the deaths of others, somehow we don't seem to relate this final event for the human body to our selves.

Death is the last of the Great Taboos. It's not chatted about over the garden fence, over lattés or glasses of wine. It's not given a seat at our tables – no, in our so-called civilised world, death waits somewhere over the events horizon, unseen, unacknowledged, denied or ignored. It's something that happens to other people, the old, the ill or the unfortunate. It is scary, even terrifying, to the everyday ego personality, living its life as it does, in the narrow band of perception over which it is master. These days our lives are rarely marked by truly soulful rites of passage celebrating and acknowledging the stations we pass on our journey through the human experience. The Hatches, Matches and Despatches columns are just about the only evidence of the major events in peoples' lives, and even these announcements seem to have less attention paid to them than even a couple of decades ago. These landmarks for the soul require serious celebration. How could a soul's arrival, union with another and departure from the stage have become hardly worth serious mention? What a distance we have put between ourselves and the natural cycles of life, the vital juice for the expression of our souls and so crucial to the maintenance of our connection with the Earth.

"I'm too busy living to think about dying." But what sort of living is this?

Allowing death – your own death – to sit quietly at your table means that your life will be lived differently. This is not a suggestion for morbid preoccupation, but an opportunity to connect more deeply with your soul. Touch Death gently – it won't bite you – to discover how it deepens the soulfulness of your life. Sooner or later a meeting with Death is inevitable, and for the soul it is a much less difficult transition than coming down to Earth and engaging with a dense little physical body that is subject to the Laws of the Material Universe. No wonder the first thing a baby does when it arrives from the womb is wail about how unsafe it feels.

Birth and Death are the noblest expressions of bravery.
Kahlil Gibran

Imagine you, the soul, have signed up for an uncertain sentence in an unpredictable world where you sit in the back seat of an individual's life, dying to express your unique qualities, marginalized by conditioning and ignored by the driver who keeps reinforcing the glass partition that separates him from his 'Passenger'. In the beginning you can whisper to the driver, and your whispers will be heard, but gradually the glass divide between you becomes like a two-way mirror. You can see him but he is no longer aware of you. Tapping on the glass, you try to give direction, ask him to stop and notice the magnificence of a blazing sunset, a ladybird, or the power of a smile or touch – the things that make you feel alive and present in the driver's drama. You may get fleeting moments of attention, but he seems hell-bent on getting to some unknown destination, or is so preoccupied with pain, power, fear, guilt, anger, or pointlessness that he is deaf to your tapping. The more the driver continues on his journey, the more he seems to become boxed in.

What might happen if he slid to one side the partition that separates him from the one who is seated behind? What would happen if *your* driver did the same? We can't wait for Death to tear down the divide between our soulfulness and our everyday ego selves. Time is getting short.

We may, however, be touched by Death through its visit to someone we love. When someone close to us dies, the shock can lock away our feelings into numbness with the incomprehensibility of such an event. Or the pain will rage through us like a tsunami, breaking open our hearts with grief, grief that tries to fill this huge yawning chasm that has appeared in our lives. Or perhaps there is a different type of grief, one that comes from the deep regret about matters unresolved.

The bitterest tears shed over graves
are for words left unsaid
and deeds left undone.
Harriet Beecher Stowe

These are the moments when soul is present in our lives. Our everyday personalities have to change places with the Passenger as we are overtaken by feelings so strong that it feels as if the jigsaw of our daily lives has been thrown in the air. In the agony of loss we might begin to wonder about our own mortality and where the essence of the one whose body is now 'empty' has gone. People often consult mediums and psychics at these times in a desperate attempt to retain some form of contact, or find out if their loved one's passage to the 'other side' has gone peacefully, whether they are alright and still 'alive' somewhere out there. Particularly difficult are deaths of our children. Seemingly snatched away before their time, the level of grief, pain and anger can scar those left behind for the rest of their lives.

Evelyn, a woman in her sixties, came for a regression to try and help her move beyond grief. Her son, Michael, had suddenly died from a severe asthma attack, leaving a wife and daughter bereft, and Evelyn still quite beside herself four years later. Her life had completely stopped. She was unable to manage the pain or find solace or comfort from any source and feared that she was on the verge of becoming obsessional. She and her son had been extremely close, and she felt that they had had previous incarnations together where they had been close companions, lovers, siblings and also rivals. She felt that understanding their past 'stories' would help her come to terms with this seemingly endless ocean of grief and pain and help her pick up the threads of a life again.

The story that unfolded was a classic tale of love and loss. She had been the daughter of a minor European nobleman and was betrothed to a man whom she had loved since she was small. He was part of her father's household, so the situation was unusual, but her father had seen and understood that the connection between his daughter – whom he loved – and this boy, was something remarkable. Inseparable as children, their friendship blossomed into love and deep passion. It was almost is if their souls were fused together. Soulmates, certainly – twin souls? Perhaps. But soulmates come together to learn and learning in this case was not about a Happily Ever After ending, but the long drawn out pain of separation, yearning and loss. War tore their lives apart, as it has done to countless millions of others. Her beloved had left with others of her father's men to join forces against the Gauls. The agonising months of uncertainty crawled by without news. The pain of longing, increased by their separation, flickered on the edge of hysteria when each day the horizon that she searched remained empty of what it was she longed to see. Her health began to fail, but there was still a seed of hope in her heart. And then the fateful day arrived when an exhausted horseman brought the news that whilst the campaign had succeeded, her beloved had paid for this with his life. Her heart now broken in her already frail body, it was only days before she died herself. As her soul departs, she makes a statement "When I find him, I will never leave his side again". Leaving her body was like coming out of a prison, and within minutes the souls were reunited. At that moment it was as if the whole room was filled with an energy that I can't describe. This is the time in a deep memory process session where insights and understanding are connected to the here and now.

Having given them time for their reunion on another plane of consciousness, I quietly ask the question "What does the essence of this woman have to say to Evelyn in the 21st century? How can she help her with her grief over Michael's death?"

Evelyn responds "She says that love never dies. It is eternal and exists beyond the dramas played out on Earth. I must not continue to live like a broken reed but learn to trust in the knowledge that our souls are never far apart..... My beloved is saying that we, as souls, contracted for his early death to occur again in the 21st century – as it had in this other lifetime. It was repeated to give me the opportunity to move beyond my grief and to bring understanding of the temporary nature of human experience. I must not lead the rest of my life feeling half dead, but find joy with his daughter and his wife. He is only ever a thought away."

Those who will not slip beneath
the still surface of the well of grief

turning downward through its black water
to the place we cannot breathe

will never know the source from which we drink,
the secret water, cold and clear,

nor find in the darkness glimmering
the small round coins
thrown by those who wished for something else.
David Whyte: The Well of Grief in *Where Many Rivers Meet*

If we begin to understand what Death is about, it will help to relieve at least some of the fear and anguish that surrounds it. Grief is about our own feelings at the loss of someone who was an important part of our lives, and whilst of course it needs to be felt and expressed, it can have the effect of keeping a soul earthbound, as this story tells us. The daughter of a friend of mine died tragically at the age of 14, and it hit her family like an atom bomb. Her younger brother felt somehow implicated in this awful event because he had been helpless to save her. 10 years after her death, her bedroom was exactly the same as the day she died. Her mother religiously opened and closed the curtains each morning and evening and spent time in the room, which had become a shrine to her daughter's memory. Moustapha and I were staying with them one summer, and the brother asked him to go to the churchyard and put flowers on her grave, as it was the anniversary of her death. Moustapha is a Muslim as well as being extremely psychic. He took off his shoes at the entrance to the churchyard in accordance with his belief about respect for the dead, and went to the girl's grave. As he knelt beside it, he took some earth from its surface, closed his eyes and then said "She is asking me to tell you please not to come here with your grief. It is difficult for her to move on because she feels responsible for your pain. When you visit this place, bring joy with you."

In the last few decades there have been some positive advances in our dealings with Death and our understanding of its role as a teacher and presence in life. Pioneering work by Dr Elizabeth Kubler-Ross with the dying has helped millions cope with departure, their own or of others. She also proposed the now well-known *5 Stages of Grief and Tragedy*, a sort of '12-step programme' identifying the different phases that may be gone through. Briefly, they are Denial (this isn't happening), Anger (why me/him/her/them – it's not fair), Bargain (Just let me live to see/do …). Depression (I can't bear this. I can't cope with it all) and Acceptance (I'm not going to struggle any more. I'm ready …). The Hospice movement, too, has given dying decency and dignity and spared countless souls from clinical hospital departures or lonely exits in solitary bedrooms.

And then there are those who have technically died, but who return to tell the tale. Again over the last few decades the Near-Death Experience

(NDE) has become a well-documented fact and one that changes the lives of those who have been through this remarkable experience. The writings and research into NDEs by two men are largely responsible for a shift in the understanding that death is not an end. It is a transition from one reality to another. Dr Kenneth Ring is Professor Emeritus of Psychology at the University of Connecticut and co-founder of the International Association for Near-Death Studies (IANDS) that was set up in 1978 to investigate and research all aspects of NDEs. Dr Raymond Moody is a parapsychologist and holds the Chair of Consciousness Studies at the University of Nevada. His book *Life After Life* has become a classic on the subject, and his independent studies of 150 people who had been through a NDE showed a commonality in their experience. Interestingly, their experiences are very much in line with Tibetan Buddhist teachings on the first stages of the transition which takes place when the physical body ceases to function.

The first thing that happens is a buzzing sound in the head, followed by a feeling of peace and painlessness. Then the experience of being out of the body and looking down on it which is in turn followed by the sensation of travelling through a tunnel and rising to the heavens. Here there are meetings with others – often dead relatives or friends – and a spiritual or light being. A review of their life – an action re-play – is run during which experience of the effects of actions is understood. Sometimes an option about whether or not to return to the physical body is made, and if it is, it is often made with reluctance as there is a general feeling of being immersed in both light and love. Remembering little Tommy's experience, mentioned in chapter 8, obviously he had not had enough life experience to run a re-play, but went straight to the meeting with the 'guy from Star Wars' who was there to assist his transition.

Having made the decision to return to Earth and their bodies, however, all NDErs report that life is never the same again. It has been changed radically and forever. Most report that death has been redefined and is not something to be fearful of any more; there are changes in how the world is viewed; a greater appreciation of life and its meaning; a sense of purpose and self-understanding, higher self-esteem and greater compassion; an increase in intuitive and psychic abilities and a letting go of the need to fill life with trivia. It's almost as if the driver of the cab and his Passenger have now changed places.

So, if the flight of a bird is so beautiful,
So strange and so sweet
How more beautiful yet must be the flight of the soul toward God,
What a glory and a sweeping on the wind
Of the wings of the spirit toward Light.
Source Unknown (Found in my uncle Ralph's papers after his death)

Birth and death have much in common. Both are miraculous and both are part of a continuous cycle. The birth canal itself mirrors the tunnel through which the soul passes on its transition from the body to its next destination. As Roger Woolger suggests in his book *Other Lives, Other Selves*, the manner in which we are born is often a mirror of how we have died in a previous lifetime – to use a simplistic example, a person born with the umbilical cord round their neck regressed spontaneously and remembered a previous incarnation that ended by his being hanged. Those who have experienced difficult births have also experienced difficult deaths. Many more babies come into the world through caesarean section these days – a relatively trauma-free entrance which perhaps reflects the numbers who, since the last World War, have died less traumatically.

So what we call death is really a birth; what we think of as an ending is actually a beginning. Departures are all part of the continuum of consciousness, the natural flow or spiral of expanding awareness to which each soul's experience is contributing. When we set off from the realm of spirit – Home for the soul – we have already drawn up the contracts for our earthly experience. We ourselves decide which parents will provide us with our body. Encoded in this earthly vehicle is the DNA containing genetic and ancestral patterns - key components for what we have decided needs to be brought into balance under the Law of Attraction. Descending through the ring-pass-not of forgetfulness, we enter our soul drama, a one-act play with only a handful of key players on a minute stage. But each of these miniscule nano-dot dramas is like a piece of a vast interlocking puzzle; each has significance and affects the colours of the whole.

If we remembered where we came from and why we were here, life on Earth would be different to say the least but this explains why it is said that there are always roughly 75% of us who are asleep at any one time. This figure makes up a consensus of people, which would include religious fanatics in my view, who do not realise who they really are. This is why being more friendly with death will open the partition to the Passenger and take us to the wisdom of the soul, knowing as it does that juice and passion and connection with natural cycles put meaning and significance into this single frame on an infinite reel. Yes, we have assigned ourselves to an already encoded vehicle, but – Bruce Lipton once again – we are not our genes.

For navigating the human experience we need our Everyday Personality and the ego that belongs to it. The problem is, like the cab driver, the ego shuts out the soul and can become a little dictator. It has a very narrow and finite view of life and is responsible for our limitations, our fears, judgements, busyness, self-importance and lack of self-worth. So perhaps we can see now how important the presence of Death is in life. It knocks the ego off its perch and rather than casting a long dark shadow, it can actually illuminate our perspective.

He who dies before he dies, does not die when he dies.
Abraham of Santa Clara

This 'dying before we die' which is so often referred to by the mystics and Gnostics throughout the ages, is the death of the ego's structures. It's the opening of the partition so the Passenger can advise the driver. It's the liquidation of the caterpillar to allow those imaginal buds to create the butterfly. It's understanding that nothing dies – it transforms. The death of the little self enhances life's qualities. It simplifies life; it magnifies and amplifies what is natural and real and is not seduced by what is plastic and empty; and it means that when we confront our own death, we will already have let go of much of the 'stuff' that keeps us recycling earthly experiences. Death and dying is all so much 'bigger' than we might imagine, until it arrives. But it does offer us the most powerful opportunity to understand life and the living of it in a different way. It's an opportunity to transform the matters of our everyday personalities into what *really* matters, as the following story reminds us.

First let me introduce you to Abigail Robinson, a most remarkable woman, who has had an extremely challenging soul journey this lifetime, with huge obstacles on her flight path to Love. In spite of their magnitude, these obstacles have not made her shut down her feelings – on the contrary; she is someone who is intensely alive and present to every moment. A very unusual woman, her work is equally unusual. She is a music-thanatologist. *Thanatos* is the Greek word for death and the musical part comes from a harp and the voice, which are used at the bedside of patients approaching death. Music-thanatologists lovingly serve the needs of the dying and their loved ones with what they call prescriptive music, which is music that changes in response to the physiological changes of the patient. This music, played on the harp, is matched to the changes in breathing and shifting emotions of the dying. It not only eases physical distress, but provides a kind of 'wave form' of sound, serenity, intimacy and reverence to ease the soul's transition, and calm the everyday personality to a place of trust and surrender. Music-thanatology, although an age-old sacred practice, has been developed over the last three decades through the vision and dedication of Therese Schroeder-Sheker, founder of the Chalice of Repose Project. Here she offers a rigorous two-year training programme in what she refers to as 'musical-sacramental midwifery'. Birthing into dying, lovingly held, and accompanied by exquisite soul music.

Abigail has many wonderful stories about her music vigils, but this personal account of the last days of her 100 year old grandmother speaks about another crucial component in the soul's journey from life to death on Earth, and that is Love ....

A Tale from the Heart

I lived in a basement in Montana. My grandmother 'Muti' had recently died across the Atlantic, but I sensed her in the wind. I was overcome at the loss of her. There was a marked irony in why I was not at her side. Instead, in close imitation of a mediaeval novitiate, my twelve hour days were immersed in study and prayer in preparation for work with the dying.

One night I had a dream. The basement ceiling now had windows which my one-hundred-year-old grandmother had cast open. With the mischievous look of a young child, she was now blowing bubbles through a plastic ring downwards towards me with the words "I'm sending you some light."

On another occasion I was lying on a table receiving a cranio-sacral treatment when much to my delighted surprise she granted me a visit so apparently substantive I could hardly believe I was still in Montana .... I saw my grandmother on a long road sloping upwards towards Highgate Hill ... she looked as she did in her sports car days, her white hair flowing stylishly out of her head scarf and dark glasses adding to the exuberance and outrageousness – long before Alzheimer's tempered her soul. I asked her what she was doing here and she said "I'm sending you healing."

Responding to my puzzlement at what seemed to me something incongruous with those days of vodka, speeding fines and an abundance of chocolates, she retorted, "You gave me healing, I'm simply returning the favour."

I didn't know she knew.

I recalled my visits to the nursing home where, at 99, she became a resident. I was saddened and disturbed by this transition. I prepared myself with the spiritual discipline drawn from my work as a healer. I would step into myself as fully as possible, knowing that my total presence was all I had to offer her. She was too far away to reach with a simple word. Absent and unmoving in her chair, only love would pull her back, would allow her to meet my gaze as I crouched in front of her.

Puzzled, she would say "I don't know you" and I would reply "It doesn't matter who I am, all that matters is that I love you."

On some occasions our conversation had to be shouted above the exaggerated drama of loud soap operas and in front of staff and residents..

"I don't know who you are....."

"It doesn't matter who I am, all that matters is that I love you."

"I don't know why I am so old and still alive."

"You are dying piece by piece, a little bit at a time."

"It's difficult dying."

".......it's difficult living."

"I don't remember anything."

"You don't need to remember anything, all that matters is that I love you."

"Somebody once told me .... That this is the one thing that is important to remember; All...That...Matters...Is...Love."

Dream as if you'll live forever
Live as if you'll die today.
James Dean

Soul Focus
There is no birth or death for the soul,
only transition

REMINDERS ....
- What do you feel when you think about Death?
- Sparing a thought for Death – your own – will also raise questions about your life and what it is that really matters.

- If you were going to die soon, who would you contact and what would you say? Why are you waiting?
- Living as if each day were your last means you live more authentically, with a different Person in the driving seat of your life.
- Death is an ending for the body, but not the soul.
- It helps us let go of the dramas of life; takes away the 'shoulds' and 'oughts' that are the barriers we erect between each other.

Resources

On Death and Dying: **Elizabeth Kubler-Ross** (Routledge)

The Tibetan Book of Living and Dying: **Sogyal Rinpoche** (Rider)

Heading Towards Omega: In Search of the Meaning of the Near-Death Experience: **Kenneth Ring** (New York: Quill)

International Association for Near-Death Studies (IANDS): www.iands.org

Life After Life: **Raymond Moody** (New York Bantam) www.lifeafter-life.com

Testimony of Light: **Helen Greaves**

What Happens When we Die?: **Dr Sam Parnia** (Hay House)

www.music-thanatologyassociation.com

www.chaliceofrepose.org

To contact **Abigail Robinson**: abigailr_uk@yahoo.co.uk

chapter 13

getting to the heart of It

All you need is Love

Those who don't feel this Love
Pulling them like a river,
Those who don't drink dawn
Like a cup of springwater
Or take in sunset like supper,
Those who don't want to change,
Let them sleep.
Jalaluddin Rumi (1207 – 1273 AD)

The heart of *any*thing is where we find the key to its essence, and for us humans it is this key that will unlock another mystery, the mystery contained in three four-letter words, body, love and soul. Love goes hand in hand with hearts – they belong together, and their union illuminates the body. Love waits to take us beyond all our samskaras, our soul dramas with their karmic backlog, our deep insecurities, our expectations, fears and disappointments. Everything we encounter in our lives, which appears as an obstacle, is in fact a signpost on the flight path to Love. One of the difficulties we have is with the word itself, which is used in these homogenised times to describe everything from the mundane to the deeply spiritual. The people in Greenland have 49 different words to describe the nature of snow and ice, because precise understanding of the quality of snow is vital to their survival. Even the Greeks managed to find four words to describe the different aspects of love. The fact that we can produce only one to express the feeling we may have for our favourite TV soap, a poem, our grandmother or cat, speaks reams. Our understanding

of love can come only through our *hearts*. Or why wouldn't I love someone with all my liver?

I wonder if you could pause for a moment, close your eyes and imagine yourself in a garden. And when you are there, just notice what sort of
garden it is, whether there are walls and fences around it, whether it is
orderly or unkempt, and if there are flowers or trees. And what about
wildness? Does it look as if someone has come in and trampled on it, or
pruned the shrubs too hard, or there has been storm damage? Never mind,
somewhere in the heart of it you'll find a perfect flower. At the heart of
everyone's garden is the flower of the soul. It may be buried under a tan-
gle of undergrowth, or trying to grow in an orderly bed of roses where it
keeps on getting cut back because it doesn't quite seem to 'fit'. But it is
there. Everyone's garden needs to be closed to the public at some time so
that it can restore itself in peace and quiet. The seasons need to be
observed, too. So there are times when it seems as if there are no leaves
on the trees, or flowers anywhere. But that's because things are happening on the *inside*, unseen and in the dark. It's gestation time. There are
days when the gate to the garden must be closed so that you can walk in
it alone, to feel and enjoy the solitude, listen to what it might want to tell
you, and wonder at that one incredible flower that is at the heart of it all.
As Rumi suggests:

> *Oh heart, sit with someone*
> *who knows the heart;*
> *go under the tree*
> *which has fresh blossoms.*

Understanding the multidimensional nature of your heart might bring a
few surprises. For example, did you know that the heart has its own intelligence? This has been demonstrated many times by the stories of trans-
plantees who tell of feeling the presence of their donor. A born-again
Christian woke up after his transplant operation swearing and cursing
having received the heart of a raunchy biker; a woman who had received

the heart of a sailor killed in a boating accident found that her terror of water had vanished, and she had a great desire to go sailing and swimming; another tells of meeting her donor in a dream, who explains that her out-of-character desire to eat Chicken McNuggets washed down by a beer is because this was his favourite meal, and the last one he had eaten before he was killed in a road accident. The possibilities of what may happen if, God forbid, we start to use animal organs is better left alone.

The heart is an extraordinary creature. It can weep, sink, race, faint, flutter, burn, harden, burst, melt, rejoice, stop or fail. It can be broken, frozen, lost, warmed, touched or turned to stone. It may be a lonely hunter, or a gazelle that leaps and almost flies, but in the heart of the heart you will *always* find the qualities of courage, strength, gentleness, vulnerability and compassion. That sense of 'knowing' also has its source here. Knowing and information are distinct from each other, one belongs to the heart and the other the head. Even as I start to write this chapter I am aware of a shift in gear, a deepening of something, a feeling of reverence, as if I have entered a cathedral.

Whether your heart is made of gold or ice, it's clearly not just a mechanical pump. Zooming in on your heart reveals that it has a multidimensional nature. On the physical level, it beats 4,200 times an hour. Its four chambers take in old tired blood from the body's circuitry and send it off to the lungs to be re-inspired. The left side receives the new blood back from the lungs and then pushes it out (2,000 gallons a day) through 60,000 miles of tubes with a force strong enough to reach the capillaries in the big toe. It literally keeps us going moment by moment and when it stops, the soul begins to depart. It not only keeps us alive by moving our life force round our body, but it is also the source of that other life force: Love. Knowing about Love is just as important as keeping us alive, unless we opt for a half-hearted, heartless life. Hearts need to rejoice, to sing, to fly. They need to *love*. And if they get broken by grief; wounded, rejected or pierced by love's arrows, it may feel as if some form of death is imminent, but that death is the possibility of the heart's doors permanently closing. These are the times to be tender with our hearts, and ensure that they stay open in spite of the pain. A hardened heart has closed its doors to love, and therefore life itself.

A heart is for giving. It has the courage to take us into the depths of our feelings. It is the meeting place of heaven and earth; body, soul and spirit embrace each other here, in the centre of our chests. The Sanskrit symbol for the heart chakra is the six-pointed star sometimes known as the Star of David. It is a universal symbol representing two triangles, one pointing down (heaven coming to earth) and the other pointing up (earth to heaven). So if our hearts are the meeting ground for Heaven and Earth, and are the seats of our soul, how could we possibly be half-hearted about love?

Historical Hearts

The great truths can never be apprehended with the mind,
only with the heart.
Plato (d. 347 BCE)

The heart has a history of being understood as the seat of the soul, start-ing – as we have already seen – with the ancient Egyptians. Whoever they were and wherever they came from there is no doubt about the fact that they knew that the heart was a crucial compass for life on earth, with its own intelligence.

My heart ticks in my chest like a beetle ...
It resonates like the bowstring of an archer. It hums like the string of a lyre.
Love. Love. Give me love, sibilant love, thundering love.
It is myself that speaks to my heart, my ka, my double.
The heart leaps and answers to its name.
Its words are the deeds of my body.
Its deeds have been my own thoughts,
Its blood the fluid of gods, river of joy and sadness.

relates Normandi Ellis in her beautiful translation of *The Egyptian Book of the Dead.*

Since the beginning of time there have been those who have known the ways of love; spiritual masters who taught how to activate and water the latent seed within each of our hearts. They knew how to awaken this power, this longing that the soul has for its Beloved. Following in Egyptian footsteps, early Christians and Islamic Sufis used the wounded and the winged heart respectively as symbols for something deeply divine. The bleeding sacred heart of Jesus is always healing, but never healed, since the 'wound' is the gateway to heaven and must remain forever open. For Muslims, a clean heart is like a mirror, reflecting the light of Allah. The heart makes constant appearances in Islamic and mystical Sufi poetry and texts.

The journey to find love is the one referred to and eulogised by the Sufi mystics. As the Islamic saying goes: "The Sufis understand with the heart what cannot be understood with the head." It is the journey of the soul and one that was eulogised by saints and mystics whatever their religion may have been.

O servant where dost thou seek me?
Lo, I am beside thee. I am neither in the temple nor in the mosque,
Neither am I in rites and ceremonies,
Nor in yoga nor in renunciation.
If thou art a true seeker, thou shalt at once see me.
Thou shalt meet me in a moment's time
Kabir (c.1440-1518).

Kabir was an Indian mystic, a family man and a weaver who passionately sought to show people the way out of delusions including the delusion of religious labelling. This is why the role of the 'knowers' from whatever apparent religious affiliation has such relevance today. As the arguments about who or what God is and what he said to whom tears our world apart, the clear sound of sacred voices from both East and West reappear from the past, calling us to our senses. Kabir's pithy comment pokes us into reflection:

The fish in the water that is thirsty
  needs serious professional counselling.

These people speak of a journey to find a love that will not be found in the physical arms of another – and ultimately nothing else has any consequence. This love belongs to a Beloved with a capital 'B'. It is a love that transcends all others; it is the ultimate love, the love into which we may disappear and lose all sense of our earthbound personality and identity, and it starts with a love for life itself. Sufis say that we are all students in the School of Love. They know that love is the most powerful and active force in the universe, and that it cannot be compared with anything else. We know this in our heart of hearts. Why else would the words of a thirteenth-century Muslim, of Afghan origin – Jalaluddin Rumi – make him one of the most popular poets in the world today? Rumi's words hit us like telegrams from some divine source that we know about, but have forgotten. Our hearts leap and swoon as the words rise from the page to tell us about the burning, passionate madness of the lover for the Beloved.

Whatever I have said about Love
When Love comes, I am ashamed to speak .....

he says. The love that he speaks of is the love of the soul for God, Spirit, Allah, the Creator, the Source, the One or whatever name you might want to give to the power that, bafflingly, simply Is. He reminds us of the sorrow of separation, the uncontainable joy of union, of the limitless horizon of the heart and the desire of this heart to find its true Friend. This is not marshmallow, doe-eyed love (although this could be a trailer for the Real Thing); it's a reckless love, as he points out, that "makes the sea boil like a kettle."

Rumi's timeless – and timely – messages speak directly from his heart to our own. His words have the ring of truth born of experience, his own experience. Born in Afghanistan, his family was forced to flee to Turkey by the Mongol hordes of Genghis Khan. They settled in Konya, where he remained for the rest of his life. He became a professor of theology and one day on his way home from school (in 1244 CE) something happened that would change his life – and many others' – for ever. He met a ragged dervish named Shams of Tabriz. According to the story, Shams recited this verse to him:

If knowledge does not liberate the self from the self, then ignorance is better than such knowledge.

It was as if Shams had touched some deep truth in Rumi's heart. He fell at the dervish's feet, and from that moment a furnace of love burned in Rumi for Shams, who then one day disappeared, perhaps sensing the jealousy that their relationship had created with Rumi's students and family. Rumi heard that he was in Damascus, and sent one of his sons to bring him back. Once more Rumi fell at his feet, overwhelmed by the joy of their passionate and ecstatic reunion. They became inseparable, but again jealousy from his students and younger son ended the meeting of these two souls – and this time it was permanent. Shams was murdered, and Rumi was sent spinning down into the deepest well of grief, lost and alone in his ocean of love.

This was his epiphany. He realised the overwhelming love, passion and grief he was feeling belonged, not to Shams, but to a Beloved more magnificent, more compassionate, more powerful than any human being – the Divine Itself. His love, and loss, of Shams was the key to his understanding of divine love – it had broken open his heart - and the inspiration for his writings. Rumi's words have fanned the flame of this love in modern times, creating a forest fire. The fact that he was a Muslim also points a way through the quagmire of current assumptions about Islam based on terrorists, *jihads* and suicidal fundamentalists. It shows us that, at the heart of it all, the routes we take on our different journeys are all sourced from the same stream and have the same destination. This is love of the highest order. It does not create division or separation, it recognises that we are all human and get things wrong before we get them right. It is not a love born from fear or hope, but love inspired by the magnificence, the beauty of vast infinity and the detail of a moth's wing or the sound of a grey dove:

I was sleeping, and being comforted
By a cool breeze, when suddenly a grey dove
From a thicket sang and sobbed with longing,
And reminded me of my own passion.
I had been away from my own soul so long,
So late-sleeping, but that dove's crying
Woke me and made me cry **Praise**
To all early-waking grievers!
Adi al-Riga

This is the role of the mystical Masters – to create a desire for union with the Beloved – which when it happens, releases an atomic mystical power, something beyond the ability of words to describe. "Stand with dignity in the magnificent current of my words and they will carry you in God's arms", says Rumi. But loving someone who is everywhere and nowhere is a challenge to say the least, and most of us have probably only fleetingly glimpsed through the keyhole of its implications. At our current level of understanding, love needs an object, because perhaps the most important part of love, the part that will endure for us as a human being, is friendship. I can't sit down with God, have a cup of tea and chew over the difficulties and challenges of being human because there seems to be no input, no sharing. If I can't *touch* this being of love and feel its presence, how can I know it is really there? Once again, Rumi has been there before us:

Today, like every other day, we wake up empty

And frightened. Don't open the door to the study and
Begin reading. Take down a musical instrument.
Let the beauty we love be what we do.
There are hundreds of ways to kneel and kiss the ground.

Perhaps it is not such an impossible task, after all. Our Beloved is beside us, in us and around us, but we have forgotten how to notice Its presence in the same way that we are not aware of our hearts beating in our chests, or a grandfather clock ticking in the background, unless we make it the focus of our attention. In our search for this union, we look into the faces of others, but our human lovers are cardboard cutouts for the Real Thing. We know that there is this Other somewhere, out there. The truth of the matter is that it is not *out* there but *in* here after all and our hearts, like Rumi's, can be the receivers of divine telegrams informing us of this love. Many teachings, books and scriptures say this, in slightly different ways.

Christianity says *"For behold, the kingdom of God is within you."* (Luke 17:21)

Islam says *"In that glory is no 'I' or 'We' or 'Thou'. 'I', 'We', 'Thou' and 'He' are all one thing."* (Mansur al Hallaj)

Buddhism says *"You are all Buddhas. There is nothing you need to achieve. Just open your eyes."* (Siddhartha Gautama)

Taoism says *"Great knowledge sees all in one. Small knowledge breaks down into the many."* (Chuang Tzu)

and to bring it right up to the minute,

Science, to quote Fritjof Capra, is saying *"...... the universe is fundamentally interconnected, interdependent, and inseparable."*

Whilst one branch of science is educating us as to the nature of the universe, another is bringing to light information that may help you change your mind about your heart. A non-profit-making organisation in the US, the Institute of HeartMath, was set up over fifteen years ago to investigate and find a solution for the rising levels of personal stress experienced by people throughout the world. They have been studying the effects that 'mismanaged' emotions have on every aspect of our life and producing educational packages for children, institutions and corporations to help people learn more about their hearts and minds, how to manage their emotions and thus reduce stress. Their work has grown out of earlier research showing that the heart appeared to be sending meaningful messages to the brain that were not only understood, but obeyed. A small band of cardiovascular researchers and neurophysiologists amalgamated their work which is now known as neurocardiology; study of the heart brain. This is what Dr Christiane Northrup, author of *Women's Bodies, Women's Wisdom* has to say:

Nearly every disease or illness I've seen or treated in two decades of medical practice could have been improved or even cured had my patients or I known how to access the physical power of our heart's intelligence. HeartMath is the owner's manual we've been waiting for to help us recognize and use our heart's energy to help heal our bodies and our lives.

Our hearts apparently have a complex intrinsic nervous system that is sophisticated enough to qualify as a 'little brain' in its own right, and its elaborate circuitry enables it to act independently of the cranial brain – to learn, remember, and even feel and sense. HeartMath research revealed, amongst other things, that the heart seemed to have its own peculiar logic that frequently diverged from the direction of the autonomic nervous system. Your heart is the most powerful generator of rhythmic information patterns in your body. It is a sophisticated information encoding and processing centre and has a far more developed communication system with the brain than most of the body's major organs. Think about it. With every beat, with every squeeze of its four chambers our own liquid crystal super information highway – the bloodstream – is not only pumped right out to our extremities, but is also imprinted with electromagnetic information from the heart itself. The heart, then, is the headquarters of the communication network connecting body, mind, emotions and soul.

Further HeartMath research showed that when heart rhythm patterns are coherent, we are more creative, think more clearly, perceive and feel more positively. In other words our hearts are actively involved in our lives. The Institute goes so far as to say:

> *The answers to many of our original questions now provide a scientific basis to explain how and why the heart affects mental clarity, creativity, emotional balance and personal effectiveness. Our research and that of others indicate that the heart is far more than a simple pump. The heart is, in fact, a highly complex, self-organized information processing center with its own functional 'brain' that communicates with and influences the cranial brain via the nervous system, hormonal system and other pathways. These influences profoundly affect brain function and most of the body's major organs, and ultimately determine the quality of life.*

So the heart and brain carry on a two-way dialogue, each influencing the other's functioning. They also tell us that the heart produces by far the most powerful rhythmic electromagnetic field in the body, and this field changes measurably according to the different emotions being experienced. The heart's electrical field is about 60 times greater than that of the brain, and its magnetic field more then 5,000 times larger. This heart field not only envelops every cell of our bodies, but also expands out in all directions. It can actually be measured several feet away from the body. No wonder people in love – whether it's with life or another – radiate. And no wonder that the ancient Egyptians pulled the brains out of their corpses to leave the heart to 'mind' the body.

The researchers at HeartMath have also proved that the electromagnetic signal produced by our hearts registers on the brain waves of those around us, and is a key mediator of energy exchanges between people. In fact our hearts are actually chatting to each other – a heart-to-heart conversation – whenever we are engaged energetically with somebody. The

Institute has also proved the existence of that link between positive emotions and improved brainpower. Once again the ancient Egyptians with their 'Think with the heart and feel with the mind' knew exactly what they were talking about. So, apparently, did Blaise Pascal, a French mathematician and physicist (1623 – 1662 AD) when he wrote "The heart has its reasons, that reason does not know".

Our computerised lives with digital everything have taken our ears away from birdsong and our eyes from observing the wonder of nature and those connections that make the heart sing. We have been blanked out, dumbed down and switched off to the astonishing world created for us, and have become entranced instead by the plastic world we have created for ourselves.

This guide started with the body – and has ended there – right at the heart of it all.

We shall not cease from exploration
And the end of all our exploring
Will be to arrive where we started
And know the place for the first time.
T S Eliot (The Four Quartets)

There are a few challenges ahead for all of us, and questions to answer about what really matters. But remember that help is always close at hand. Just close your eyes once more, and enter your garden. Sit with that perfect flower at the heart of it. If you asked what it needed of you, I wonder what that might be? It is the most precious thing that you have; it knows you by heart. Perhaps there's something you would like to say to it about your life and all that's in it? You will feel its tender wisdom and loving kindness respond.

On behalf of our souls, each other and all we hold dear, time must be found to be still. So even if it's only for a few moments each day, spend time here in your garden in the presence of this flower. See how it changes as you breathe life into it. Notice how it is affected by simple acts of kindness, natural beauty, compassion and wild love.

Soul Focus

The heart is the soul's compass for the human experience

REMINDERS

- The energy waveforms of loving-kindness not only make others feel good, but they also keep you and your body well and healthy.
- Love radiates.
- Your heart is a multidimensional interface between the realms of The All That Is, the physical world and your soul.
- Give your mind a break for a change and think with your heart. See how it might be if you trusted your heart, and not your head's intelligence in your relationships with others and the world around you.
- Hearts speak with each other, so what comes from the heart is heard by the heart.
- There is an infinite Source of Love – it's not like a bank account.
- Do whatever makes your heart sing.

Resources

The Essential Rumi: Translated by **Coleman Barks** (Penguin)
Rumi: The Book of Love: Translated by **Coleman Barks** (Harper SanFrancisco)
The Book of the Heart: **Louisa Young** (Flamingo)
Love Poems from God: **Daniel Ladinsky** (Penguin Compass)
Soulmates: **Sue Minns** (Hodder Mobius)
The Heartmath Solution: **Doc Childre** (Harper SanFrancisco)
www.heartmath.org

Work of the eyes is done.
Now go and do the heart-work.
Rainer Maria Rilke

O books

O is a symbol of the world, of oneness and unity. In different cultures it also means the "eye", symbolizing knowledge and insight, and in Old English it means "place of love or home". O books explores the many paths of understanding which different traditions have developed down the ages, particularly those today that express respect for the planet and all of life. In philosophy, metaphysics and aesthetics O as zero relates to infinity, indivisibility and fate. In Zero Books we are developing a list of provocative shorter titles that cross different specializations and challenge conventional academic or majority opinion.

For more information on the full list of over 300 titles please visit our website **www.O-books.net**

myspiritradio is an exciting web, internet, podcast and mobile phone global broadcast network for all those interested in teaching and learning in the fields of body, mind, spirit and self development. Listeners can hear the show online via computer or mobile phone, and even download their favourite shows to listen to on MP3 players whilst driving, working, or relaxing.

Feed your mind, change your life with O Books,
The O Books radio programme carries interviews with most authors, sharing their wisdom on life, the universe and everything...e mail questions and co-create the show with O Books and myspiritradio.

Just visit **www.myspiritradio.com** for more information.

SOME RECENT O BOOKS

Back to the Truth
5,000 years of Advaita
Dennis Waite

A wonderful book. Encyclopedic in nature, and destined to become a classic. **James Braha**

Absolutely brilliant...an ease of writing with a water-tight argument outlining the great universal truths. This book will become a modern classic. A milestone in the history of Advaita. **Paula Marvelly**
1905047614 500pp **£19.95 $29.95**

Beyond Photography
Encounters with orbs, angels and mysterious light forms
Katie Hall and John Pickering

The authors invite you to join them on a fascinating quest; a voyage of discovery into the nature of a phenomenon, manifestations of which are shown as being historical and global as well as contemporary and intently personal.

At journey's end you may find yourself a believer, a doubter or simply an intrigued wonderer... Whatever the outcome, the process of journeying is likely prove provocative and stimulating and - as with the mysterious images fleetingly captured by the authors' cameras - inspiring and potentially enlightening. **Brian Sibley**, author and broadcaster.
1905047908 272pp 50 b/w photos +8pp colour insert **£12.99 $24.95**

Don't Get MAD Get Wise
Why no one ever makes you angry, ever!
Mike George

There is a journey we all need to make, from anger, to peace, to forgiveness. Anger always destroys, peace always restores, and forgiveness always heals. This explains the journey, the steps you can take to make it happen for you.

1905047827 160pp **£7.99 $14.95**

IF You Fall...
It's a new beginning
Karen Darke

Karen Darke's story is about the indomitability of spirit, from one of life's cruel vagaries of fortune to what is insight and inspiration. She has over-come the limitations of paralysis and discovered a life of challenge and adventure that many of us only dream about. It is all about the mind, the spirit and the desire that some of us find, but which all of us possess. **Joe Simpson**, mountaineer and author of *Touching the Void*

1905047886 240pp **£9.99 $19.95**

Love, Healing and Happiness
Spiritual wisdom for a post-secular era
Larry Culliford

This will become a classic book on spirituality. It is immensely practical and grounded. It mirrors the author's compassion and lays the foundation for a higher understanding of human suffering and hope. **Reinhard Kowalski** Consultant Clinical Psychologist

1905047916 304pp **£10.99 $19.95**

A Map to God
Awakening Spiritual Integrity
Susie Anthony

This describes an ancient hermetic pathway, representing a golden thread running through many traditions, which offers all we need to understand and do to actually become our best selves.

1846940443 260pp **£10.99 $21.95**